...nd EDITION

The ... HIGHLY COMMENDED
...Edinburgh's English-Speaking Union
...n Language Award 2004

Skills in English

Level 3

Listening

Teacher's Book

Terry Phillips
and
Anna Phillips

Garnet
EDUCATION

Published by
Garnet Publishing Ltd.
8 Southern Court
South Street
Reading RG1 4QS, UK

First edition, copyright © 2004 Garnet Publishing Ltd.
Second edition, copyright © 2004 Garnet Publishing Ltd.
Reprinted with corrections 2005.

ISBN 1 85964 794 4

British Library Cataloguing-in-Publication Data
A catalogue record for this book is available from the British Library.

Production

Project manager:	Richard Peacock
Editorial team:	Nicky Platt, Lucy Thompson, Katharine Mendelsohn
Art director:	David Rose
Design:	Mark Slader
Typesetting:	Samantha Barden
Illustration:	Beehive Illustration (Simon Rumble/ RogerWade-Walker), Janette Hill, Doug Nash, Karen Rose
Photography:	Corbis, Digital Vision, Mary Evans Picture Library, NOAA Photo Library, Photodisc

Garnet Publishing wishes to thank the following for their assistance in the development of this project:
Dr Abdullah Al Khanbashi, Abderrazak Ben Hamida, Maxine Gillway, Susan Boylan and the Level 3 team at UGRU, UAE University

Every effort has been made to trace the copyright holders and we apologize in advance for any unintentional omissions. We will be happy to insert the appropriate acknowledgements in any subsequent editions.

Audio production: Matinée Sound & Vision Ltd.;
John Green TEFL Tapes

Printed and bound
in Lebanon by International Press

Skills in English

Level 3

Listening

Contents

Book Map

Theme	Listening text type	Aural skills
1 **Education,** How Do We Learn?	Lecture	• Revision
2 **Daily Life,** Growing Up	Lecture	• Fixed phrases • Using abbreviations in notes • Taking notes of stories, ideas, etc.
3 **Work and Business,** Why Do People Work Hard?	Lecture	• Using symbols in notes • Recognising digressions
4 **Science and Nature,** Tornadoes and Hurricanes	Talk	• Signposts – reminders • Mini-signposts • Leaving space in notes for missing information
5 **The Physical World,** Natural Disasters	Lecture	• Rhetorical questions • Two-sided signposts
6 **Culture and Civilization,** What Is Society?	Lecture	• Distinguishing fact from opinion • Participating in discussions
7 **They Made Our World,** The Greatest Advance in History	Talk	• Understanding a speaker's argument
8 **Art and Literature,** Gulliver and Robinson Crusoe	Talk	• Guessing the spelling of proper nouns • Understanding dramatic language
9 **Sports and Leisure,** $5,000,000,000,000 p.a.	Lecture with questions	• Understanding pros and cons • Contributing to discussions
10 **Nutrition and Health,** Food – The New Poison?	Lecture with questions	• Revision

INTRODUCTION

The series

This course is part of the four-level *Skills in English* series. The series as a whole prepares students to study wholly or partly in English medium at tertiary level.

In addition, there is a remedial/false beginner course, *Starting Skills in English*, for students who are not ready to begin Level 1.

At each level there are four courses, each dealing with a discrete skill: Listening, Speaking, Reading or Writing. The focus in a particular course is very definitely on that skill. The methodology notes below repeatedly stress the discrete skills focus, and caution against spending too much time on, for example, Speaking, in this Listening Skills course. This is not because the writer dislikes integrated skills. The insistence on the target skill is because the writer believes that some students need one or two skills more than the others, and that students should be allowed to make differential progress in the four skills rather than constantly being held to the level at which they can hear, say, read and write a common set of language items.

In all four skills books, the course is organised into 10 themes, each with particular thematic focus. The 10 themes are:

Theme 1:	Education
Theme 2:	Daily Life
Theme 3:	Work and Business
Theme 4:	Science and Nature
Theme 5:	The Physical World
Theme 6:	Culture and Civilization
Theme 7:	They Made Our World
Theme 8:	Art and Literature
Theme 9:	Sports and Leisure
Theme 10:	Nutrition and Health

If you are using other skills books in the series, we recommend that you use them in the following sequence:

Listening
Speaking
Reading
Writing

The commonality of theme across the four skills means that the more skills books you use, the deeper and wider the students' linguistic ability to communicate in that thematic area becomes.

This course

This is the Listening Skills course at Level 3. The aim is to help students with an intermediate level of general English to improve their skills in understanding lectures in English.

The course comprises the Student's Book, this Teacher's Book, five CDs or four cassettes containing all the listening material, and a Test Booklet.

The course stands alone – in other words, it is not necessary for students to have studied any of the other skills courses in order to benefit from this course. Similarly, it is not necessary for students to have studied Level 2 of the same skill. However, there are obvious advantages if students have followed this path, since the materials are organised into the same themes, and the work in this course on a particular theme often continues on from that in Level 2. If your students have studied Level 2, consider doing a quick revision or test of the information and vocabulary in the relevant theme at that level before launching into the new work on that theme in this course.

The Test Booklet contains one test for each theme, a revision test after Themes 1 to 5 and a final test. The tests are sold in packs of ten, with an answer and marking guide. In addition, when you purchase a pack of ten booklets, you get access to an alternative final test on the skillsinenglish.com website. Methodology notes on administering the tests are provided in the answer and marking guide.

Organisation of the course

Each theme contains four lessons. Each lesson has a clear focus and purpose, as follows:

Lesson	Focus	Purpose and methodology points
1	Vocabulary	To ensure that students understand and can recognise basic vocabulary that will be needed for the theme.
2	Listening	To practise the listening skill; this lesson revises the aural skills and the segmental features taught in previous themes.
3	Learning new skills	To highlight specific listening skills of two types: a segmental features such as individual phonemes and minimal pairs; b broad aural skills such as *understanding signpost language.*
4	Applying new skills	To apply skills learnt in Lesson 3 to a new text – usually a parallel text to that in Lesson 2.

Vocabulary

As can be seen from the information about the organisation of the course above, the writer is firmly committed to the importance of vocabulary. This is why one lesson out of every four is devoted to vocabulary and why, in addition, the first activity in many of the other three lessons in each theme is a vocabulary revision exercise. In the case of listening, students must be able to recognise a wide range of words in isolation and, even more importantly, in the stream of speech.

In Lesson 1, key vocabulary is printed down the outer margin. The positioning is deliberate. You and the students should be able to flick back and find a thematic set easily.

There are two sets of words in each case:

The red words

These are all from Level 2. The green words from that level (see below) have become the red words for this. In other words, these are key words which it is assumed students have acquired, in addition to the basic Council of Europe Waystage-level words, from this theme. It is therefore assumed that students correctly placed at this level will know all or most of these from previous language learning. If they do not, you will need to supplement the one or two exercises provided. Students are required to manipulate the words in a number of ways, largely to prove that they understand the meaning. Thus, activities require them to discuss questions using the red words, put the red words into lexical sets or make true sentences about themselves, their family, country, etc., using the red words.

The green words

These are high-frequency words from the thematic set that will be required for the listening texts in Lessons 2 or 4. It is essential that, by the end of this lesson, the students understand the meaning of these words *and* can correctly pick them out from the stream of speech, so that they do not cause problems with comprehension in the later lessons.

In Lessons 2, 3 and 4, there are additional words that will almost certainly be new to the students. Some of these require pre-teaching, in which case there are additional vocabulary activities at the start of the relevant lesson. In most cases, however, these new words are defined in the listening texts themselves or deducible from context. Clearly, the ability to wait for definitions in a text and to work out meaning from spoken context are key listening skills; therefore, these new items should not be pre-taught. However, once the students have had the opportunity to understand the items in context, it is quite reasonable to focus on the new vocabulary and try to ensure that some, at least, is remembered in the future.

To enable you and the students to keep track of the thematic sets, these are reproduced at the back of this book and the Students' Book. In addition, they are organised alphabetically with their origins (i.e., as a red or green word) retained.

Skills Checks

These are a key feature of the course. In every theme, there is at least one Skills Check box. The naming of this feature is significant. It is assumed that the students will have heard about most, if not all, of the skills points in these boxes – i.e., they are skills *checks*, not skills *presentations*. It is the writer's experience that many students who have gone through a modern language course have *heard of* the majority of skills points but cannot make practical use of them. If you feel in a particular case that the students have no idea about the point in question, spend considerably longer on a full presentation.

In most cases, the students are given an activity to do before looking at the Skills Check box. Thus, a test-teach-test approach is used. This is quite deliberate. With this approach, there is a good chance that the students will be sensitised to the particular point before being asked to understand it intellectually. This is likely to be more effective than talking about the point and then asking the students to try to apply it.

Specific activities

Certain types of activity are repeated on several occasions throughout the book. This is because these activities are particularly valuable in language learning.

Crosswords and puzzles

One of the keys to vocabulary learning is repetition. However, the repetition must be active. It is no good if students are simply going through the motions. The course uses crosswords and other kinds of puzzles to bring words back into consciousness through an engaging activity.

Odd one out

The ability to see the connections between linguistic items – and, therefore, the odd one out – is a key indicator of comprehension. However, it is often easier to see the odd one out than it is to explain why that item is different. This is why reasons are sometimes given. Where they are not, consider writing the reasons on the board, in jumbled order, if you feel your students will struggle without them.

Gap fill

Filling in missing words or phrases in a sentence or a text, or labelling a map or diagram, indicates comprehension of both the missing items and the context in which they correctly fit. It is generally better to provide the missing items to ensure that all the required items are available to all the students. In the case of Lesson 1, the words are usually available in the word list on the right. In other cases, you might prefer to supply the words or phrases on the board.

In addition, you can vary the approach to gap fills by sometimes going through the activity with the whole class, orally, pens down, then setting the same task individually. Gap fills or labelling activities can be photocopied and set as revision at the end of the unit or later, with or without the missing items box.

Two-column activities

This type of activity is generally better than open-ended questions or gap fill with no box of missing items, as it ensures that all the target language is available to the students. However, the activity is only fully effective if the two columns are dealt with in the following way:

1 Ask students to match the two parts from each column.
2 Ask students to cover column 2 and remember these parts from the items in column 1.
3 Ask students to cover column 1 and remember these parts from the items in column 2.

Additional activities are:

- Students test each other in pairs.
- Teacher reads out column 1 – students complete with items from column 2, books closed.
- With books closed, students write as many of the items as they can remember.

Ordering

Several different kinds of linguistic element can be given out of order for students to arrange correctly. The ability to put things in the correct order strongly indicates comprehension of the items.

This type of activity is sometimes given before students listen; the first listening task is then to check the order. To make the exercise more enjoyable, and slightly easier, it is a good idea to photocopy the items (or write them out again) and cut them into strips or single words. Students can then physically move the items and try different ordering. The teacher can even make a blackboard / whiteboard set of sentences and encourage students to arrange or direct the arrangement of the items on the board.

Tables and charts

Students are often asked to transfer information into a table by ticking the correct box, or writing notes or single words in the boxes. This activity is a good way of testing comprehension of listening, as it does not require much linguistic output from the students at a time when they should be concentrating on comprehension. Once the table has been completed, it can form the basis of:

1 a checking activity – students compare their tables, and note and discuss differences;
2 a reconstruction activity – students give the information in the table in full, in speech or writing.

The second should be used with caution, bearing in mind the focus on the listening skill in the course rather than on written or spoken production.

Error correction

It was once thought that showing students an error reinforced the error – the students would be even more likely to make that error in the future. We now know that recognising errors is a vital part of language learning. Rather than reinforcing the error, showing it can serve to highlight the problem much better than any number of explanatory words. Students must be able to recognise errors – principally in their own work – and correct them. For this reason, error recognition and correction activities are occasionally used.

Methodology points

Setting up tasks

The teaching notes for many activities begin with the word 'Set …'

This single word covers a number of vital functions for the teacher, as follows:

1 Refer students to the rubric – or instructions.
2 Check that they understand **what** to do – get one or two students to explain the task in their own words.
3 Tell the students **how** they are to do the task, if this is not clear in the rubric – as individual work, pairwork, or in groups.
4 Go through the example if there is one. If not, make it clear what the target output is – full sentences, short answers, notes, etc.
5 Go through one or two of the actual prompts, working with a good student to elicit the required output.

Use of visuals

There is a large amount of visual material in the book. This should be exploited in a number of ways:

1 before an activity, to orientate the students, to get them thinking about the situation or the activity, and to provide an opportunity for a small amount of pre-teaching of vocabulary;
2 during the activity, to remind students of important language;
3 after the activity, to help with related work or to revise the target language.

Pronunciation

The focus of this listening course is on a receptive skill rather than a productive one. Therefore, pronunciation of individual phonemes is not focused on directly in the book. However, it is important that students can hear all the target items correctly. In addition, it is arguable that saying a phoneme helps with ear training; therefore, some practice of the pronunciation may be desirable.

Comparing answers in pairs

This activity is suggested on almost every occasion when the students have completed an activity individually. This provides all students with a chance to give and explain their answers, which is not possible if the teacher immediately goes through the answers with the whole class.

Monitoring

Pairwork and group activities are, of course, an opportunity for the students to produce spoken language. As mentioned above, this is not the main focus of this course. But the second benefit of these interactional patterns is that they provide an opportunity for the teacher to check three points:

1 that the students are performing the correct task, in the correct way;
2 that the students understand the language of the task they are performing;
3 the elements that need to be covered again for the benefit of the whole class, and the points that need to be dealt with on an individual basis with particular students.

Feedback

At the end of each activity, there should be a feedback stage. During this stage, the correct answers (or a model answer in the case of freer activities) are given, alternative correct answers (if any) are accepted, and wrong answers are discussed.

Note: If no answers are provided, answers depend on students.

Feedback can be:

a high-speed, whole-class, oral – this method is suitable for cases where short answers with no possible variations are required;
b individual, oral – this method is suitable where answers are longer and / or where variations are possible;
c individual, onto the board – this method is suitable when the teacher will want to look closely at the correct answers to highlight points of interest or confusion.

Remember – learning does not usually take place when a student gets something right. Learning generally takes place after a student has got something wrong, and begins to understand why it is wrong.

Confirmation and correction

Many activities benefit from a learning tension, i.e., a period of time when students are not sure whether something is right or wrong. The advantages of this tension are:

a a chance for all students to become involved in an activity before the correct answers are given;
b a higher level of concentration from students – (tension is quite enjoyable!);
c a greater focus on the item as students wait for the correct answer;
d a greater involvement in the process – students become committed to their answers and want to know if they are right and, if not, why not.

In cases where learning tension of this type is desirable, the detailed teachers' notes say, 'Do not confirm or correct (at this point).'

Highlighting grammar

This course is not organised on a grammatical syllabus and does not focus on grammar specifically. However, on occasion, the expression *Highlight the grammar* is used in the teachers' notes. This expression means:

1 focus the students' attention on the grammar point, e.g., *Look at the verb in the first sentence;*
2 write an example of the target grammar on the board;
3 ask a student to read out the sentence / phrase;
4 demonstrate the grammar point in an appropriate way (see below);
5 refer to the board throughout the activity if students are making mistakes.

Ways of dealing with different kinds of grammar point:

- for **word order**, show the order of items in the sentence by numbering them, e.g.,

1	2	3	4
They	often	have	a special party.

- for **paradigms**, show the changes with different persons of the verb.

I	go
He	go **es**

According to recent corpora research, the main tense that appears in academic text is the simple present. This tense alone accounts for the vast majority of sentences. At the other extreme, in one corpus of four million words, there was only one example of the present perfect continuous. This suggests that we should not spend a huge amount of time on verb tenses in an EAP course. Instead, we need to ensure that students can understand and produce compound and complex sentences in the simple present tense. Rather than in verb tenses, difficulty in academic texts often lies in the use of complex noun phrases with a great deal of pre- and post-modification of the head word, and in the use of long subordinate clauses at the start of sentences. For this reason, *Skills in English* first ensures that students can understand and produce basic SVO patterns and then, gradually, can understand and produce expansion of the S and O and combinations of SVO sentences in various ways.

Self-checking

On a few occasions during the course, the teachers' notes encourage you to ask the students to check their own work. This can be done by referring students to the full tapescript at the end of the book. This is an excellent way to develop the students' recognition and correction of error. Listening, in particular, obviously happens inside someone's head – in the end, each student has to understand his or her *own* error or misunderstanding.

Many of the Language and culture notes in this edition are written for students whose first language is Arabic. If you have students from a different language group, check with the skillsinenglish.com website to see if there are relevant notes. We are constantly increasing the range of languages covered.

Lesson 1: Vocabulary

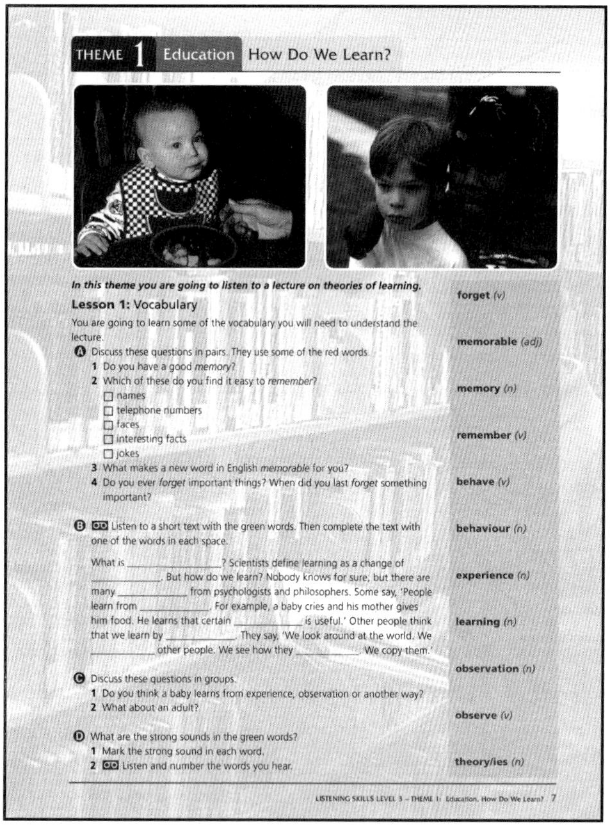
THEME 1 Education How Do We Learn?

In this theme you are going to listen to a lecture on theories of learning.

Lesson 1: Vocabulary

You are going to learn some of the vocabulary you will need to understand the lecture.

A Discuss these questions in pairs. They use some of the red words.

1 Do you have a good *memory*?
2 Which of these do you find it easy to *remember*?
- ☐ names
- ☐ telephone numbers
- ☐ faces
- ☐ interesting facts
- ☐ jokes

3 What makes a new word in English *memorable* for you?
4 Do you ever *forget* important things? When did you last *forget* something important?

B Listen to a short text with the green words. Then complete the text with one of the words in each space.

What is __________? Scientists define learning as a change of __________. But how do we learn? Nobody knows for sure, but there are many __________ from psychologists and philosophers. Some say, 'People learn from __________. For example, a baby cries and his mother gives him food. He learns that certain __________ is useful.' Other people think that we learn by __________. They say, 'We look around at the world. We __________ other people. We see how they __________. We copy them.'

C Discuss these questions in groups.

1 Do you think a baby learns from experience, observation or another way?
2 What about an adult?

D What are the strong sounds in the green words?

1 Mark the strong sound in each word.
2 Listen and number the words you hear.

forget *(v)*
memorable *(adj)*
memory *(n)*
remember *(v)*
behave *(v)*
behaviour *(n)*
experience *(n)*
learning *(n)*
observation *(n)*
observe *(v)*
theory/ies *(n)*

LISTENING SKILLS LEVEL 3 – THEME 1: Education, How Do We Learn? 7

General note

Students who studied Level 2 will remember the red words as target items from the corresponding theme at that level. Point this out. If your students didn't study Level 2, just spend a little longer on Exercise A, ensuring that they understand the meaning of the words.

Introduction

If students studied Level 2, do a quick revision of the main points of this theme. Write the words below on the board. Remind students that in Level 2 the topic was 'How do we remember?' and that these are the ways that people remember things. Elicit what each one means – the definitions are on the right. Do further work on the two-column activity.

frequency	how often, e.g., you hear, read or do something
activity	doing something, e.g., with information
variety	different things
association	linking, e.g., one piece of information with another
mnemonics	something strange or memorable about information that you use to help you remember

If students didn't study Level 2, just go straight to A as the introduction.

Exercise A

Set for pairwork. Feed back orally. It is worth spending quite a long time on this because of the high value of these words in talking about education.

Extend the words with *remind / reminder* if you would like to. These occur later in the theme.

Methodology note

In this course, words from the same 'family' are given, rather than relying on students building, e.g., *memorable* from *memory*. This is because the rules for building words in English are complex and not really productive. For example, we can build the adjective *memorable* from the related noun on this occasion, but the converse *forgettable* is built from a related verb.

The students should be encouraged to learn the words by rote – which they should be good at.

Exercise B

Exploit the visuals. Ask students to tell you what is happening in the pictures and what it has got to do with learning. Give students time to read the text. Set for individual work then pairwork checking. Play the recording. Feed back orally.

Answers

What is *learning*? Scientists define learning as a change of *behaviour*. But how do we learn? Nobody knows for sure, but there are many *theories* from psychologists and philosophers. Some say, 'People learn from *experience*. For example, a baby cries and his mother gives him food. He learns that certain *behaviour* is useful.' Other people think that we learn by *observation*. They say, 'We look around at the world. We *observe* other people. We see how they *behave*. We copy them.'

Exercise C

Set for groupwork. Feed back as general discussion. This could be quite a long discussion if students become interested in it, so don't cut it short if it develops well.

Exercise D

Remind students (or tell them for the first time if they did not study Level 2) that all long words in English have one strong sound. Give examples from the red words as follows:

for'get
'memorable
'memory
re'member

Exaggerate the stressed syllable and swallow the other sounds. Remind / tell students that they may only hear the strong sound in a long word.

Set for individual work then pairwork checking. Play the recording.

Answers

	sound	as in this word:
1	serve	ob'serve
2	pe	ex'perience
3	have	be'have / be'haviour
4	lear	'learning
5	the	'theory / ies
6	va	obser'vation

Language and culture note

The rules for stressing words in Arabic are very strict. You can work out where the stress will fall in a new word. For example, all long vowels are stressed.

This, of course, is not true in English. Therefore, students need to identify the stressed syllable in all new words and have practice in identifying the word from the stressed sound alone.

Language and culture note

Throughout this course, the word *college* is used to mean tertiary-level institution. This is a common use of the word in the English-speaking world. The Arabic word *kulia* is almost co-extensive with *college*, i.e., it can mean a faculty or school of a university or an academy of higher learning. However, it can also mean a secondary school, so you will need to stress that in this course *college* is interchangeable with *university* and not with *secondary school*. The fictional Greenhill College is a tertiary establishment with degree-level courses.

Closure

Say sentences ending with one of the target words from this lesson. Exaggerate the stressed sound and swallow the other sounds in the word, e.g.:

Some people believe you can learn by
_____*va*_____.

See if students can identify the word (observation).

Lesson 2: Listening

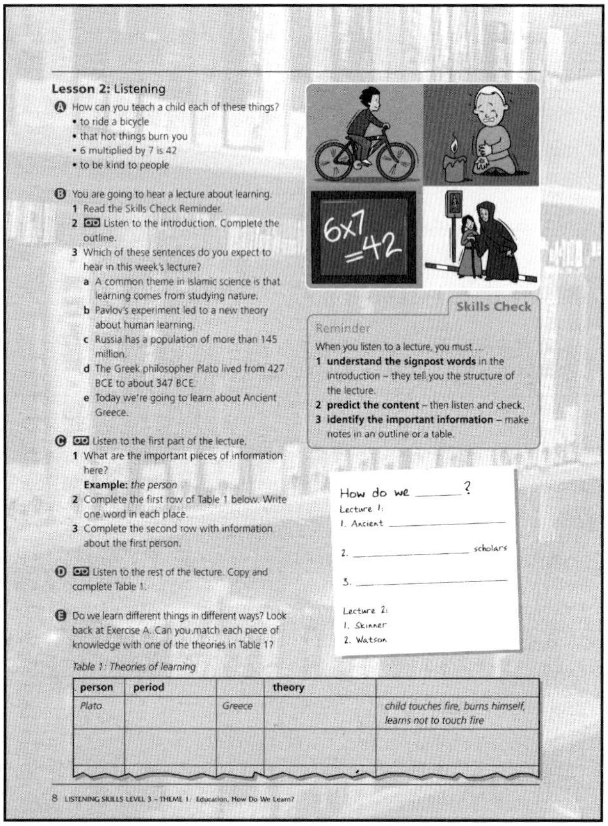

Lesson 2: Listening

A How can you teach a child each of these things?
- to ride a bicycle
- that hot things burn you
- 6 multiplied by 7 is 42
- to be kind to people

B You are going to hear a lecture about learning.
1 Read the Skills Check Reminder.
2 Listen to the introduction. Complete the outline.
3 Which of these sentences do you expect to hear in this week's lecture?
   a A common theme in Islamic science is that learning comes from studying nature.
   b Pavlov's experiment led to a new theory about human learning.
   c Russia has a population of more than 145 million.
   d The Greek philosopher Plato lived from 427 BCE to about 347 BCE.
   e Today we're going to learn about Ancient Greece.

C Listen to the first part of the lecture.
1 What are the important pieces of information here?
   Example: *the person*
2 Complete the first row of Table 1 below. Write one word in each place.
3 Complete the second row with information about the first person.

D Listen to the rest of the lecture. Copy and complete Table 1.

E Do we learn different things in different ways? Look back at Exercise A. Can you match each piece of knowledge with one of the theories in Table 1?

Table 1: Theories of learning

person	period		theory	
Plato		*Greece*		*child touches fire, burns himself, learns not to touch fire*

Introduction

Remind students of the information in the text in Lesson 1. Say the first part of each sentence or phrase and get students to try to complete it, e.g.:

> *What is learning? Scientists define learning as* (a change of behaviour).
> *But how do we* (learn)?
> *Nobody knows for* (sure)
> *but there are many* (theories)
> *from psychologists and* (philosophers).

Methodology note

You know your students better than anybody, certainly better than the writer of this course. Listen to each lecture while you are preparing your lesson and decide if you need to pre-teach some more words. Clearly, you should not pre-teach words which are the target of listening activities, but you may well feel that other words in the text will cause students to stumble and thus need pre-teaching.

Exercise A

Set for pairwork. Feed back orally. Allow the activity to continue if students are enjoying it and coming to interesting conclusions.

Answers

Answers depend on students, but they may decide the following:

to ride a bicycle	you've got to do it
that hot things burn you	experience, observation
6 times 7 is 42	memory
to be kind to people	experience, observation?

Exercise B

Work through the Skills Check Reminder. Write the points on the board. Tick them off as you work through them in this lesson.

1 Set for individual work then pairwork checking.
2 Play the introduction. Feed back, building up the outline on the board.
3 Do as a whole-class activity. Get students to explain their choices.

Answers

2 Model answer
   <u>*How do we learn?*</u>
   Lecture 1:
   1. *Ancient Greece*
   2. *Islamic scholars*
   3. *Russia*

3 *Probable:*
   a A common theme in Islamic science is that learning comes from studying nature. *A theory about learning – which fits with the topic of the lecture.*
   b Pavlov's experiment led to a new theory about human learning. *As above.*
   d The Greek philosopher Plato lived from 427 BCE to about 347 BCE. *When lecturers talk about famous people from history, they usually give their nationality and the date of their birth and death.*

Unlikely:

c Russia has a population of more than 145 million. *So what? Not relevant to a lecture about learning.*

e Today we're going to learn about Ancient Greece. *No we aren't; we're going to learn about learning.*

Exercise C

Explain that students must build up the headings of the table. Set for individual work then pairwork checking. Play Part 1. Elicit the headings and build up the blank table on the board. Students should be able to identify that the following information is important and, from that, work out the possible headings:

- the name of each person = person
- the period when he lived = period
- the place where he lived = place
- his theory of learning = theory
- an example of his theory = example

Play Part 1 again for students to complete the information about Plato. Feed back onto the board. Note that students only need to say a few words for the example – just enough for them to remember later.

Exercise D

Set for individual work then pairwork checking. Play Part 2. Feed back into the table on the board.

Deal with new vocabulary you need for this exercise. Don't worry about the rest – there will be time for more exploitation next lesson.

Language and culture note

Plato (*aflatoon*) and Aristotle (*arstoo*) are extremely famous in the Arab World. In Arabic, Plato is called the owner of power and light, and Aristotle is called the first master. Al Farabi is the second master.

Exercise E and Closure

Set for groupwork.

Answers

Possible answers:
to ride a bicycle = learning by experience
hot things burn you = knowing why and / or experience and / or conditioning
6 multiplied by 7 is 42 = memory
to be kind to people = conditioning

Answers

person	period	place	theory	example
Plato	427–347 BCE	Greece	learning is remembering; experience	child touches fire, burns himself, learns not to touch fire
Aristotle	384–322 BCE	Greece	learning is knowing why	child sees the pattern – hot things = burn you
Al Farabi	9th C	Arab World	learning is observing	child sees another child get burnt – does not touch the fire himself
Ibn Sina	10th C	Arab World	learning is observing	
Ibn Rushd	12th C	Arab World	learning is observing	
Pavlov	19th C	Russia	learning is conditioning	child is frightened by mother's reaction and does not act the same way again

Lesson 3: Checking skills

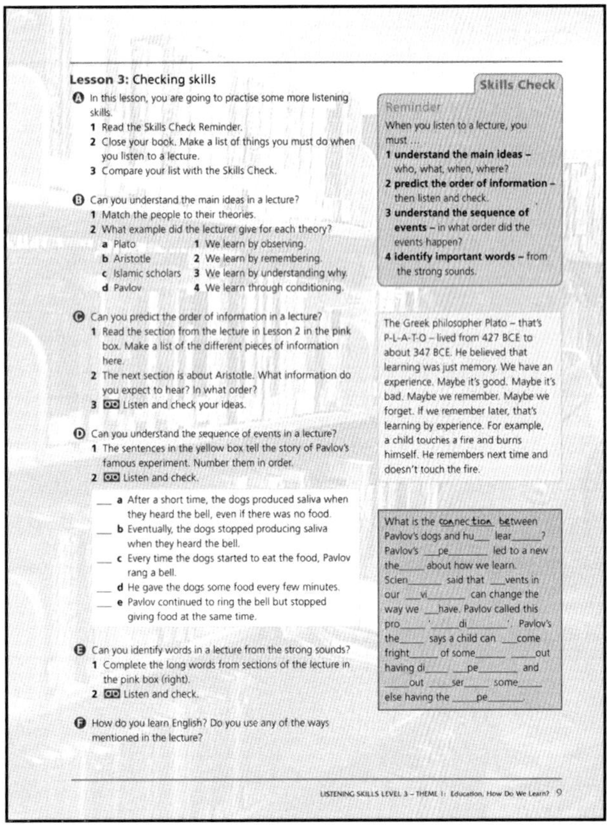

Lesson 3: Checking skills

A In this lesson, you are going to practise some more listening skills.
1 Read the Skills Check Reminder.
2 Close your book. Make a list of things you must do when you listen to a lecture.
3 Compare your list with the Skills Check.

B Can you understand the main ideas in a lecture?
1 Match the people to their theories.
2 What example did the lecturer give for each theory?

a Plato	1 We learn by observing.
b Aristotle	2 We learn by remembering.
c Islamic scholars	3 We learn by understanding why.
d Pavlov	4 We learn through conditioning.

C Can you predict the order of information in a lecture?
1 Read the section from the lecture in Lesson 2 in the pink box. Make a list of the different pieces of information here.
2 The next section is about Aristotle. What information do you expect to hear? In what order?
3 Listen and check your ideas.

D Can you understand the sequence of events in a lecture?
1 The sentences in the yellow box tell the story of Pavlov's famous experiment. Number them in order.
2 Listen and check.

___ a After a short time, the dogs produced saliva when they heard the bell, even if there was no food.
___ b Eventually, the dogs stopped producing saliva when they heard the bell.
___ c Every time the dogs started to eat the food, Pavlov rang a bell.
___ d He gave the dogs some food every few minutes.
___ e Pavlov continued to ring the bell but stopped giving food at the same time.

E Can you identify words in a lecture from the strong sounds?
1 Complete the long words from sections of the lecture in the pink box (right).
2 Listen and check.

F How do you learn English? Do you use any of the ways mentioned in the lecture?

Skills Check

Reminder

When you listen to a lecture, you must ...
1 **understand the main ideas** – who, what, when, where?
2 **predict the order of information** – then listen and check.
3 **understand the sequence of events** – in what order did the events happen?
4 **identify important words** – from the strong sounds.

The Greek philosopher Plato – that's P-L-A-T-O – lived from 427 BCE to about 347 BCE. He believed that learning was just memory. We have an experience. Maybe it's good. Maybe it's bad. Maybe we remember. Maybe we forget. If we remember later, that's learning by experience. For example, a child touches a fire and burns himself. He remembers next time and doesn't touch the fire.

What is the connection between Pavlov's dogs and hu___ lear_____? Pavlov's ___pe_______ led to a new the_____ about how we learn. Scien______ said that ___vents in our ___vi_______ can change the way we ___have. Pavlov called this pro_____ '_____di_______'. Pavlov's the_____ says a child can ___come fright_____ of some______ _____out having di_____ ___pe_______ and _____out ___ser_____ some_____ else having the _____pe_______.

LISTENING SKILLS LEVEL 3 – THEME 1: Education, How Do We Learn? 9

Introduction

Elicit the listening skills from the previous lesson (Skills Check Reminder 1). Write them on the board again.

Exercise A

Point out there are more listening skills.

1 Work through the Skills Check.
2 Set for individual work then pairwork checking.
3 Get students to self-check, then feed back, adding the new points to the list on the board. As before, tick them off as you work through them in this lesson.

Exercise B

Set for pairwork. Feed back orally.

Answers

Plato	We learn by remembering.	child has experience
Aristotle	We learn by understanding why.	child realises that hot things burn
Islamic scholars	We learn by observing.	child sees other child getting burnt
Pavlov	We learn through conditioning.	child's mother makes him afraid of fire

Exercise C

Ideally, work with an OHT of this part of the lecture.

1 Set for pairwork. Feed back onto the board as follows:
   - How to spell Plato.
   - Plato's dates.
   - What Plato believed about learning.
   - An explanation of Plato's ideas.
   - An example.
2 Prediction based on analysis above. Elicit that the chances are that the information in the next part will be in the same order.
3 Play Part 2 again for students to self-check. Note that the dates precede the spelling of the name this time.

Exercise D

Set for pairwork. Ideally, use cut-ups so students can actually move the pieces of paper around. Play the recording. Feed back orally.

Answers

Correct order:

d He gave the dogs some food every few minutes.
c Every time the dogs started to eat the food, Pavlov rang a bell.
b After a short time, the dogs produced saliva when they heard the bell, even if there was no food.

e Pavlov continued to ring the bell but stopped giving food at the same time.

a Eventually, the dogs stopped producing saliva when they heard the bell.

Exercise E

Set for individual work then pairwork checking. Go through the text, saying the stressed syllable each time so students are clear what exactly it is. This is sometimes not obvious, because sound–sight is not always predictable, e.g.,

hu = /hjuː/
lear = /lɜː/
pe = /pɪə/

Play the recording for self-checking.

Answers

What is the con*nection* *bet*ween Pavlov's dogs and hu*man* lear*ning*? Pavlov's *experiment* led to a new the*ory* about how we learn. Scien*tists* said that *e*vents in our *en*viro*nment* can change the way we *be*have.

Pavlov called this pro*cess* '*con*di*tioning*'. Pavlov's the*ory* says a child can *be*come fright*ened* of some*thing* *with*out having di*rect* *ex*pe*rience* and *with*out *ob*ser*ving* some*one* else having the *ex*pe*rience*.

Closure

Deal with new vocabulary from these parts of the lecture.

Lesson 4: Applying skills

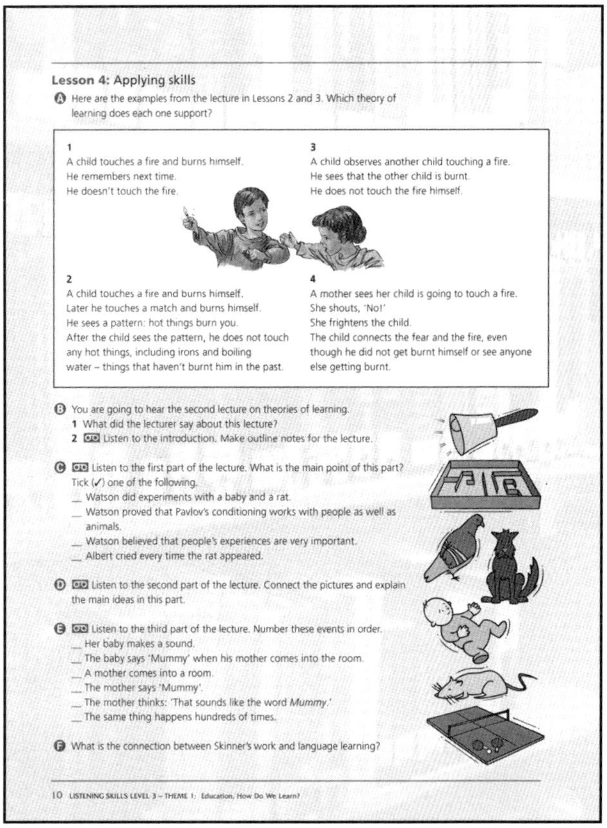

Lesson 4: Applying skills

A Here are the examples from the lecture in Lessons 2 and 3. Which theory of learning does each one support?

1
A child touches a fire and burns himself.
He remembers next time.
He doesn't touch the fire.

2
A child touches a fire and burns himself.
Later he touches a match and burns himself.
He sees a pattern: hot things burn you.
After the child sees the pattern, he does not touch any hot things, including irons and boiling water – things that haven't burnt him in the past.

3
A child observes another child touching a fire.
He sees that the other child is burnt.
He does not touch the fire himself.

4
A mother sees her child is going to touch a fire.
She shouts, 'No!'
She frightens the child.
The child connects the fear and the fire, even though he did not get burnt himself or see anyone else getting burnt.

B You are going to hear the second lecture on theories of learning.
1 What did the lecturer say about this lecture?
2 Listen to the introduction. Make outline notes for the lecture.

C Listen to the first part of the lecture. What is the main point of this part? Tick (✓) one of the following.
__ Watson did experiments with a baby and a rat.
__ Watson proved that Pavlov's conditioning works with people as well as animals.
__ Watson believed that people's experiences are very important.
__ Albert cried every time the rat appeared.

D Listen to the second part of the lecture. Connect the pictures and explain the main ideas in this part.

E Listen to the third part of the lecture. Number these events in order.
__ Her baby makes a sound.
__ The baby says 'Mummy' when his mother comes into the room.
__ A mother comes into a room.
__ The mother says 'Mummy'.
__ The mother thinks: 'That sounds like the word *Mummy*.'
__ The same thing happens hundreds of times.

F What is the connection between Skinner's work and language learning?

10 LISTENING SKILLS LEVEL 3 – THEME 1: Education, How Do We Learn?

Introduction

Exploit the visual. What is happening here?
OR
Ask the students: *What is the basic situation in all the examples of learning?* Write the words *child* and *fire* on the board.

Exercise A

Set for pairwork. Feed back orally.

Answers

1 We learn by remembering / experience.
2 We learn by understanding why.
3 We learn by observing.
4 We learn through conditioning.

Exercise B

Remind students that the lecturer talked about two lectures.

1 Refer students back to the outline notes. What is she going to talk about this week? Elicit, but don't confirm or correct.
2 Set for individual work then pairwork checking. Play the introduction. Feed back, writing the outline on the board.

Answers

Model outline:
<u>How do we learn?</u>
Theories from the 20th C
1 Watson
2 Skinner

Methodology notes

1 This is a short practice in listening for key information. Most of this information is not relevant to the task. Students must ignore this and only write about this week's lecture.
2 On this occasion, the names of the scientists are not spelt out. This is deliberate. The students should be able to guess the spelling.

Exercise C

Set for individual work then pairwork checking. Play Part 1. Feed back orally. Deal with why the other summaries are wrong.

Answers

Watson proved that Pavlov's conditioning works with people as well as animals.

Exercise D

Exploit the visuals. Check / teach the words *rat, maze, pigeon, table tennis, bell, baby.* Ask students to connect items from the first part of the lecture – they should connect *baby* and *rat*. One picture should be used twice. Set for pairwork. Play Part 2. Feed back orally.

Answers

a dog + a bell = Pavlov's theory
a baby + a rat = Watson
a maze + a rat = Skinner 1
a pigeon + a table tennis table = Skinner 2

Exercise E

Don't let the students look at the sentences before you play the recording. Set for pairwork. Play Part 3. Feed back onto the board.

Answers

1 A mother comes into a room.
2 Her baby makes a sound.
3 The mother thinks: 'That sounds like the word *Mummy*.'
4 The mother says 'Mummy'.
5 The same thing happens hundreds of times.
6 The baby says 'Mummy' when his mother comes into the room.

Methodology note

On this occasion, it is best if students don't look at the sentences before listening. Then they can use logic and aural memory to put them into the right order. Otherwise, they will use logic and reading, and the listening will just be a final check, if even that.

Exercise F

Whole-class discussion. If students have interesting things to say – about rote learning and drilling, for example – let the discussion continue. Otherwise, just give a few examples of the effect of Skinner's ideas on language learning in the 1960s.

Closure

Further exploit the text with comprehension questions.
AND / OR
Play some of the parts again and pause for students to supply the next word or phrase.

Lesson 1: Vocabulary

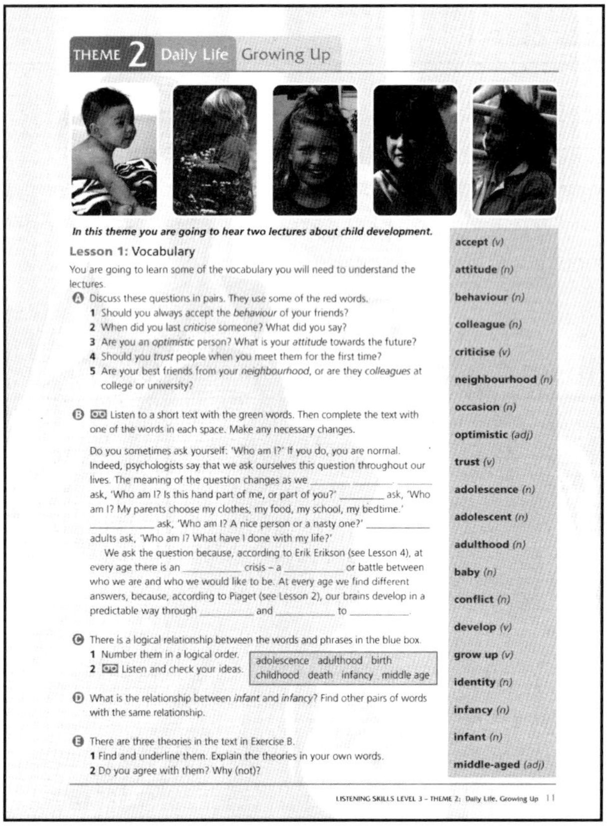

THEME 2 Daily Life Growing Up

In this theme you are going to hear two lectures about child development.

Lesson 1: Vocabulary

You are going to learn some of the vocabulary you will need to understand the lectures.

A Discuss these questions in pairs. They use some of the red words.
1 Should you always accept the *behaviour* of your friends?
2 When did you last *criticise* someone? What did you say?
3 Are you an *optimistic* person? What is your *attitude* towards the future?
4 Should you *trust* people when you meet them for the first time?
5 Are your best friends from your *neighbourhood*, or are they *colleagues* at college or university?

B Listen to a short text with the green words. Then complete the text with one of the words in each space. Make any necessary changes.

Do you sometimes ask yourself: 'Who am I?' If you do, you are normal. Indeed, psychologists say that we ask ourselves this question throughout our lives. The meaning of the question changes as we _____ _____. _____ ask, 'Who am I? Is this hand part of me, or part of you?' _____ ask, 'Who am I? My parents choose my clothes, my food, my school, my bedtime.' _____ ask, 'Who am I? A nice person or a nasty one?' _____ adults ask, 'Who am I? What have I done with my life?'

We ask the question because, according to Erik Erikson (see Lesson 4), at every age there is an _____ crisis – a _____ or battle between who we are and who we would like to be. At every age we find different answers, because, according to Piaget (see Lesson 2), our brains develop in a predictable way through _____ and _____ to _____.

C There is a logical relationship between the words and phrases in the blue box.
1 Number them in a logical order.
2 Listen and check your ideas.

adolescence adulthood birth childhood death infancy middle age

D What is the relationship between *infant* and *infancy*? Find other pairs of words with the same relationship.

E There are three theories in the text in Exercise B.
1 Find and underline them. Explain the theories in your own words.
2 Do you agree with them? Why (not)?

accept (v)
attitude (n)
behaviour (n)
colleague (n)
criticise (v)
neighbourhood (n)
occasion (n)
optimistic (adj)
trust (v)
adolescence (n)
adolescent (n)
adulthood (n)
baby (n)
conflict (n)
develop (v)
grow up (v)
identity (n)
infancy (n)
infant (n)
middle-aged (adj)

LISTENING SKILLS LEVEL 3 – THEME 2: Daily Life, Growing Up 11

General note

Students who studied Level 2 will remember the red words as target items from the corresponding theme at that level. Point this out. If your students didn't study Level 2, just spend a little longer on Exercise A, ensuring that they understand the meaning of the words.

Introduction

Write the title on the board. Elicit / explain that it means the process of changing from a baby into an adult. See if students can name any of the stages from birth to adulthood. Point out that one of the problems of growing up is making friends.

Exercise A

Set for pairwork. Feed back orally.

Exercise B

Give students time to look at the text and think about the possible words for each space. Set for individual work then pairwork checking. Play the recording. Feed back orally. Check that students understand the idea of *identity*. Perhaps use an *identity card* to demonstrate the point that it means *who you are*. Don't do any more work on the content – the next exercises cover this.

Answers

Do you sometimes ask yourself: 'Who am I?' If you do, you are normal. Indeed, psychologists say that we ask ourselves this question throughout our lives. The meaning of the question changes as we *grow up*. *Babies* ask, 'Who am I? Is this hand part of me, or part of you?' *Infants* ask, 'Who am I? My parents choose my clothes, my food, my school, my bedtime.' *Adolescents* ask, 'Who am I? A nice person or a nasty one?' *Middle-aged* adults ask, 'Who am I? What have I done with my life?'

We ask the question because, according to Erik Erikson (see Lesson 4), at every age there is an *identity* crisis – a *conflict* or battle between who we are and who we would like to be. At every age we find different answers, because, according to Piaget (see Lesson 2), our brains develop in a predictable way through *infancy* and *adolescence* to *adulthood*.

Exercise C

Write the words from the box on the board. Ask students what the logical relationship is – stages of life. Set for pairwork. Play the recording. Feed back onto the board. Check the pronunciation. Ask students to mark the stressed syllable on multi-syllable words.

Answers

1 birth
2 'infancy
3 'childhood
4 ado'lescence
5 'adulthood
6 middle 'age
7 death

Exercise D

Write the words *infant* and *infancy* on the board. Elicit that one is the noun for person and the other is the noun for stage. Add these above – see the table in Answers. Set for pairwork. Feed back onto the board.

Answers

person	stage
infant	infancy
adolescent	adolescence
child	childhood
adult	adulthood

Exercise E

Explain the rubric. You may have to teach the word *theory*. Teach the pronunciation as well. Help students find the first theory.

1 Set for pairwork. Feed back orally.
2 General discussion.

Answers

The theories are:

1 We ask ourselves, 'Who am I?' throughout our lives.
2 There are identity crises at every age. (Erikson)
3 Brains develop in a predictable way during stages of life. (Piaget)

Closure

Point out that you are going to look at Erikson's and Piaget's theories in more detail in the rest of this theme. Check that students can recognise the green words from the stressed syllables, e.g., you say *les* and the students say *adolescent / adolescence*.

Lesson 2: Listening

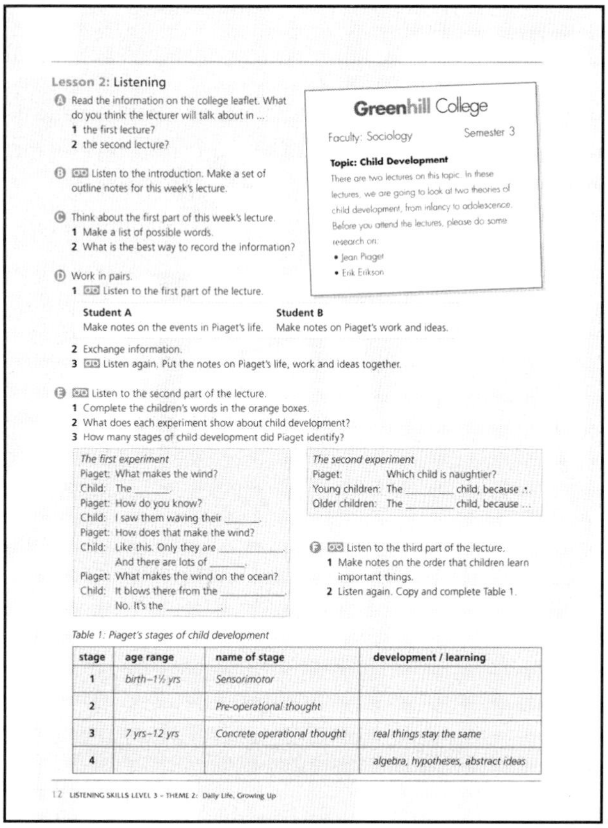

Lesson 2: Listening

A Read the information on the college leaflet. What do you think the lecturer will talk about in ...
1 the first lecture?
2 the second lecture?

Greenhill College
Faculty: Sociology Semester 3
Topic: Child Development
There are two lectures on this topic. In these lectures, we are going to look at two theories of child development, from infancy to adolescence. Before you attend the lectures, please do some research on:
• Jean Piaget
• Erik Erikson

B Listen to the introduction. Make a set of outline notes for this week's lecture.

C Think about the first part of this week's lecture.
1 Make a list of possible words.
2 What is the best way to record the information?

D Work in pairs.
1 Listen to the first part of the lecture.

Student A
Make notes on the events in Piaget's life.

Student B
Make notes on Piaget's work and ideas.

2 Exchange information.
3 Listen again. Put the notes on Piaget's life, work and ideas together.

E Listen to the second part of the lecture.
1 Complete the children's words in the orange boxes.
2 What does each experiment show about child development?
3 How many stages of child development did Piaget identify?

The first experiment
Piaget: What makes the wind?
Child: The ______.
Piaget: How do you know?
Child: I saw them waving their ______.
Piaget: How does that make the wind?
Child: Like this. Only they are ______.
And there are lots of ______.
Piaget: What makes the wind on the ocean?
Child: It blows there from the ______.
No. It's the ______.

The second experiment
Piaget: Which child is naughtier?
Young children: The ______ child, because ...
Older children: The ______ child, because ...

F Listen to the third part of the lecture.
1 Make notes on the order that children learn important things.
2 Listen again. Copy and complete Table 1.

Table 1: Piaget's stages of child development

stage	age range	name of stage	development / learning
1	*birth–1½ yrs*	*Sensorimotor*	
2		*Pre-operational thought*	
3	*7 yrs–12 yrs*	*Concrete operational thought*	*real things stay the same*
4			*algebra, hypotheses, abstract ideas*

12 LISTENING SKILLS LEVEL 3 – THEME 2: Daily Life, Growing Up

Introduction

Revise the theories from Lesson 1.

Exercise A

Refer students to the leaflet. Set for pairwork. Feed back orally. Elicit the predictable facts.

Answers

First lecture = Piaget's theory of child development from infancy to adolescence.
Second lecture = Erikson's theory of child development from infancy to adolescence.

Exercise B

Remind students about the importance of predicting content and the order of content in a lecture. Set for individual work then pairwork checking. Play the introduction. Feed back, writing the notes onto the board.

Answers

Model answer:

<u>Child development</u>

Jean Piaget

1 Life
2 Development of ideas
3 Four stages

Exercise C

1 You might like to do this as a class discussion, writing the words on the board.
2 Elicit some ideas; confirm or correct.

Answers

1 Life stages words – *born*, *school*, etc.
2 Chronologically with dates

Exercise D

1 Put students into pairs. Remind students that you often have to listen for specific pieces of information – and ignore other information. Make sure they understand the difference between Piaget's life – the dates of life events – and his work and ideas – theories, beliefs. Play Part 1.
2 Give students time to exchange the information.
3 Play the recording again for checking.

Answers

Model answers – note that it is not important at this stage that the students' notes follow a standard form. This is covered in the next lesson.

Student A	
9/8/1896	b. Sw
uni. (Neuchatel)	natural sciences
work in Fr.	in a school
1921	returned to Sw.
	became director of studies of inst. (Geneva)
2 yrs later	m., 3 ch.
next 40 yrs	uni, research inst.
16/9/1980	d. (Geneva)

Student B
interested in birds
interested in shellfish
developed intelligence test for 5–8-year-olds
how brain develops
the biological explanation of knowledge
children solve problems at different ages
studied development of his own children

Exercise E

Give students time to read the conversations in the orange box. Don't give students any specific instructions for listening to stories like this in the middle of a lecture – see Lesson 3. You might like to pre-teach the word *naughty*. Set for individual work then pairwork checking. Play Part 2. Feed back orally.

Answers

1 Answers in italics
(The first experiment)
Piaget: What makes the wind?
Child: The *trees*.
Piaget: How do you know?
Child: I saw them waving their *arms*.
Piaget: How does that make the wind?
Child: Like this. Only they are *bigger*. And there are lots of *trees*.
Piaget: What makes the wind on the ocean?
Child: It blows there from the *land*. No. It's the *waves* ...
(The second experiment)
Piaget: Which child is naughtier?
Young children: The *first* child, because ...
Older children: The *second* child, because ...

2 Children can understand certain things at different stages of development. The first experiment shows that children only really understand things that they invent themselves. The second experiment shows that ideas of right and wrong change with age.

3 four

Exercise F

Write *speech* on the board. Ask students at what age they think children learn to understand this. Elicit answers but do not confirm or correct. Write more points on the board as follows and repeat the procedure:

an idea of the past and the future
the consequences of an action – if I drop this glass, it will break
abstract ideas like algebra
a litre of water is the same in a big bottle or a small bottle
What does metal feel like? What does a bell sound like?

1 Set for individual work and pairwork checking. Play Part 3. Feed back, numbering the items on the board in order.
2 Set for pairwork. Play Part 3 again. Feed back, building up the table on the board. Be prepared to play parts of the recording again, if students are struggling.

Answers

Model answer:

Table 1: Piaget's stages of child development

stage	age range	name of stage	development / learning
1	birth–18 months / 2 yrs	Sensorimotor	experiment – shaking things, putting things in mouth, throwing
2	18–24 months–7 yrs	Pre-operational thought	learn to speak, pretend, understand past and future
3	7 yrs–12 yrs	Concrete operational thought	real things stay the same
4	12 yrs +	Formal operational thought	algebra, hypotheses, abstract ideas

Closure

Allow students to read the tapescript on pages 52 and 53 of the Student's Book. If you like, play the recording of the whole lecture while they read. Ask some more general comprehension questions and deal with new vocabulary.

Lesson 3: Learning new skills

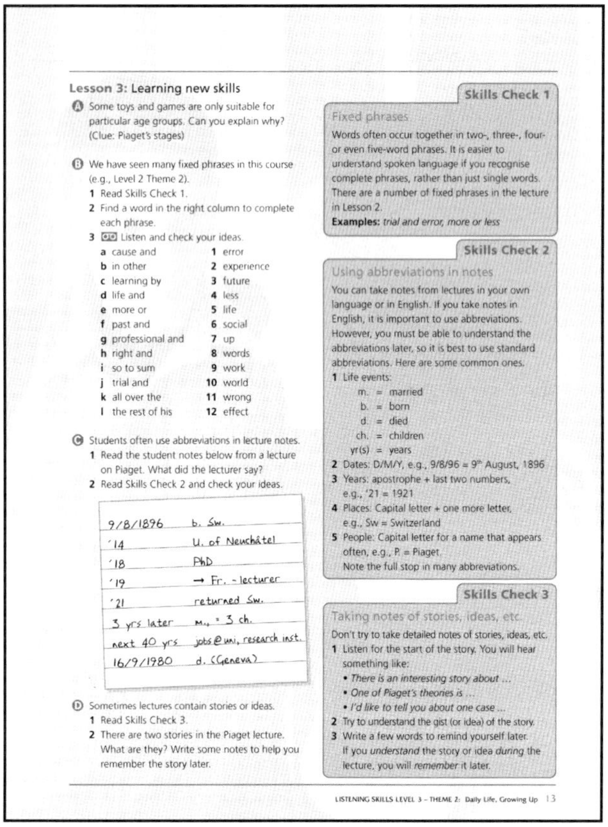

Lesson 3: Learning new skills

A Some toys and games are only suitable for particular age groups. Can you explain why? (Clue: Piaget's stages)

B We have seen many fixed phrases in this course (e.g., Level 2 Theme 2).

1 Read Skills Check 1.
2 Find a word in the right column to complete each phrase.
3 Listen and check your ideas.

a cause and	**1** error
b in other	**2** experience
c learning by	**3** future
d life and	**4** less
e more or	**5** life
f past and	**6** social
g professional and	**7** up
h right and	**8** words
i so to sum	**9** work
j trial and	**10** world
k all over the	**11** wrong
l the rest of his	**12** effect

C Students often use abbreviations in lecture notes.

1 Read the student notes below from a lecture on Piaget. What did the lecturer say?
2 Read Skills Check 2 and check your ideas.

9/8/1896	b. Sw.
'14	U. of Neuchâtel
'18	PhD
'19	→ Fr. - lecturer
'21	returned Sw.
3 yrs later	m., = 3 ch.
next 40 yrs	jobs @ uni, research inst.
16/9/1980	d. (Geneva)

D Sometimes lectures contain stories or ideas.

1 Read Skills Check 3.
2 There are two stories in the Piaget lecture. What are they? Write some notes to help you remember the story later.

Skills Check 1

Fixed phrases

Words often occur together in two-, three-, four- or even five-word phrases. It is easier to understand spoken language if you recognise complete phrases, rather than just single words. There are a number of fixed phrases in the lecture in Lesson 2.

Examples: *trial and error, more or less*

Skills Check 2

Using abbreviations in notes

You can take notes from lectures in your own language or in English. If you take notes in English, it is important to use abbreviations. However, you must be able to understand the abbreviations later, so it is best to use standard abbreviations. Here are some common ones.

1 Life events:
m. = married
b. = born
d. = died
ch. = children
yr(s) = years

2 Dates: D/M/Y, e.g., 9/8/96 = 9th August, 1896
3 Years: apostrophe + last two numbers, e.g., '21 = 1921
4 Places: Capital letter + one more letter, e.g., Sw = Switzerland
5 People: Capital letter for a name that appears often, e.g., P. = Piaget.
Note the full stop in many abbreviations.

Skills Check 3

Taking notes of stories, ideas, etc.

Don't try to take detailed notes of stories, ideas, etc.

1 Listen for the start of the story. You will hear something like:
- *There is an interesting story about ...*
- *One of Piaget's theories is ...*
- *I'd like to tell you about one case ...*

2 Try to understand the gist (or idea) of the story.
3 Write a few words to remind yourself later.
If you *understand* the story or idea *during* the lecture, you will *remember* it later.

LISTENING SKILLS LEVEL 3 – THEME 2: Daily Life, Growing Up 13

Introduction

Elicit the four stages of Piaget's theory and what happens in each one.

Exercise A

Explain that a rattle (demonstrate) is good for a baby because babies like shaking things. Elicit some more ideas for different stages. Ask students if they have brothers / sisters and ask for personal anecdotes that fit (or don't fit) into the Piaget stages, e.g., *My brother is nearly two and he likes throwing things out of his pram.*

Exercise B

Ask students if they remember these phrases from the previous lesson. Start saying some of the fixed phrases from Exercise B – but mix them up. Change the order of balanced phrases or change the final word, e.g.,

effect and cause
wrong and right
in other phrases
less or more
so to sum together

After a while, ask the students if they have noticed anything strange about the phrases. Elicit the fact that you have changed part of each phrase, and give a couple of examples of the correct structure and the phrase you originally said.

1 and 2 Set for individual work then pairwork checking.

3 Play the recording. Feed back orally. Then put students into pairs to do further work on the two-column activity.

Methodology note

There are a lot of fixed phrases in English. If students can learn these as they arise, it will help them enormously with their listening. This is because once they hear the start of the phrase, they will be able to identify it and move on to listening to the next point.

Answers

a	cause and *effect*	12
b	in other *words*	8
c	learning by *experience*	2
d	life and *work*	9
e	more or *less*	4
f	past and *future*	3
g	professional and *social*	6
h	right and *wrong*	11
i	so to sum *up*	7
j	trial and *error*	1
k	all over the *world*	10
l	the rest of his *life*	5

Exercise C

Ask students how they prefer to take notes – in English or their own language. Point out that once listening skills are good, it is often easier to take notes in English rather than a first language.

1 Set for pairwork. Don't feed back at this point.
2 Set for pairwork. Feed back orally. Check that students can quickly associate each month with a number – do a test. Make the following additional points:
   - if we don't know the exact date or number, we can put *c.* (for *circa*, a Latin word that means 'about').
   - some countries have a ready-made abbreviation – e.g., UK, US, UAE.

Answers

Ensure that students can say sentences like this during feedback:

Piaget was born on the 9th August, 1896, in Switzerland.

Exercise D

Remind students about the stories in the Piaget lecture. They are stories of two experiments he did.

1 Set for individual work then pairwork checking.
2 Make sure students know what the stories were, then set for pairwork. Feed back orally, telling each story but making mistakes for the students to correct. Then ask for suggestions for notes to help you remember the story in a few weeks' time. Reinforce the point in Skills Check 3 that the notes only have to jog your memory. It is not like a fact that has to be recorded exactly. Elicit names for the stories.

Answers

Possible names for stories:

- The wind
- The boys and the glasses

Closure

Check the fixed phrases again.

Lesson 4: Applying new skills

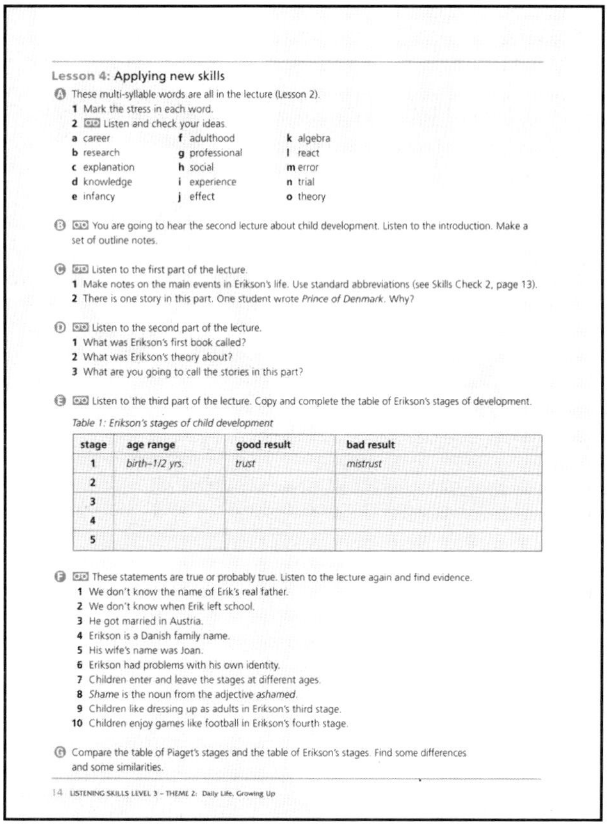

Lesson 4: Applying new skills

A These multi-syllable words are all in the lecture (Lesson 2).
1 Mark the stress in each word.
2 Listen and check your ideas.

a career	f adulthood	k algebra
b research	g professional	l react
c explanation	h social	m error
d knowledge	i experience	n trial
e infancy	j effect	o theory

B You are going to hear the second lecture about child development. Listen to the introduction. Make a set of outline notes.

C Listen to the first part of the lecture.
1 Make notes on the main events in Erikson's life. Use standard abbreviations (see Skills Check 2, page 13).
2 There is one story in this part. One student wrote *Prince of Denmark*. Why?

D Listen to the second part of the lecture.
1 What was Erikson's first book called?
2 What was Erikson's theory about?
3 What are you going to call the stories in this part?

E Listen to the third part of the lecture. Copy and complete the table of Erikson's stages of development.

Table 1: Erikson's stages of child development

stage	age range	good result	bad result
1	*birth–1/2 yrs.*	*trust*	*mistrust*
2			
3			
4			
5			

F These statements are true or probably true. Listen to the lecture again and find evidence.
1 We don't know the name of Erik's real father.
2 We don't know when Erik left school.
3 He got married in Austria.
4 Erikson is a Danish family name.
5 His wife's name was Joan.
6 Erikson had problems with his own identity.
7 Children enter and leave the stages at different ages.
8 *Shame* is the noun from the adjective *ashamed*.
9 Children like dressing up as adults in Erikson's third stage.
10 Children enjoy games like football in Erikson's fourth stage.

G Compare the table of Piaget's stages and the table of Erikson's stages. Find some differences and some similarities.

14 LISTENING SKILLS LEVEL 3 – THEME 2: Daily Life, Growing Up

Introduction

Elicit some of the fixed phrases again. Ask students to put some of them into sentences – either from the lecture or new ones.

Exercise A

Remind students that stress in multi-syllable words is not predictable.

1 Set for individual work then pairwork checking.
2 Play the recording. Feed back orally.

Answers

a ca'reer
b re'search
c expla'nation
d 'knowledge
e 'infancy
f 'adulthood
g pro'fessional
h 'social
i ex'perience
j e'ffect
k 'algebra
l re'act
m 'error
n 'trial
o 'theory

Exercise B

Students should be able to do this easily now. Play the introduction. Feed back, writing the outline on the board. Ask students what sort of information they expect in each section and in what order (ideas in brackets below).

Answers

Model answers:
Erik Erikson
1 Life (life events in chronological order)
2 Theories (stages 1, 2, 3, etc., from infancy to adulthood)

Exercise C

1 Set for individual work then pairwork checking. Play Part 1. Feed back, writing a model set of notes on the board.
2 Because Erikson thought he was from the Danish royal family (and Hamlet was Prince of Denmark – see Level 1 Theme 8).

Answers

Model answer:

15/06/02	b. Ge.
'05	mother m. Homberger = Erik H.
'20	left sch. = artist then teacher
	then ch. psy. in Au.
	m.
'33	→ U.S.
	taught @ Yale, Harvard

'39	→ Ca. = Uni.
	studied Nat. Am. ch.
	Am. citizen → Erikson
	Prince of Denmark story
'50	→ E. coast
'70	retired
12/05/94	d.

Exercise D

Give students time to read the three questions. Set for individual work then pairwork checking. Play Part 2. Feed back orally.

Answers

1 *Childhood and Society*
2 Identity crises at each stage of development.
3 Possible answers:
- How are you?
- The unexpected food

Exercise E

Follow the procedure as with the similar information about Piaget. Play Part 3, once for general understanding and again for students to complete the table. Feed back, building up the table on the board.

Answers

Model answer:

Table 1: Erikson's stages of child development

stage	age range	good result	bad result
1	birth–1/2 yrs	trust	mistrust
2	2–4 yrs	self-confidence	shame
3	4–5/6 yrs	initiative	guilt
4	early sch.	structured play	inferiority
5	adol. 13/14–20 yrs	identity	diffusion

Methodology note

This part of the lecture is difficult, but the students only have to pick out some key words.

Exercise F

Remind students about making inferences (covered in Level 2). Give them time to read all the statements, and elicit a few ideas for the first two or three. Set for pairwork. Feed back onto the board and then play the whole lecture again. Pause after the students have heard the key information and feed back orally.

Answers

Model answers:

1 It says there is no record of the name.
2 It says in *about* 1920.
3 He got married at the time he was studying in Austria.
4 It asks if that is why he gave himself a Danish family name.
5 It actually says *his wife*, then *Joan*.
6 The two stories are about his own identity crisis.
7 It says *about* in every case.
8 One word is used to define the other.
9 It says they like make-believe at this stage.
10 It says they like teamwork games at this stage.

Exercise G

Do this as a general discussion, drawing out the similar ages of the stages in some cases, etc.

Closure

Ask students to imagine they want to tell a friend about these lectures. How can they summarise the information in two sentences per lecture?

Lesson 1: Vocabulary

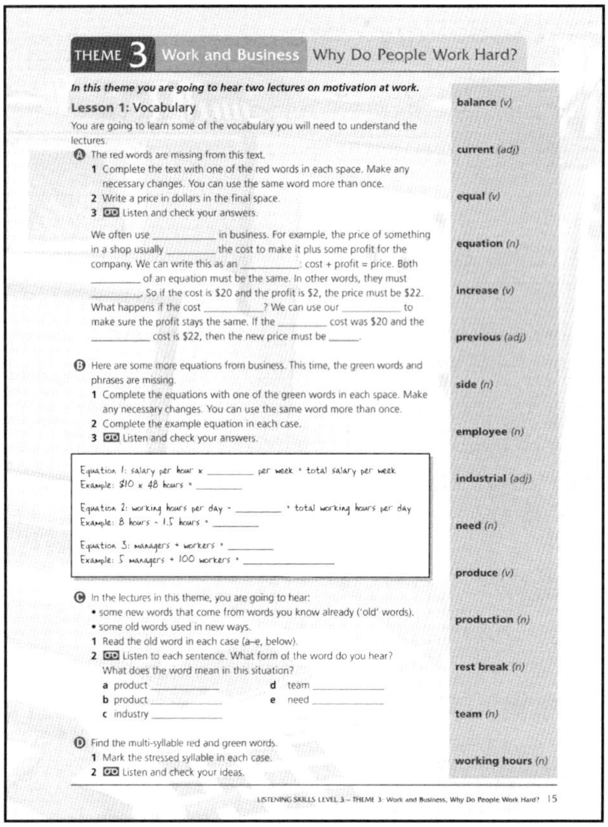

THEME 3 Work and Business Why Do People Work Hard?

In this theme you are going to hear two lectures on motivation at work.

Lesson 1: Vocabulary

You are going to learn some of the vocabulary you will need to understand the lectures.

A The red words are missing from this text.

1 Complete the text with one of the red words in each space. Make any necessary changes. You can use the same word more than once.

2 Write a price in dollars in the final space.

3 Listen and check your answers.

We often use ________ in business. For example, the price of something in a shop usually ________ the cost to make it plus some profit for the company. We can write this as an ________: cost + profit = price. Both ________ of an equation must be the same. In other words, they must ________. So if the cost is $20 and the profit is $2, the price must be $22. What happens if the cost ________? We can use our ________ to make sure the profit stays the same. If the ________ cost was $20 and the ________ cost is $22, then the new price must be ______.

B Here are some more equations from business. This time, the green words and phrases are missing.

1 Complete the equations with one of the green words in each space. Make any necessary changes. You can use the same word more than once.

2 Complete the example equation in each case.

3 Listen and check your answers.

Equation 1: salary per hour x ________ per week = total salary per week
Example: $10 x 48 hours = ________

Equation 2: working hours per day - ________ = total working hours per day
Example: 8 hours - 1.5 hours = ________

Equation 3: managers + workers = ________
Example: 5 managers + 100 workers = ________

C In the lectures in this theme, you are going to hear:

- some new words that come from words you know already ('old' words).
- some old words used in new ways.

1 Read the old word in each case (a–e, below).

2 Listen to each sentence. What form of the word do you hear? What does the word mean in this situation?

a product ________ **d** team ________
b product ________ **e** need ________
c industry ________

D Find the multi-syllable red and green words.

1 Mark the stressed syllable in each case.

2 Listen and check your ideas.

balance *(v)*
current *(adj)*
equal *(v)*
equation *(n)*
increase *(v)*
previous *(adj)*
side *(n)*
employee *(n)*
industrial *(adj)*
need *(n)*
produce *(v)*
production *(n)*
rest break *(n)*
team *(n)*
working hours *(n)*

LISTENING SKILLS LEVEL 3 – THEME 3: Work and Business, Why Do People Work Hard? 15

Introduction

Write the title of the theme on the board and pose the question – *Why do people work hard?* If students don't know, point out that sometimes people work hard in a particular situation and sometimes they don't. Ask what makes the difference. Elicit a few ideas but don't confirm or correct. Point out that during this theme they will hear some theories about this. Anybody in the class who wants to be a manager at some time in the future should work hard in this theme … otherwise they might not be a very good manager – they might not be able to get people to work hard for them.

Exercise A

Remind students of the ideas about managing yourself from Level 2 Theme 3, if they did this. Otherwise, go straight into the activity.

Write the following on the board: *10 + 17 = 27*

Ask students what it is. Check / teach the word *equation*. Point out that the word comes from *equal* because the two sides must be equal.

Set for individual work then pairwork checking. Make sure students understand that they are not looking for a green word for the final space. They must actually solve the equation. Play the recording.

Feed back orally. Do some more work on the points in this text, e.g., make incorrect statements for students to correct.

You might like to point out that profit is not normally expressed as a fixed amount, e.g., $2, but as a percentage, e.g., 10%. Elicit why this might be the case – because you want to keep a relationship between the cost and profit. If you think the students would be interested, show them a different equation with a different result, as follows:

cost + 10% profit = price, therefore 20 + 2 = 22, but 22 + 2.20 = 24.20.

Answers

We often use *equations* in business. For example, the price of something in a shop usually *equals* the *cost* to make it plus some *profit* for the company. We can write this as an *equation*: cost + profit = price. Both *sides* of an equation must be the same. In other words, they must *balance*. So if the cost is $20 and the profit is $2, the price must be $22. What happens if the cost *increases*? We can use our *equation* to make sure the profit stays the same. If the *previous* cost was $20 and the *current* cost is $22, then the new price must be *$24*.

Exercise B

Make sure students realise that the missing words are the green ones this time – but that they don't have to use *all* the green words. Make sure also that they realise they actually have to solve the equations in the examples. Set for individual work then pairwork checking. Play the recording. Feed back, building up the questions on the board. If you wish, do some more equations for the students to solve; then feed back orally, to fix the new words.

Answers

Equation 1: salary per hour x *working hours* per week = total salary per week
Example: $10 x 48 hours = *$480*

Equation 2: working hours per day – *rest breaks* = total working hours per day
Example: 8 hours – 1.5 hours = *6.5 hours*

Equation 3: managers + workers = *employees*
Example: 5 managers + 100 workers = *105 employees*

Exercise C

This is a new exercise. Set it up carefully. Point out that **b** is not a mistake. They are going to hear a different derived word in this case. Set for pairwork. Play the recording. Feed back orally.

Answers

a This is Mr Jones. He is the *production* manager.
b Good morning, Mr Jones. What do you actually *produce* here?
c This is the *industrial* part of the city. All the factories are here.
d The workers have started to work as a *team*. They are producing a lot more now.
e We all have a number of *needs*. We need food and drink and love, for example.

Methodology note

The ability to understand a derived word from its root is a key skill. It is important that students learn to do this automatically and not to panic because they do not recognise the whole word.

Language and culture note

It is very unusual for an Arabic word to have two completely unrelated meanings, e.g., *table* = furniture *or* columns and rows. In fact, the new meanings of old words here are related, i.e., *team* and *need*, so they should have little difficulty working out what each word must mean in context. However, the ability to make this mental shift is a key skill. It is what the English philosopher, Billows, called *Effort after meaning*, e.g., *The workers have started to work as a team* **cannot** mean that they have started a football team in the factory. Students ask themselves what it could mean and then come to a sensible conclusion.

Exercise D

Set for individual work then pairwork checking. Play the recording. Feed back, getting the words on the board and marking the stressed syllable.

Answers

'balance	em'ployee
'current	in'dustrial
'equal	pro'duce
e'quation	pro'duction
in'crease	'working
'previous	

Closure

Say some of the red and green multi-syllable words. Exaggerate the stressed syllable and 'swallow' the rest of the word. See if students can identify the words.

Lesson 2: Listening

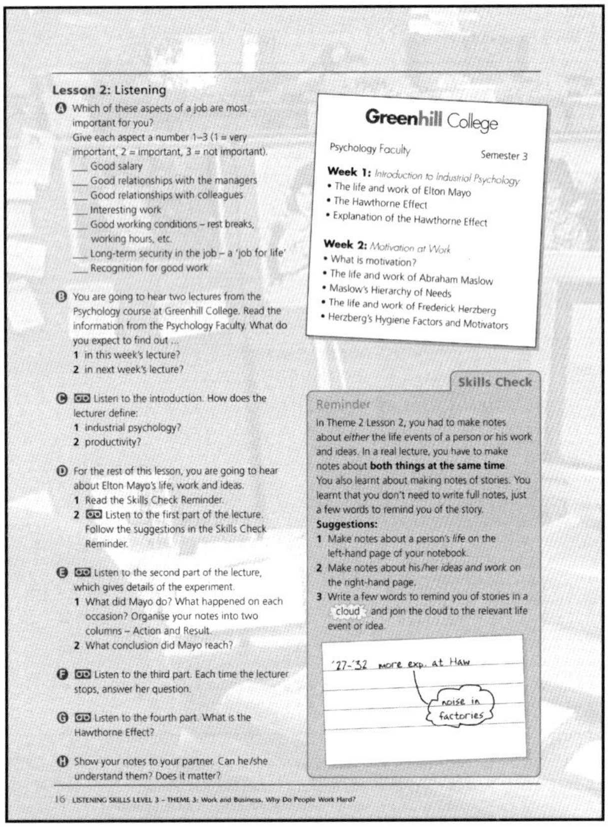

Lesson 2: Listening

A. Which of these aspects of a job are most important for you?
Give each aspect a number 1–3 (1 = very important, 2 = important, 3 = not important).
__ Good salary
__ Good relationships with the managers
__ Good relationships with colleagues
__ Interesting work
__ Good working conditions – rest breaks, working hours, etc.
__ Long-term security in the job – a 'job for life'
__ Recognition for good work

B. You are going to hear two lectures from the Psychology course at Greenhill College. Read the information from the Psychology Faculty. What do you expect to find out ...
1 in this week's lecture?
2 in next week's lecture?

C. Listen to the introduction. How does the lecturer define:
1 industrial psychology?
2 productivity?

D. For the rest of this lesson, you are going to hear about Elton Mayo's life, work and ideas.
1 Read the Skills Check Reminder.
2 Listen to the first part of the lecture. Follow the suggestions in the Skills Check Reminder.

E. Listen to the second part of the lecture, which gives details of the experiment.
1 What did Mayo do? What happened on each occasion? Organise your notes into two columns – Action and Result.
2 What conclusion did Mayo reach?

F. Listen to the third part. Each time the lecturer stops, answer her question.

G. Listen to the fourth part. What is the Hawthorne Effect?

H. Show your notes to your partner. Can he/she understand them? Does it matter?

Greenhill College
Psychology Faculty — Semester 3

Week 1: *Introduction to Industrial Psychology*
- The life and work of Elton Mayo
- The Hawthorne Effect
- Explanation of the Hawthorne Effect

Week 2: *Motivation at Work*
- What is motivation?
- The life and work of Abraham Maslow
- Maslow's Hierarchy of Needs
- The life and work of Frederick Herzberg
- Herzberg's Hygiene Factors and Motivators

Skills Check

Reminder

In Theme 2 Lesson 2, you had to make notes about *either* the life events of a person *or* his work and ideas. In a real lecture, you have to make notes about **both things at the same time**.
You also learnt about making notes of stories. You learnt that you don't need to write full notes, just a few words to remind you of the story.

Suggestions:
1 Make notes about a person's *life* on the left-hand page of your notebook.
2 Make notes about his/her *ideas and work* on the right-hand page.
3 Write a few words to remind you of stories in a cloud and join the cloud to the relevant life event or idea.

'27–'32 more exp. at Haw
noise in factories

16 LISTENING SKILLS LEVEL 3 – THEME 3: Work and Business, Why Do People Work Hard?

Methodology notes

1 From this point onwards, the lectures are quite challenging in terms of length and complexity. This is because students at this level should be able to cope with this degree of complexity. Also, it is to prepare students for the inevitable loss of understanding that will happen to them in a real-life lecture. The idea is to give students lots of practice in getting lost and then finding an entry point back into the lecture. Point out that the structure of the lecture – which can be deduced from outlines and from the introduction – gives the students lots of access points in case they get lost. For example, in this case they know the lecture will be about the life and work of Elton Mayo first and then about the Hawthorne Effect. If they get lost in the information about his life, they can wait and get back into the lecture when the topic switches to the Hawthorne Effect – so they should listen for the key word *Hawthorne*.

2 There are easy and more difficult parts of this lecture and the one in Lesson 4. If you feel your students will really struggle with the difficult bits (the hypothesis and theory content), focus mainly on the factual (the lives of the theorists and the experiment in Lecture 1) and spend far less time on the theory. You might even let students follow these parts with the transcripts.

Introduction

Remind students of some of the green words from the previous lesson. Elicit example sentences with each one.

Exercise A

Set for pairwork or group work. Make sure students understand each item. Feed back onto the board, trying to reach a consensus. If you can't reach one, point this out – different people think different things are important. Leave the results on the board and return to it in the Closure.

Answers

There are no right answers, of course, but you might like to point out that in surveys, men often put salary and security top, whereas women often put good relationships and recognition top.

Exercise B

Exploit the college handout. Make sure students can find their way around it, e.g., *What does this document show?* but do not, of course, pre-teach any of the items.

Set for pairwork. Feed back orally. Elicit the fact that this document helps you to predict the order of information in the lecture – a vital skill (see Methodology note 2 above).

Possible answers

1 about Mayo, Hawthorne Effect
2 about Maslow and Herzberg and their ideas, i.e., Hierarchy of Needs, Hygiene Factors and Motivators

Exercise C

Set for individual work then pairwork checking. Play the introduction. Feed back, writing the definitions on the board. Also, make sure that students realise that the introduction gives them the order of content in the lecture.

Elicit the example the lecturer gives of productivity. If you wish, work out with the students the percentage, i.e., 6 items instead of 5 items = 1 item more = 1 out of 5 = 1/5 = 20% more productivity.

Answers

1 the study of the way people think about work and the effects of working conditions on productivity
2 the amount of work that a person does in one time period, e.g., one day

Language and culture note

Many scientific terms derived from Greek are the same in Arabic. For example, the word *psychology* should not cause any problems here (Arabic = *sikolo'gia*).

Exercise D

1 Set for individual work then pairwork checking. Work through the Skills Check carefully, showing the ideas on the board. Make sure students realise they have to add to each side throughout the lecture, i.e., not all the information about Mayo's life is grouped into one section of the lecture.
2 Set for individual work then pairwork checking. Play Part 1. Feed back, building up a model set of notes on the board. Elicit the story (actually a digression – see Lesson 3) and the possible notes you could write in a cloud.

Answers

Possible layout in students' notebooks:

left-hand page		right-hand page
26/12/1880	b. Austral.	
1901	moved to UK	
1923	moved to USA	
	teacher at U. of Penn.	
	became prof. at Ha. Bus. Sch.	
1924–1927	exp. at Haw.	Does light affect level of prod.? Found there was no change
'27–'32	more exp. at Haw.	Does tiredness affect level of prod.?
		noise in factories

Exercise E

1 Set for individual work then pairwork checking. Point out that students only have to get the gist of the experiment – they don't have to remember the details the first time through. Play Part 2. Elicit the gist. Play Part 2 again and elicit the details.
2 Elicit the conclusion Mayo reached. Ask students if they can remember exactly what the lecturer said about the conclusion. If necessary, play this part of the recording again. Finally, elicit *at this point*. Ask students what it means or suggests – that he changed his mind later.

Answers

1 Model answer:

Action	Result
5 min breaks, 1 a.m., 1 p.m.	prod. ↑ .
→ 10 min	prod. ↑ . ↑ .
+ 4 breaks	rhythm broken; prod. ↘
– 4 breaks	prod. ↑ .
leave @ 4.30 (not 5.00)	prod. ↑ .
leave @ 4.00	prod. ≠ ↘

2 He concluded that tiredness had an effect on productivity / that a shorter working day and regular rest breaks were the key to increasing productivity.

Exercise F

Set for individual work. Play Part 3. At each pause, elicit some ideas from students, then continue. In particular, elicit ideas at the end to answer the final question.

Answers

The answers are on the recording in each case, except of course the last question, which is answered in the next part.

Methodology note

Students may find Exercise F very difficult. Do not put anyone on the spot by asking them to actually answer the questions, if they are not ready to do so. After all, they would not be put on the spot in most cases in a real lecture. Treat the questions as rhetorical in this case and do not hold the pause. However, if students want to answer, it is a good way of checking comprehension and giving them a chance to show their reasoning powers.

Exercise G

Set for individual work then pairwork checking. Make sure students are still taking notes onto the double page of their notebook. Play Part 4. Elicit and write the effect on the board. Elicit the secondary idea as well.

Answers

Hawthorne Effect = Workers increase productivity because managers value their work.
Secondary idea = People need to organise their own work in a way that will be interesting to them.

Exercise H

Set for pairwork. Monitor and feed back on any general points.

Closure

1 Look again at the order they gave to points in Exercise A. Elicit any ideas from Mayo's work about this list. They should notice that the Hawthorne girls wanted recognition for good work more than they wanted good working conditions. You might like to point out that this might be a temporary effect!
2 Allow students to read the tapescript. Elicit some of the key words from the lecture.

Lesson 3: Learning new skills

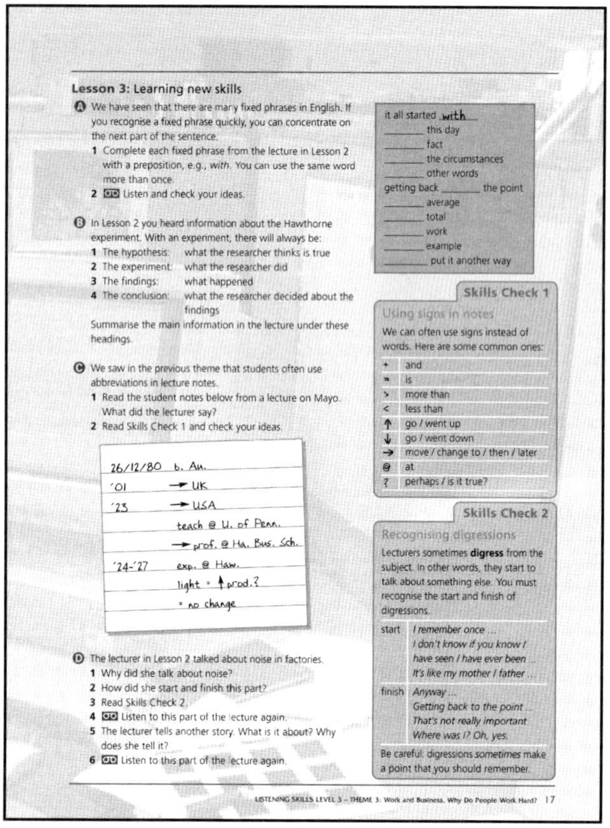

Lesson 3: Learning new skills

A We have seen that there are many fixed phrases in English. If you recognise a fixed phrase quickly, you can concentrate on the next part of the sentence.

1 Complete each fixed phrase from the lecture in Lesson 2 with a preposition, e.g., *with*. You can use the same word more than once.

2 Listen and check your ideas.

it all started with
_______ this day
_______ fact
_______ the circumstances
_______ other words
getting back _______ the point
_______ average
_______ total
_______ work
_______ example
_______ put it another way

B In Lesson 2 you heard information about the Hawthorne experiment. With an experiment, there will always be:

1 The hypothesis: what the researcher thinks is true
2 The experiment: what the researcher did
3 The findings: what happened
4 The conclusion: what the researcher decided about the findings

Summarise the main information in the lecture under these headings.

C We saw in the previous theme that students often use abbreviations in lecture notes.

1 Read the student notes below from a lecture on Mayo. What did the lecturer say?
2 Read Skills Check 1 and check your ideas.

26/12/80 b. Au.
'01 → UK
'23 → USA
teach @ U. of Penn.
→ prof. @ Ha. Bus. Sch.
'24–'27 exp. @ Haw.
light = ↑ prod.?
= no change

Skills Check 1

Using signs in notes

We can often use signs instead of words. Here are some common ones:

+	and
=	is
>	more than
<	less than
↑	go / went up
↓	go / went down
→	move / change to / then / later
@	at
?	perhaps / is it true?

D The lecturer in Lesson 2 talked about noise in factories.

1 Why did she talk about noise?
2 How did she start and finish this part?
3 Read Skills Check 2.
4 Listen to this part of the lecture again.
5 The lecturer tells another story. What is it about? Why does she tell it?
6 Listen to this part of the lecture again.

Skills Check 2

Recognising digressions

Lecturers sometimes **digress** from the subject. In other words, they start to talk about something else. You must recognise the start and finish of digressions.

start	*I remember once ...* *I don't know if you know / have seen / have ever been ...* *It's like my mother / father ...*
finish	*Anyway ...* *Getting back to the point ...* *That's not really important* *Where was I? Oh, yes.*

Be careful: digressions *sometimes* make a point that you should remember.

LISTENING SKILLS LEVEL 3 – THEME 3: Work and Business, Why Do People Work Hard? 17

Introduction

Say the stressed syllables of some of the multi-syllable words from the previous lesson. Ask students to identify the word in each case. Deal with the two key words from the lecture – *affect (v)* and *effect (n)*.

Exercise A

Remind students about fixed phrases. Make sure they understand that they need to hear a fixed phrase as a phrase and not have to understand the individual words and then put them together. Set for individual work then pairwork checking. Play the recording.

Answers

it all started *with*
to this day
in fact
in the circumstances
in other words
getting back *to* the point
on average
in total
at work
for example
to put it another way

Methodology note

Because the target words here are all prepositions / particles, they are unstressed and make hardly any additional sound in themselves. However, they often have an effect on the other words around them, e.g., *in other words* can sound like *another word*; *for example* can sound like *rexampa* and not be recognised at all; similarly, *at work* can sound like *twerk*.

Exercise B

Write the four parts of any report on an experiment on the board. Spend a reasonable amount of time making sure that they understand the four items clearly. In particular, they must be able to identify the difference between *hypothesis, findings* and *conclusion*. Work with the table as a two-column activity. Get the four parts on the board. Set for pairwork. Feed back onto the board.

Model answer

1	The hypothesis:	Tiredness affects productivity.
2	The experiment:	He increased the rest breaks, cut working hours and checked productivity. It went up. Then he returned everything to the original conditions and productivity went up again.
3	The findings:	Productivity increased even when the original conditions were replaced.
4	The conclusion:	Productivity increased because people were noticing their work.

Exercise C

Remind students of the abbreviations from the previous theme. Set for pairwork. Feed back orally. Make sure students are making full sentences like a lecturer would, e.g., *Mayo was born on the 26th December, 1880.*

Exercise D

1 and 2 Work through the questions with the students as a group. Elicit points from a number of students each time, but do not confirm or correct.

3 Set for individual work.

4 Play the part of the lecture again for self-checking.

5 and 6 Read the questions with the students then set for individual work. Play the part of the lecture again.

Do further work on the phrases in Skills Check 2, e.g., start each one and get students to complete it.

Answers

1 Because noise all day makes you tired, so maybe noise affects factory workers.

2 I remember once ... / So, anyway, getting back to the point ...

5 About girls working in a jam tart factory. She tells the story to illustrate the point that people need to organise their own work in a way that will be interesting to them.

Closure

Dictate the words / phrases from Skills Check 1 for students to write the signs, e.g., you say *and*, the students write + .

Lesson 4: Applying new skills

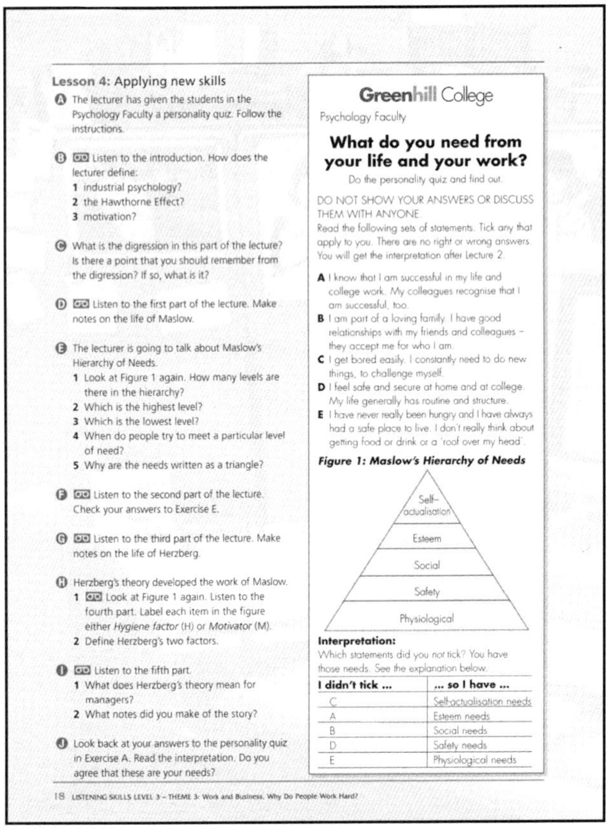

Lesson 4: Applying new skills

A The lecturer has given the students in the Psychology Faculty a personality quiz. Follow the instructions.

B Listen to the introduction. How does the lecturer define:
1 industrial psychology?
2 the Hawthorne Effect?
3 motivation?

C What is the digression in this part of the lecture? Is there a point that you should remember from the digression? If so, what is it?

D Listen to the first part of the lecture. Make notes on the life of Maslow.

E The lecturer is going to talk about Maslow's Hierarchy of Needs.
1 Look at Figure 1 again. How many levels are there in the hierarchy?
2 Which is the highest level?
3 Which is the lowest level?
4 When do people try to meet a particular level of need?
5 Why are the needs written as a triangle?

F Listen to the second part of the lecture. Check your answers to Exercise E.

G Listen to the third part of the lecture. Make notes on the life of Herzberg.

H Herzberg's theory developed the work of Maslow.
1 Look at Figure 1 again. Listen to the fourth part. Label each item in the figure either *Hygiene factor* (H) or *Motivator* (M).
2 Define Herzberg's two factors.

I Listen to the fifth part.
1 What does Herzberg's theory mean for managers?
2 What notes did you make of the story?

J Look back at your answers to the personality quiz in Exercise A. Read the interpretation. Do you agree that these are your needs?

Greenhill College
Psychology Faculty

What do you need from your life and your work?

Do the personality quiz and find out.

DO NOT SHOW YOUR ANSWERS OR DISCUSS THEM WITH ANYONE.
Read the following sets of statements. Tick any that apply to you. There are no right or wrong answers. You will get the interpretation after Lecture 2.

A I know that I am successful in my life and college work. My colleagues recognise that I am successful, too.
B I am part of a loving family. I have good relationships with my friends and colleagues – they accept me for who I am.
C I get bored easily. I constantly need to do new things, to challenge myself.
D I feel safe and secure at home and at college. My life generally has routine and structure.
E I have never really been hungry and I have always had a safe place to live. I don't really think about getting food or drink or a 'roof over my head'.

Figure 1: Maslow's Hierarchy of Needs

Interpretation:
Which statements did you *not* tick? You have those needs. See the explanation below.

I didn't tick ...	... so I have ...
C	Self-actualisation needs
A	Esteem needs
B	Social needs
D	Safety needs
E	Physiological needs

18 LISTENING SKILLS LEVEL 3 – THEME 3: Work and Business, Why Do People Work Hard?

Methodology note

As before, this lecture is quite complex but the structure is very clear, so if students get lost on one point, they can get back into the lecture later. This is good practice in tolerance of ambiguity, which they will need in a real lecture room.

Introduction

Revise the note-taking aids to date. Combine the signs from this theme with the single letters and two-letter codes from the previous lesson. Dictate words and phrases for students to render as notes.

Exercise A

Draw a triangle on the board. Elicit that it is a triangle. Divide it into sections, as in Maslow's hierarchy.

Explain that this is a triangle of needs – things people try to get in their lives. Write *physiological* in the bottom section and explain that this means *somewhere to live, something to eat and drink* – the most basic needs. Point out that when people have satisfied these needs (when they have got these things) they start to think about *safety* for now and in the future (things like a safe house and a pension). Move up through the triangle, explaining it as you go, then test students on their understanding of the triangle. *Self-actualisation* = getting everything you are capable of = total success in your life.

Explain that when you put things in order like this, with the most important at the top, it is called a *hierarchy*.

Refer students to the personality quiz. Make sure students understand that they only have to do the quiz. They don't have to look at the interpretation at this point.

You can spend a long time on this personality quiz, as the questions orient the students to think about these areas, which will be discussed in the lecture. Note the instruction not to show or discuss the answers with anyone. Point out that you are not going to ask the students to reveal their answers. It would be very difficult for a student to answer honestly in public, e.g., *I know that I am successful* or *I am* **not** *part of a loving family.*

Set for individual work. Monitor and assist as necessary. Feed back on any problems with the words but not on the students' answers.

Remind students that you will return to this later.

Exercise B

Set for individual work then pairwork checking. Play the introduction. Feed back, writing the definitions on the board.

Answers

industrial psychology = the study of how people think about work

the Hawthorne Effect = people work better when they feel valued

motivation = a way of satisfying needs through action and behaviour*

*There are many other definitions. You might like to set the students to research this point.

Exercise C

Set for pairwork. Feed back orally.

Answers

Collecting train numbers – the point, perhaps, is that people can motivate themselves to do things that other people would find boring.

Exercise D

Remind students about making notes on facing pages. Play Part 1. Feed back, writing some model notes on the board.

Exercise E

Work through the questions as a whole class. Try to ensure that students understand the correct answer to each point before moving on. It is essential for them to understand Maslow's hierarchy if they are to understand the next part of the lecture.

Exercise F

Play Part 2. Set for pairwork. Feed back orally.

Answers

Model answers to Exercise E:

1 Five
2 Self-actualisation
3 Physiological
4 When they have satisfied the level below.
5 Because most people do not manage to satisfy all their needs – they only satisfy the first two or three, perhaps.

Exercise G

Repeat the procedure for Exercise D. Play Part 3.

Exercise H

Set for individual work then pairwork checking. Play Part 4. Feed back onto a sketch of the pyramid on the board. Elicit definitions of the two factors.

Possible answers

1 H = Physiological and safety
  M = Esteem and self-actualisation
  The lecturer does not mention *Social* – it could be either. What do the students think?
2 hygiene factor = prevents workers being dissatisfied
  motivator = makes people work harder

Exercise I

Set the first question and elicit a few ideas before playing the recording. Point out that a key job for a manager is motivating people – or rather, perhaps, getting them to motivate themselves. Do not confirm or correct. Play Part 5. Go round and see what people have written as notes on the story. Feed back orally.

Answers

1 It means they must make sure all the hygiene factors are in place, but they must also make sure that employees are valued as people.
2 They should have written something like *the three builders* or *the three men and the mosque*. The story shows that it is important for people to see

the value of their work. If they see the value, they will work harder.

Exercise J

Remind students that you are not going to ask them to read out their answers. Just let them look at the interpretation and feed back on whether they agree, NOT on what it says.

Closure

Get the students to tell each other, and then you, the train numbers story and the story of the three men and the mosque, and to explain their significance.

Lesson 1: Vocabulary

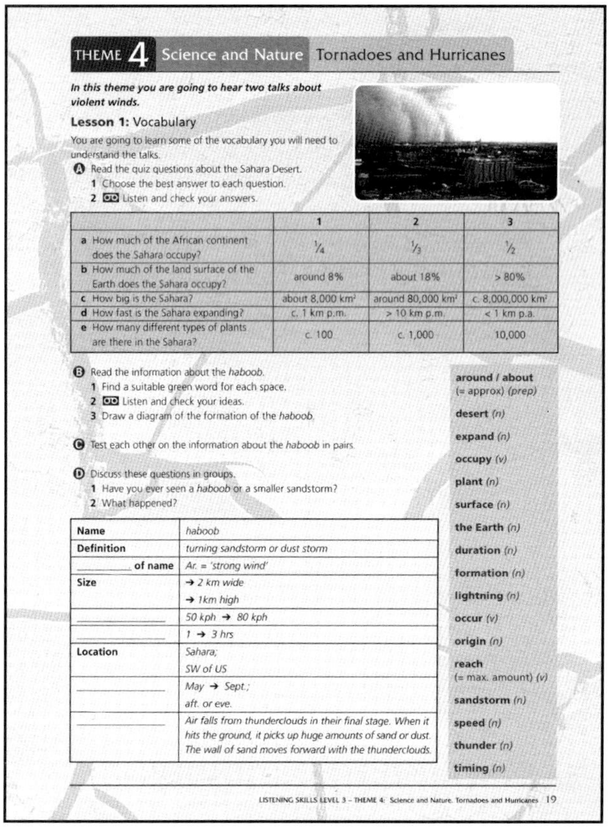

THEME 4 Science and Nature Tornadoes and Hurricanes

In this theme you are going to hear two talks about violent winds.

Lesson 1: Vocabulary

You are going to learn some of the vocabulary you will need to understand the talks.

A Read the quiz questions about the Sahara Desert.
1 Choose the best answer to each question.
2 Listen and check your answers.

	1	2	3
a How much of the African continent does the Sahara occupy?	¼	⅓	½
b How much of the land surface of the Earth does the Sahara occupy?	around 8%	about 18%	> 80%
c How big is the Sahara?	about 8,000 km²	around 80,000 km²	c. 8,000,000 km²
d How fast is the Sahara expanding?	c. 1 km p.m.	> 10 km p.m.	< 1 km p.a.
e How many different types of plants are there in the Sahara?	c. 100	c. 1,000	10,000

B Read the information about the *haboob*.
1 Find a suitable green word for each space.
2 Listen and check your ideas.
3 Draw a diagram of the formation of the *haboob*.

C Test each other on the information about the *haboob* in pairs.

D Discuss these questions in groups.
1 Have you ever seen a *haboob* or a smaller sandstorm?
2 What happened?

Name	*haboob*
Definition	*turning sandstorm or dust storm*
________ **of name**	*Ar. = 'strong wind'*
Size	*→ 2 km wide* *→ 1km high*
________	*50 kph → 80 kph*
________	*1 → 3 hrs*
Location	*Sahara;* *SW of US*
________	*May → Sept.;* *aft. or eve.*
________	*Air falls from thunderclouds in their final stage. When it hits the ground, it picks up huge amounts of sand or dust. The wall of sand moves forward with the thunderclouds.*

around / about (= approx) *(prep)*
desert *(n)*
expand *(n)*
occupy *(v)*
plant *(n)*
surface *(n)*
the Earth *(n)*
duration *(n)*
formation *(n)*
lightning *(n)*
occur *(v)*
origin *(n)*
reach (= max. amount) *(v)*
sandstorm *(n)*
speed *(n)*
thunder *(n)*
timing *(n)*

LISTENING SKILLS LEVEL 3 – THEME 4: Science and Nature, Tornadoes and Hurricanes 19

Introduction

Write the title of the theme on the board. Ask students if they know what either of the words means. Elicit as much information as you can about these types of storm, but do not confirm or correct at this stage – the aim of this is just to raise questions in the students' minds.

Language and culture note

In Arabic, there is one word, *iSaar*, which can mean *tornado* or *hurricane*. To distinguish, Arabs can say *iSaar a-tornaadoo* or *iSaar alhurkeen*. By itself, the root word from *iSaar* can mean *twist* or *wring*, so the idea of a turning storm should not be too difficult for Arabic speakers to understand.

Exercise A

If students did Level 2, they might actually remember the answers. Even if they did not, they should be able to work out what is the most likely answer.

1 Set for individual work then pairwork checking. Make sure students understand the abbreviations – these are deliberately used to revise and prepare for use in this theme.
  Note: p.m. = per month; p.a. = per annum (per year); > = greater than; < = less than.
2 Play the recording to allow students to check. Feed back, eliciting the correct answers in full sentences. This forces students to expand the notes.

Answers

a ⅓
b around 8%
c c. 8,000,000 km²
d c. 1 km p.m.
e c. 1,000

Exercise B

Refer students to the illustration. Ask students what they can see. Elicit the word *haboob*.

1 Set for pairwork. Do not feed back.
2 Play the recording. Feed back on the green words in the table. Say one of the words and get students to tell you the relevant information, e.g., *What is the speed of a haboob? The speed is from 50 kilometres per hour to 80 kilometres per hour.* Once again, this forces the students to understand and expand the notes.
3 Set for pairwork. Feed back onto the board. Elicit the meaning of the green words *occur* and *reach,* which appear in the listening but not in the table.

Answers

Name	haboob
Definition	turning sandstorm or dust storm
Origin of name	Ar. = 'strong wind'
Size	→ 2 km wide → 1 km high
Speed	50 kph → 80 kph
Duration	1 → 3 hrs
Location	Sahara; SW of US
Timing	May → Sept.; aft. or eve.
Formation	Air falls from thunderclouds in their final stage. When it hits the ground, it picks up huge amounts of sand or dust. The wall of sand moves forward with the thunderclouds.

Note: The students' diagrams should show the thunderclouds, with lightning coming out of them, then air coming down from the front of the storm and forcing sand / dust up. The thunderclouds should be moving with the sand / dust as a wall at the front of the movement.

Language and culture note

Students might recognise the word *haboob* in its specialist meaning here, or at least recognise the derivation from *habba = to blow.* Of course, the English expression *hubbub* has the same derivation.

Exercise C

Set for pairwork. Monitor and assist.

Exercise D

Set for groupwork. Feed back on storm stories orally.

Closure

Say the stressed syllable of the multi-syllable green words and elicit the full word in each case.

Lesson 2: Listening

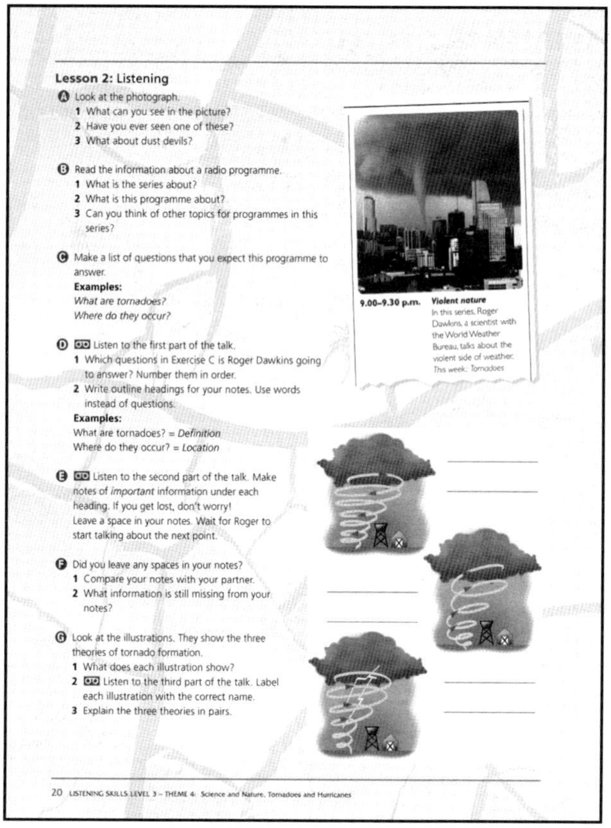
Lesson 2: Listening

A Look at the photograph.
1 What can you see in the picture?
2 Have you ever seen one of these?
3 What about dust devils?

B Read the information about a radio programme.
1 What is the series about?
2 What is this programme about?
3 Can you think of other topics for programmes in this series?

C Make a list of questions that you expect this programme to answer.
Examples:
What are tornadoes?
Where do they occur?

D Listen to the first part of the talk.
1 Which questions in Exercise C is Roger Dawkins going to answer? Number them in order.
2 Write outline headings for your notes. Use words instead of questions.
Examples:
What are tornadoes? = *Definition*
Where do they occur? = *Location*

E Listen to the second part of the talk. Make notes of *important* information under each heading. If you get lost, don't worry! Leave a space in your notes. Wait for Roger to start talking about the next point.

F Did you leave any spaces in your notes?
1 Compare your notes with your partner.
2 What information is still missing from your notes?

G Look at the illustrations. They show the three theories of tornado formation.
1 What does each illustration show?
2 Listen to the third part of the talk. Label each illustration with the correct name.
3 Explain the three theories in pairs.

9.00–9.30 p.m. **Violent nature**
In this series, Roger Dawkins, a scientist with the World Weather Bureau, talks about the violent side of weather.
This week: Tornadoes

20 LISTENING SKILLS LEVEL 3 – THEME 4: Science and Nature, Tornadoes and Hurricanes

Introduction

Test students on the *haboob*, without letting them look back at the information in Lesson 1. Use the nouns from the table in each case, e.g., *What are the **origins** of the name?*

Exercise A

Exploit the photograph. Elicit any stories about tornadoes and dust devils the students have seen.

Language and culture note

It is unlikely that any students will have seen a true tornado, but they will all have seen dust devils, little swirling clouds of dust or sand, called in Arabic *iSaar arimla* = wind of the sand.

Exercise B

Set for pairwork. Feed back orally. Check the meaning of *violent*. Elicit at least *hurricanes* for a topic of another programme in the series.

Answers

1 Violent nature
2 Tornadoes
3 Hurricanes – perhaps also the *haboob*, thunderstorms, floods, landslides; not things like volcanoes and earthquakes because the series is about the violent side of *weather*.

Exercise C

Work through the examples. Elicit another couple of examples. The students should be able to think of several, based on their experience talking about the *haboob*. Feed back, getting a list of questions on the board.

Answers

Model questions:
What are tornadoes?
Where does the name come from?
Where do they occur?
How big are they? / What size can they reach?
How fast do they travel?
How long do they last?
When do they occur?
How do they form?

Methodology note

It is important that students should be able to associate, e.g., *Where do they occur?* with *Location*, since they are likely to hear:

1 the rhetorical question, e.g., *Where do they occur?*
2 the interrogative relative, e.g., … *where they occur*;
3 the noun, e.g., *location.*

Exercise D

1 Set for individual work then pairwork checking. Play Part 1 of the talk. Feed back, numbering the relevant questions on the board.
2 Set for individual work then pairwork checking. Monitor and assist. Feed back, getting a model outline on the board. (See Answers after F.)

Exercise E

Get students to read out the rubric. Check comprehension. You might like to go through the Skills Check reminder from the next lesson at this point. Students who did Level 1 and Level 2 will be familiar with this; students who did not do these levels or an equivalent need to understand this signpost language if they are to follow the instruction to *Wait for Roger to start talking about the next point.* Remind students also about note-making points covered already (see Theme 2, Lesson 3, Skills Check 2 and Theme 3, Lesson 3, Skills Check 1). Remind them also about taking notes of stories with a word or two in a cloud connected to the point, and about recognising digression.

Set for individual work. Play Part 2. Check that students are making notes correctly. If not, explain again and restart the part. Do not feed back – see Exercise F.

Exercise F

Demonstrate how you can make questions to get missing information, e.g.,

What's the maximum turning speed?
How long do tornadoes last for?
How far can they travel?
What was the point of the toads story?

Set for pairwork. Monitor and assist. Feed back, getting a model set of notes on the board. Don't let students add to their notes, however. This is very important, as you are going to return to these notes in the next lesson. During the feedback, make sure all pens are down. At the end, ask students to make sure they bring their incomplete notes to the next lesson.

Answers

Model answer:

1. Definition
= a turning column of wind

2. Origins
Sp. = 'thunderstorm'

3. Size, speed, duration
across = 100 m → 1 km
turn = 500 kph → 800 kph
speed = 50 kph → 150 kph – (car story)
few mins. → 2 hrs
distance = 7 km → > 200 km – (toads story)

4. Location
all over world but dest. = US
central plain = T. Alley.
US = 500 p.a.
also W. Eur., Ind., Ch., Jap., Aus.

5. Timing
any time of day / m. / yr.
US = 3/4 March → July
maj. = May

6. Measurement
Fujita 0 → 5
Torro 0 → 12
1 = mild = blow down small trees
12 = super T. = move cars 100 m; damage buildings

7. Formation

Methodology note

Although this is a Listening module, not a Speaking one, asking for missing information after a lecture is a key listening skill. Don't worry too much about the accuracy of the questions, as long as the student can make clear the point that he / she needs clarified.

Exercise G

Refer students to the illustrations.

1 Elicit some ideas of what they show. Make sure students understand that each diagram shows farm buildings from the central plains of the US, e.g., Kansas. Pre-teach *spiral*. Check / teach *upward* and *downward* and the word *column* in this meaning.

2 Set for individual work then pairwork checking. Play Part 3. Feed back onto an OHT of the diagrams, or by doing a sketch of each diagram on the board and labelling it.

3 Get students to explain the theories in pairs.

Answers

1 The Downward Spiral theory

2 The Electrical Storm theory

3 The Rising Air theory

Closure

1 Ask some inference questions about the information in the talk, as follows. Say, *These sentences are true or probably true. What evidence is there in the talk?*

sentence	evidence
Tornadoes make a noise like thunder.	The Spanish word for thunderstorm is used.
Tornadoes can sometimes go faster than cars.	The tornado caught up with the car in the story.
There are sometimes tornadoes in Mexico.	The story about the toads came from Mexico.
There is no wind in the centre of a tornado.	The farmer was able to look up and see the lightning.

2 Refer students to the tapescript to check words or expressions they didn't understand / hear properly.

Lesson 3: Learning new skills

Lesson 3: Learning new skills

A Many fixed phrases are pairs of words. Complete these pairs. The first three are from the talk in Lesson 2.

1 summer or *winter*
2 daytime or ______
3 morning or ______
4 wind and ______
5 rain or ______
6 thunder and ______
7 cold and ______
8 warm and ______

B Read Skills Check 1.

1 Memorise the phrases.
2 Test each other in pairs.

How can you introduce the topic?

Today I'm going to talk about …

C Find your notes from the talk in Lesson 2. What information is still missing? Ask your teacher for the information.

Example:
You: *How fast can tornadoes turn?*
T: *From 500 to 800 kilometres per hour.*

D Read Skills Check 2.

1 Read these sentences from the talk in Lesson 2.
2 What is the missing word / phrase in each case?

a ______ don't confuse the turning speed with the travelling speed …
b ______ have seen that film of people trying to outrun a tornado …
c ______ most of them happen in just one part of the United States …
d ______ the duration of tornadoes covers a wide range …
e ______ we don't really know the exact cause of tornadoes …
f ______ where was I? Oh, yes, size and speed can vary …

E What is the most interesting / surprising thing you have learnt about tornadoes in this theme?

Skills Check 1

Signposts – reminder

Lecturers use **signpost language** to help you to understand the order of information.
Lecturers use signposts to:

introduce the topic	*Today I'm going to talk about …*
explain the structure of the lecture	*Firstly, I'm going to explain …* *Then, I'm going to describe …* *Finally, I'll give you …*
end a section	*So, we've seen that …*
begin a new section	*Now, let's consider …*
help listeners to organise notes	*There are three types of …* *Firstly / Secondly / Finally …*

If you get lost in a lecture, don't worry!

1 Leave a space in your notes.
2 Wait for the start of the next section.
3 Ask your colleagues for the missing information at the end of the lecture – or ask the lecturer if there is an opportunity at the end.

Skills Check 2

Mini-signposts

Major signposts tell you the organisation of the lecture / talk and of each section. **Mini-signposts** tell you something about the next piece of information – if you understand them.

Mini-signposts	***I'm going to …***
I don't know if you … (saw / read / heard)	tell a story / give an example
By the way, / Incidentally,	give an extra piece of information or a piece of advice
Similarly, / Again,	say something that is like a previous piece of information
In fact, / Actually,	give more detail about this information
Anyway,	go back to my previous subject
To sum up,	summarise the information from the previous section / the whole lecture

LISTENING SKILLS LEVEL 2 – THEME 4: Science and Nature, Tornadoes and Hurricanes 21

Introduction

See how many facts students can remember about tornadoes. Prompt with an area, e.g., *Speed*, and elicit information.

Exercise A

Write the first pair of words on the board. Remind students about the importance of recognising fixed phrases – as soon as you recognise the phrase, you can move on to the next part of the listening.

Set for pairwork. Feed back orally. Point out that in English many of these can only go this way, e.g., *lightning and thunder* sounds strange to an English-speaking person.

Answers

1	summer or	winter
2	daytime or	night-time
3	morning or	evening
4	wind and	rain
5	rain or	shine
6	thunder and	lightning
7	cold and	wet
8	warm and	dry

Exercise B

Refer students to Skills Check 1.

1 Set for individual work. Go round and check that students are learning the phrases.
2 Set for pairwork. Feed back orally.

Exercise C

Refer students to their incomplete notes from the previous lesson. Elicit questions from individual students. Use the model notes from the previous lesson (after Exercise F) to answer any of the questions.

Exercise D

Follow the procedure as written. If you feel the activity may be too difficult, play the talk from Lesson 2 before the students do the exercise.

During the feedback, say the mini-signposts several times so that the students get to hear them in context.

Methodology note

As this is a Listening module, there is no specific need for the students to be able to say words or phrases, such as the signposts and mini-signposts, accurately. However, since the ear monitors the voice, saying something more and more accurately may help the ear to hear it more efficiently.

Answers

a *By the way, / Incidentally,* don't confuse the turning speed with the travelling speed ...

b *I don't know if you* have seen that film of people trying to outrun a tornado ...

c *In fact, / Actually,* most of them happen in just one part of the United States ...

d *Similarly, / Again,* the duration of tornadoes covers a wide range ...

e *To sum up,* we don't really know the exact cause of tornadoes ...

f *Anyway,* where was I? Oh, yes, size and speed can vary ...

Exercise E

Whole-class discussion.

Closure

Say only the stressed syllable of key vocabulary items and get students to tell you the full word as follows:

na	tor'nado
vio	'violent
dent	inci'dentally
lec	e'lectrical
class	'classify
dam	'damaged
ser	'seriously
struc	de'structive
vel	de'velop
va	'vary
fects	e'ffects

Lesson 4: Applying new skills

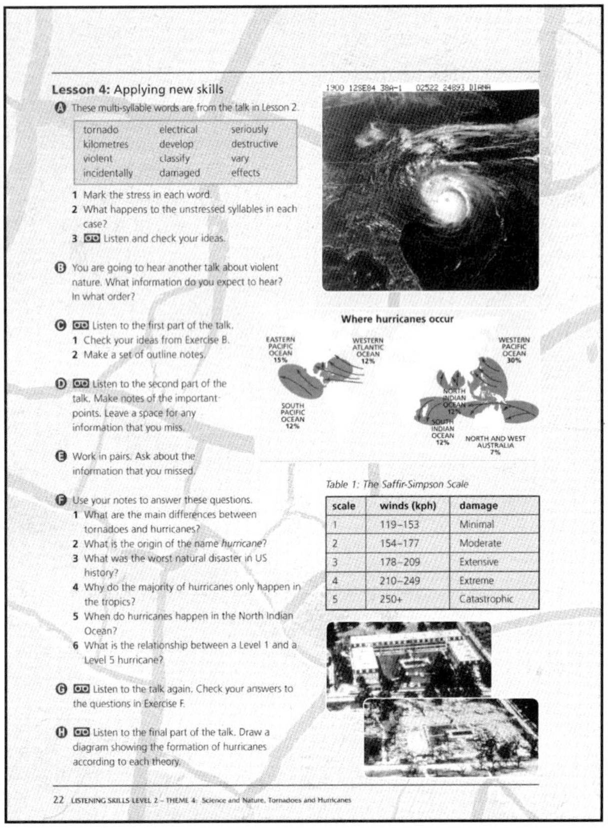
Lesson 4: Applying new skills

A These multi-syllable words are from the talk in Lesson 2.

tornado	electrical	seriously
kilometres	develop	destructive
violent	classify	vary
incidentally	damaged	effects

1 Mark the stress in each word.
2 What happens to the unstressed syllables in each case?
3 Listen and check your ideas.

B You are going to hear another talk about violent nature. What information do you expect to hear? In what order?

C Listen to the first part of the talk.
1 Check your ideas from Exercise B.
2 Make a set of outline notes.

D Listen to the second part of the talk. Make notes of the important points. Leave a space for any information that you miss.

E Work in pairs. Ask about the information that you missed.

F Use your notes to answer these questions.
1 What are the main differences between tornadoes and hurricanes?
2 What is the origin of the name *hurricane*?
3 What was the worst natural disaster in US history?
4 Why do the majority of hurricanes only happen in the tropics?
5 When do hurricanes happen in the North Indian Ocean?
6 What is the relationship between a Level 1 and a Level 5 hurricane?

G Listen to the talk again. Check your answers to the questions in Exercise F.

H Listen to the final part of the talk. Draw a diagram showing the formation of hurricanes according to each theory.

Table 1: The Saffir-Simpson Scale

scale	winds (kph)	damage
1	119–153	Minimal
2	154–177	Moderate
3	178–209	Extensive
4	210–249	Extreme
5	250+	Catastrophic

22 LISTENING SKILLS LEVEL 2 – THEME 4: Science and Nature, Tornadoes and Hurricanes

Introduction

Give some false information about tornadoes for students to correct, e.g.,

Tornadoes travel at 500 kilometres per hour.
They are 20 kilometres wide.
They bring huge amounts of rain.
They pick up cats and dogs from the US and drop them in Mexico.

Exercise A

1 and 2 Set for individual work then pairwork checking.
3 Play the recording. Feed back, getting the marked-up words on the board.

Answers

tor'nado	unstressed vowels keep full value
ki'lometres	schwa (/ə/) at end
'violent	schwa (/ə/) at end
inci'dentally	silent *a*
e'lectrical	*e* = /ɪ/; schwa (/ə/) at end
de'velop	*e* = /ɪ/; schwa (/ə/) at end
'classify	some people say *i* as schwa (/ə/)
'damaged	/ɪ/ at end; no extra syllable for *ed*
'seriously	*ou* = schwa (/ə/)
de'structive	*e* = /ɪ/
'vary	*y* = /ɪ/
e'ffects	*e* = /ɪ/

Exercise B

Students should be able to give you the full list of headings from their notes on tornadoes, e.g.,

Definition
Origins of the name, etc.

Methodology note

Active listening is about making predictions of content and then checking with the incoming message. If a student goes into a lecture on, e.g., *hurricanes*, and already has a list of probable points that the lecturer will cover, he / she is much better prepared than a student who is a *tabula rasa* (or *clean slate*). Point out to students that we normally know in advance what a lecturer is going to talk *about*, we just listen for what he / she will actually *say*.

Exercise C

1 Set for individual work then pairwork checking. Play Part 1.
2 Set for individual work then pairwork checking. Feed back, getting the structure on the board. It is, unsurprisingly, very similar to the structure for the talk on tornadoes.

Answers

Possible headings:

Definition	*Timing*
Origins of name	*Measurement*
Location	*Formation*

Exercise D

Refer students to the visuals. Elicit some ideas of what they show. Remind students about the importance of leaving a space in your notes that clearly indicates what you have missed. Set for individual work. Play Part 2. Pause the recording a few times, if you feel it is necessary. Do not feed back at this point.

Answers

See after Exercise E.

Exercise E

Set for pairwork. Feed back orally.

Answers

Model answers:

Definition

= turning wind = tornado but diff. ...

1 h. = over water; t. = over land

2 h = rain; t. = ~~rain~~

3 ? = h. > dest. than t. – (Galveston story = 37k people d., 3,600 build. dest.)

h = names, e.g., Andrew – list of names on web = www.fema.gov/kids/hunames.htm

Origins of name

Mayan (Mex.) = hurakan → Carib. = Hurican → Uni. Miami = Hurricane

Location

warm water = > 27°C so = tropics (W. Atl., E. Pac., S. Ind. oceans)

current hurricanes on web = www.solar.ifa.hawaii.edu.

Timing

Sum. but length of season varies

Atl. = 01 / 06 – 30 / 11 (maj. = 15 / 08 – 15 / 10)

N. Pac. = all yr.

N. Ind. = May + Nov

Measurement

Saffir-Simpson – 1 → 5

1 = 119–153 kph = min. dam.

5 = → 270 kph = cat. dam.

5 = 500 x 1

Exercise F

Set for pairwork. Do not feed back at this point.

Answers

See after Exercise G.

Exercise G

Play Part 2 again. Feed back orally.

Answers

1 Hurricanes form over water, while tornadoes form over land. Hurricanes are huge rainstorms, whereas tornadoes do not contain rain.
2 The name of a Mayan god.
3 The hurricane that hit Galveston in 1900.
4 Because this is where the water is above 27°C, and hurricanes only form over warm water.
5 The majority of hurricanes in the North Indian Ocean happen in May and November.
6 A Level 5 hurricane is 500 times as violent.

Exercise H

Set for pairwork. Play Part 3. Feed back, getting copies of the diagrams on the board.

Answers

1 The diagram should show hot air rising inside a column of turning air, with more air being sucked in at the bottom, the turning getting more and more violent.
2 The diagram should show the sun and Earth close together, with the sun producing an area of low pressure and electrical storms that start a turning wind.

Closure

Ask students what they found the most interesting / surprising fact about hurricanes.

THEME 5 The Physical World Natural Disasters

Lesson 1: Vocabulary

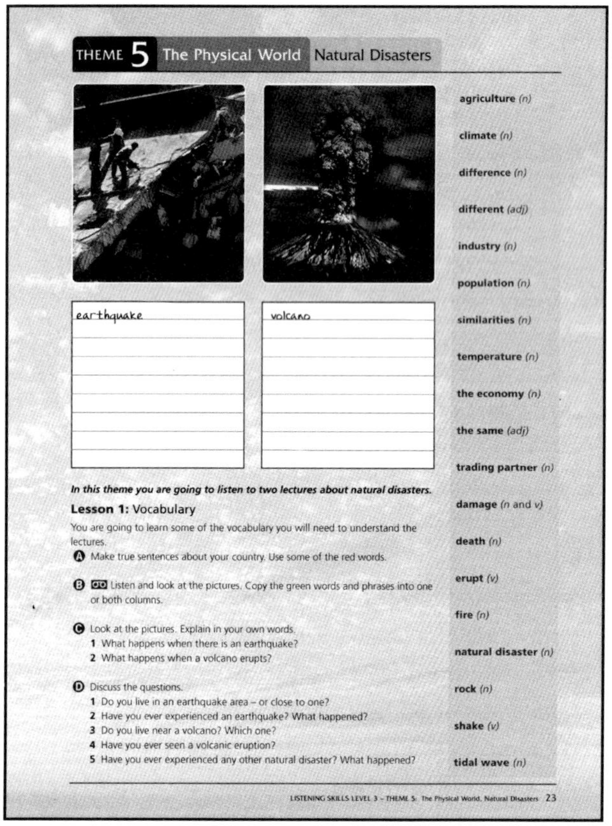

THEME 5 The Physical World Natural Disasters

agriculture *(n)*
climate *(n)*
difference *(n)*
different *(adj)*
industry *(n)*
population *(n)*
similarities *(n)*
temperature *(n)*
the economy *(n)*
the same *(adj)*
trading partner *(n)*
damage *(n* and *v)*
death *(n)*
erupt *(v)*
fire *(n)*
natural disaster *(n)*
rock *(n)*
shake *(v)*
tidal wave *(n)*

In this theme you are going to listen to two lectures about natural disasters.

Lesson 1: Vocabulary

You are going to learn some of the vocabulary you will need to understand the lectures.

A Make true sentences about your country. Use some of the red words.

B Listen and look at the pictures. Copy the green words and phrases into one or both columns.

C Look at the pictures. Explain in your own words.
1 What happens when there is an earthquake?
2 What happens when a volcano erupts?

D Discuss the questions.
1 Do you live in an earthquake area – or close to one?
2 Have you ever experienced an earthquake? What happened?
3 Do you live near a volcano? Which one?
4 Have you ever seen a volcanic eruption?
5 Have you ever experienced any other natural disaster? What happened?

LISTENING SKILLS LEVEL 3 – THEME 5: The Physical World, Natural Disasters 23

Introduction

If students have done Level 1 and / or Level 2, they should be able to say a lot about their own country now. Elicit a list of words that you can use to describe a country, before going on to Exercise A.

If they have not done either of the preceding levels, write the main title of the theme – *The Physical World* – on the board and elicit words connected with this theme.

In either case, students should be able to come up with the majority of these, with some prompting, some of which are red words (r).

agriculture (r)
border
city
climate (r) – rainfall, temperature
continent
country
desert
island
location
mountain
population (r)
region
river
the economy (r) – exports, industry (r), trading partners (r)
town

Exercise A

Set for pairwork. Feed back orally.

OR

If students in the class are from different countries, get students from the same country to work together to make a small presentation.

Exercise B

Write the subtitle of the theme on the board – *Natural Disasters* – and elicit any ideas students have about the contents. Refer students to the pictures and elicit the names of the two natural disasters depicted.

Set for individual work then pairwork checking. Play the recording. Feed back, building up the tables on the board.

Answers

earthquake
natural disaster
shakes
damage
deaths
tidal waves
fire

volcano
natural disaster
erupt
rocks
ash
damage
tidal waves
damaged
fire

Language and culture note

The Arabic word for earthquake is *zulzula*, which comes from the verb meaning 'to shake'. This means any mime involving shaking should make it clear to students what is being described. It will also be interesting when you come to the part that says that the scientific word *seismology* comes from the Greek word *seismos,* meaning 'to shake'.

The Arabic word for volcano is *burkaan*, which is clearly derived from the same source. Note: There is no /v/ in Arabic, so that phoneme had to change to another fronted consonant.

Exercise C

Set for pairwork. Feed back orally.

Exercise D

It is unlikely that any of the students can answer 'yes' to any of these questions, but they are worth asking just in case. An eyewitness account would be incredibly interesting. On the assumption that the answer will be 'no' to all the questions, though, do this as a whole-class activity, just to get the students used to hearing the target words. If you have a story to tell about the topic, tell it.

Closure

Say the text again in modified form and stop when a green word or phrase is required. See if students can complete each one appropriately, as follows:

> There are many similarities between earthquakes and volcanoes. Both can cause natural *disasters*. When an earthquake occurs in a town or city, the earth *shakes* violently and this can cause a lot of *damage* to buildings. This often leads to many *deaths*. In a similar way, when a volcano *erupts* near a town or city, the hot *rocks* and *ash* can damage buildings and kill people. Both kinds of event can also cause *tidal waves*.
>
> There are also some differences between earthquakes and volcanoes. Earthquakes usually only last for a few seconds or minutes, whereas volcanoes can *erupt* for days or even months. With a volcano, we often see *fire* shooting high into the air, while earthquakes are not usually linked with *fire* from underground. Of course, damaged buildings often catch *fire* after an *earthquake*.

Lesson 2: Listening

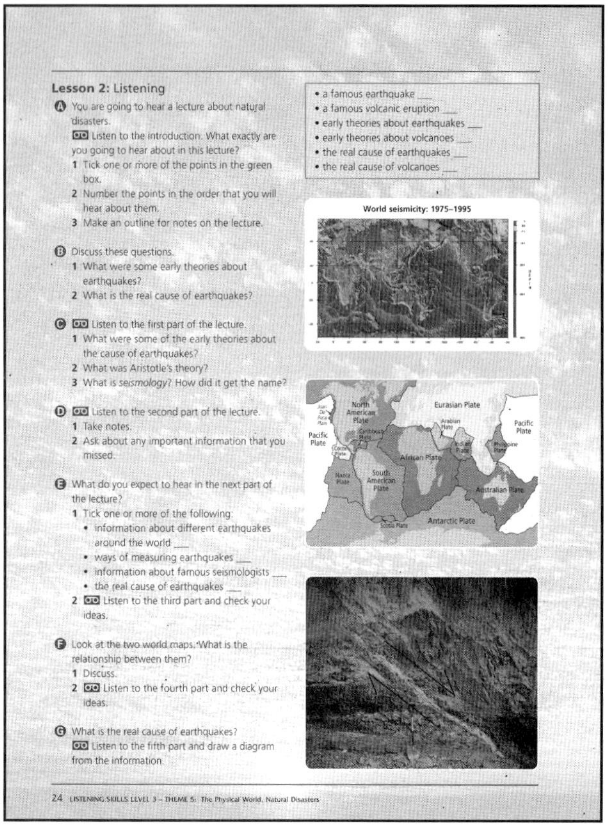
Lesson 2: Listening

A You are going to hear a lecture about natural disasters.

Listen to the introduction. What exactly are you going to hear about in this lecture?

1 Tick one or more of the points in the green box.
2 Number the points in the order that you will hear about them.
3 Make an outline for notes on the lecture.

- a famous earthquake ___
- a famous volcanic eruption ___
- early theories about earthquakes ___
- early theories about volcanoes ___
- the real cause of earthquakes ___
- the real cause of volcanoes ___

B Discuss these questions.

1 What were some early theories about earthquakes?
2 What is the real cause of earthquakes?

C Listen to the first part of the lecture.

1 What were some of the early theories about the cause of earthquakes?
2 What was Aristotle's theory?
3 What is *seismology*? How did it get the name?

D Listen to the second part of the lecture.

1 Take notes.
2 Ask about any important information that you missed.

E What do you expect to hear in the next part of the lecture?

1 Tick one or more of the following:
   - information about different earthquakes around the world ___
   - ways of measuring earthquakes ___
   - information about famous seismologists ___
   - the real cause of earthquakes ___
2 Listen to the third part and check your ideas.

F Look at the two world maps. What is the relationship between them?

1 Discuss.
2 Listen to the fourth part and check your ideas.

G What is the real cause of earthquakes?

Listen to the fifth part and draw a diagram from the information.

24 LISTENING SKILLS LEVEL 3 – THEME 5: The Physical World, Natural Disasters

Up to this point in the course, the students have learnt about the following points regarding note-taking in lectures:

- using abbreviations;
- taking brief notes of stories, ideas, etc.;
- using signs;
- recognising digressions;
- understanding signposts;
- understanding mini-signposts;
- leaving space in notes for missing information.

Remind students of these points.

Introduction

Give some 'facts' about earthquakes and volcanoes but make some mistakes. Students correct, e.g.,

[mistakes in italics]

There are *no* similarities between earthquakes and volcanoes. *They can't* cause natural disasters. When an earthquake occurs in a town or city, the *sky* shakes violently and this can cause a lot of damage to *people*. This often leads to many *volcanoes*. In a similar way, when a volcano *shakes* near a town or city, the hot *rocks* and *fire* can damage buildings and kill people. *Volcanoes* can also cause *tidal waves*.

There are *no* differences between earthquakes and volcanoes. Earthquakes usually only last for a few *years,* whereas volcanoes can erupt for *seconds or even minutes*. With *an earthquake*, we often see *fire* shooting high into the air. Of course, damaged buildings often *fall into the ground* after an earthquake.

Exercise A

Refer students to the box. Give them plenty of time to read the possible topics.

1 Set for individual work then pairwork checking. Play the introduction.
2 Set for pairwork. Feed back orally.
3 Set for individual work then pairwork checking.

Answers

Model outline – with space after 1.1, etc., for notes:

1. Earthquakes

1.1. Early theories

1.2. Famous earthquake

1.3. Real cause

Exercise B

1 Point out that the students may not have heard about any early theories yet, but what do they imagine ancient peoples thought when they heard noises under the ground and the ground started to shake? Set for group work. Feed back but do not confirm or correct.
2 Point out, similarly, that students may not have heard about the real cause yet. But what do they think is the real cause? Set for group work. Feed back but do not confirm or correct.

Methodology note

Nobody listens to a lecture about, for example, earthquakes, without thinking a little about the content. This is essential schemata activation before listening to the actual information. Allow the activity to go on for as long as students are interested in discussing the points.

Exercise C

Give students time to read the questions. Set for individual work then pairwork checking. Play Part 1 of the recording. Make sure students are making notes in the correct part of their outline. Feed back, getting model notes on the board. Make sure students understand that *shook* is the past tense of *shake*. Point out that it is the same pattern as *take / took* (but not, of course, *make*, *bake*, *wake*, etc.).

Answers

Model notes:

1. Earthquakes

1.1 Early theories

1.1.1 animals = angry so grnd shook

1.1.2 Arist. = wind (seismos = Gr 'shake' so seismology = sc. of quakes)

Language and culture note

As discussed in Theme 1 of this course, Aristotle is, of course, well known to Arab students. He is called *arstoo* and has the soubriquet 'the first master'.

Exercise D

Remind students that they have now moved on to the second part of the lecture, so the lecturer will be talking about *A famous earthquake*.

1 Set for individual work. Remind students about stories – you do not need to take full notes, just a reminder, perhaps in a cloud. Remind students also to put a clear question mark for things they miss. Play Part 2.

2 Set for pairwork. Feed back onto the board, building up model notes.

Answers

Model notes:

2.2 Famous quake

1750 Eng then – sm. quakes

1755 Lisbon (Port) = 70,000 dead - "noise, shocks, fire, smoke"

sc. in Eu. = quakes dang. so times / loc. / measure

type of rock = real cause?

Exercise E

1 Elicit ideas. Students may think that it is time for the lecturer to move on to the third part of the lecture – the real cause of earthquakes. But there are clues in Part 2 that scientists are still a long way from the real cause – they are just starting to record and measure earthquakes. Point out that recording and measuring is the stage before finding, or at least proving, the real cause. It is likely that someone will make a prediction or hypothesis and then set out to prove it.

2 Set for individual work then pairwork checking. Play Part 3. Feed back orally. Elicit the general answer – famous seismologists – and then build up some model notes. Note that the lecturer does not spell these names, so the students must just make a stab at spelling them. If you wish, play Part 3 again for students to make their own notes.

Answers

This part is about famous seismologists and an idea of the real cause.

Model notes:

1850s Mallet

1880 Milne = instr. = seismograph
US = Gilbert = lines in rock before not after quake
lines = faults

1906 Reid = fault lines after San F. quake
pressure = quake?

Exercise F

1 Refer students to the first map. Elicit where earthquakes happen. Students should be able to at least name the continents and the parts of the continents, e.g., *on the east coast of Asia*. Refer students to the second map. Students should be able to see the relationship between earthquake activity and the plates. Do not explain at this moment what the plates are, but try to elicit that earthquakes happen at the edge of the plates.

2 Set for pairwork. Play Part 4. Feed back orally.

Answers

Continents move around on plates. The plates come together in some places. Earthquakes happen at the edges of the plates – where the plates come together.

Exercise G

Refer students to the picture of the fault lines. Elicit the idea that there are two plates here, one moving under the other. Check / teach the word *friction* for the rubbing of two hard surfaces together. Tell students / elicit the fact that friction causes heat. This is important later in the theme when we talk about volcanoes.

Set for pairwork. Feed back, getting a diagram on the board.

Answers

Students should have drawn (ideally under the *Real cause* part of their notes) something like this:

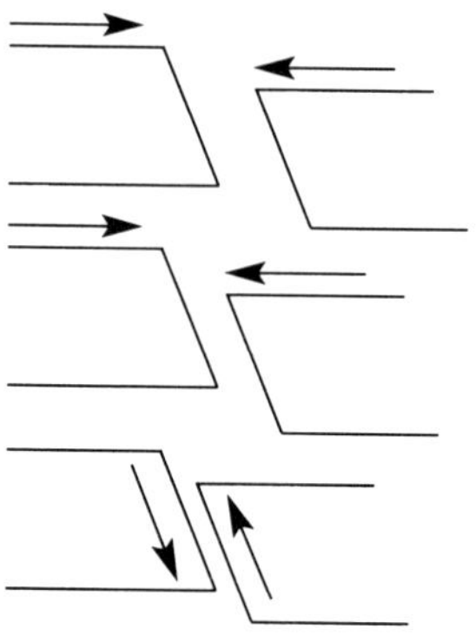

Closure

Get students to tell each other about the information in the lecture from their notes.

OR

Role-play a scene where you have not been at the lecture and you want to know the key points so you can catch up. Make lots of mistakes that the students have to correct.

Lesson 3: Learning new skills

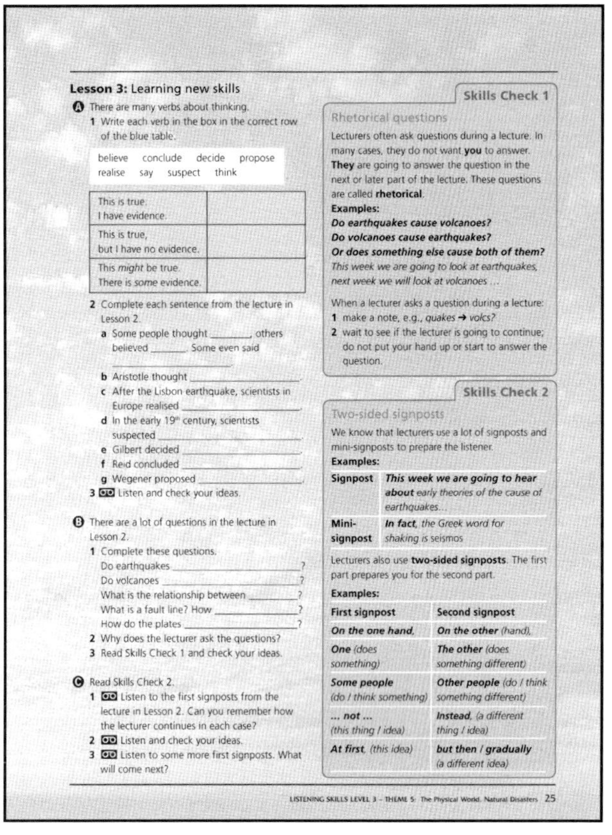

Lesson 3: Learning new skills

A There are many verbs about thinking.

1 Write each verb in the box in the correct row of the blue table.

believe conclude decide propose realise say suspect think

This is true. I have evidence.	
This is true, but I have no evidence.	
This *might* be true. There is *some* evidence.	

2 Complete each sentence from the lecture in Lesson 2.

a Some people thought ______, others believed ______. Some even said ______.

b Aristotle thought ______.

c After the Lisbon earthquake, scientists in Europe realised ______.

d In the early 19th century, scientists suspected ______.

e Gilbert decided ______.

f Reid concluded ______.

g Wegener proposed ______.

3 Listen and check your ideas.

B There are a lot of questions in the lecture in Lesson 2.

1 Complete these questions.

Do earthquakes ______?

Do volcanoes ______?

What is the relationship between ______?

What is a fault line? How ______?

How do the plates ______?

2 Why does the lecturer ask the questions?

3 Read Skills Check 1 and check your ideas.

C Read Skills Check 2.

1 Listen to the first signposts from the lecture in Lesson 2. Can you remember how the lecturer continues in each case?

2 Listen and check your ideas.

3 Listen to some more first signposts. What will come next?

Skills Check 1

Rhetorical questions

Lecturers often ask questions during a lecture. In many cases, they do not want **you** to answer. **They** are going to answer the question in the next or later part of the lecture. These questions are called **rhetorical**.

Examples:

Do earthquakes cause volcanoes?

Do volcanoes cause earthquakes?

Or does something else cause both of them?

This week we are going to look at earthquakes, next week we will look at volcanoes …

When a lecturer asks a question during a lecture:

1 make a note, e.g., *quakes → volcs?*

2 wait to see if the lecturer is going to continue; do not put your hand up or start to answer the question.

Skills Check 2

Two-sided signposts

We know that lecturers use a lot of signposts and mini-signposts to prepare the listener.

Examples:

Signpost	***This week we are going to hear about*** *early theories of the cause of earthquakes…*
Mini-signpost	***In fact****, the Greek word for shaking is* seismos

Lecturers also use **two-sided signposts**. The first part prepares you for the second part.

Examples:

First signpost	**Second signpost**
On the one hand,	***On the other*** *(hand),*
One *(does something)*	***The other*** *(does something different)*
Some people *(do / think something)*	***Other people*** *(do / think something different)*
… not … *(this thing / idea)*	***Instead,*** *(a different thing / idea)*
At first, *(this idea)*	***but then / gradually*** *(a different idea)*

LISTENING SKILLS LEVEL 3 – THEME 5: The Physical World, Natural Disasters 25

Introduction

Refer students to the maps and the drawing they made in Lesson 2. Get students to explain about plates and how they cause earthquakes. Get them to identify the nearest earthquake zone to their country.

Exercise A

Start writing the list of verbs from the box on the board. Point out that all the words come from the lecture in Lesson 2. Ask students after writing each word: *What connects all these verbs?* Elicit *thinking*.

1 Set for pairwork. Feed back onto the board, building up the table.

2 Work through the first one as an example. Make sure the students understand that these are not one-word answers. Set for individual work then pairwork checking. Play the recording. Feed back orally. Point out that lecturers use different verbs that have roughly the same meaning because they don't want to repeat words.

Answers

1

This is true. I have evidence.	*conclude; decide; realise; propose*
This is true, but I have no evidence.	*believe; think; say*
This *might* be true. There is some evidence.	*suspect*

Note: You might disagree about some of these. Point out that we can interpret some of the verbs in different ways. In the case of *think*, if we stress the verb, i.e., *I* ***think*** *it's true*, it means we are unsure.

2 a Some people thought *they were snakes*, others believed *they were turtles*. Some even said *they were giant spiders*.

b Aristotle thought *there were huge winds under the earth that sometimes caused the ground to shake*.

c After the Lisbon earthquake, scientists in Europe *realised that earthquakes could be very dangerous*.

d In the early 19th century, scientists suspected *that there was something about the geology in particular places that led to earthquakes*.

e Gilbert decided *that fault lines in rocks came* before *the earthquake, not after it*.

f Reid concluded *that pressure builds up along a fault line and is eventually released as an earthquake*.

g Wegener proposed *a startling theory*.

Exercise B

1 Elicit possible questions from the class working together.

2 Elicit ideas but do not confirm or correct.

3 Refer students to Skills Check 1.

Answers

Possible questions:

Do earthquakes cause volcanoes?

Do volcanoes cause earthquakes?

What is the relationship between them / earthquakes and volcanoes?

What is a fault line? How does it occur?

How do the plates move?

Exercise C

1 Refer students to the first part of Skills Check 2. Remind them about the signposts and, particularly, the mini-signposts from previous themes as follows:

mini-signposts	*I'm going to …*
I don't know if you (saw / read / heard) …	tell a story / give an example
By the way, / Incidentally,	give an extra piece of information or a piece of advice
Similarly, / Again,	say something that is like a previous piece of information
In fact, / Actually,	give more detail about this information
Anyway,	go back to my previous subject
To sum up,	summarise the information from the previous section / the whole lecture

Refer students to the second part of Skills Check 2. Give the first one as an example – this does not appear in the lecture in Lesson 2 or on the recording. Set for pairwork. Do not confirm or correct.

2 Play the recording. Feed back, getting the sentences on the board.

3 Set for individual work then pairwork checking. Play the recording. Elicit ideas from a number of students.

Show that other words are possible in some cases, especially:

one – the other = two possibilities
one – another = more than two possibilities
most – some = relationship in terms of numbers or importance

Answers

1 and 2

first signpost		second signpost	
One	*plate is trying to move north, for example.*	*The other*	*plate is trying to move south.*
Some people	*thought there were snakes underground.*	*Other people*	*believed there were turtles.*
The continents were **not**	*fixed in their position on the globe.*	**Instead,**	*they were moving around on huge plates.*
At first,	*other scientists laughed at Wegener's ideas,*	***but gradually***	*people found more and more evidence for his plate theory.*

3

on the recording		*possible ending …*	
1 On the one hand,	I want to go out this evening.	On the other (hand),	***I should finish my assignment.***
2 One	parent wants his son to be a doctor.	The other	***parent wants him to be a lawyer.***
3 Some people	like meat.	Other people	***prefer fish.***
4 I did not	wait for the person to call me.	Instead,	***I called the person.***
5 At first,	nobody believed him,	but gradually	***they realised he was telling the truth.***

Closure

Say the stressed syllabus of some of the key words from the lecture. See if students can work out the word. If they can't work it out at first, put it in a context.

los (/lɒs/)	*philosopher*	wit (/wɪt/)	*eyewitness*
ast (/ɑːst/)	*disaster*	mol (/mɒl/)	*seismologist*
lay (/leɪ/)	*relationship*	pre (/pre/)	*pressure*
grou (/graʊ/)	*underground*	gra (/græ/)	*gradually*
sha (/ʃeɪ/)	*shaking*	fric (/frɪk/)	*friction*

Lesson 4: Applying new skills

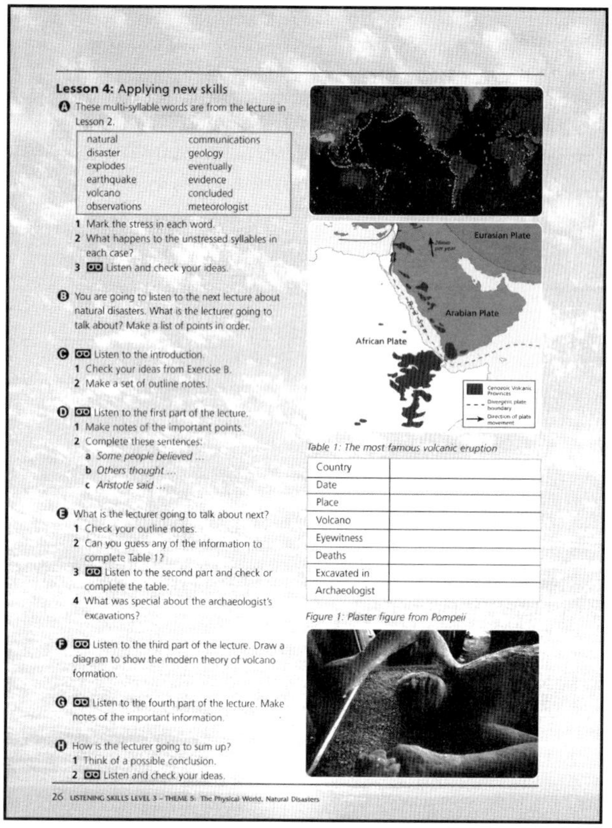

Lesson 4: Applying new skills

A These multi-syllable words are from the lecture in Lesson 2.

natural	communications
disaster	geology
explodes	eventually
earthquake	evidence
volcano	concluded
observations	meteorologist

1 Mark the stress in each word.
2 What happens to the unstressed syllables in each case?
3 Listen and check your ideas.

B You are going to listen to the next lecture about natural disasters. What is the lecturer going to talk about? Make a list of points in order.

C Listen to the introduction.
1 Check your ideas from Exercise B.
2 Make a set of outline notes.

D Listen to the first part of the lecture.
1 Make notes of the important points.
2 Complete these sentences:
a *Some people believed ...*
b *Others thought ...*
c *Aristotle said ...*

E What is the lecturer going to talk about next?
1 Check your outline notes.
2 Can you guess any of the information to complete Table 1?
3 Listen to the second part and check or complete the table.
4 What was special about the archaeologist's excavations?

F Listen to the third part of the lecture. Draw a diagram to show the modern theory of volcano formation.

G Listen to the fourth part of the lecture. Make notes of the important information.

H How is the lecturer going to sum up?
1 Think of a possible conclusion.
2 Listen and check your ideas.

Table 1: The most famous volcanic eruption

Country	
Date	
Place	
Volcano	
Eyewitness	
Deaths	
Excavated in	
Archaeologist	

Figure 1: Plaster figure from Pompeii

26 LISTENING SKILLS LEVEL 3 – THEME 5: The Physical World, Natural Disasters

Introduction

Write the first half of the two-sided signposts from Lesson 3 on the board. Elicit the second half. Elicit complete sentences with the two-sided signposts.

Exercise A

1 Set for individual work then pairwork checking.
2 Set for pairwork.
3 Play the recording. Feed back, marking the stress and pointing out the effects on other syllables.

Answers

'natural	silent letter; schwa (/ə/) in last syllable
di'saster	schwa (/ə/) in last syllable
ex'plodes	
'earthquake	
vol'cano	
obser'vations	schwa (/ə/) in last syllable
communi'cations	schwa (/ə/) in first and last syllable
ge'ology	second *o* to schwa (/ə/)
e'ventually	schwa (/ə/) in penultimate syllable
'evidence	schwa (/ə/) in last syllable
con'cluded	schwa (/ə/) in first syllable
meteo'rologist	schwa (/ə/) in penultimate syllable

Exercise B

Set for pairwork. Students should be able to remember or work out from the previous lecture the information and the order. Do not feed back.

Exercise C

Set for pairwork. Play the introduction. Feed back, getting the model outline on the board.

Answers

Model outline:

1. Volcanoes
- *1.1 Origins of name?*
- *1.2 Most famous?*
  - *1.2.1. when? / where?*
  - *1.2.2. why famous?*
- *1.3 How appear?*
- *1.4 How long to form?*
- *1.5 Relationship: Quakes + Volcanoes*

Exercise D

1 Set for individual work then pairwork checking.
2 Set for pairwork. Feed back orally.

Answers

1 Model notes:
volc = island in Med.
peo. saw fire from Vulcan's shop undergrnd
theories:

1 *fire undergrnd*
2 *fire under whole Earth*
3 *Aris = wind = broke thru' earth = volc.*

2 a Some people believed volcanoes were the flames from underground fires.
  b Others thought there was fire under the whole of the Earth.
  c Aristotle said there were winds rushing around under the Earth. These winds caused earthquakes and, when they broke through the Earth, they caused volcanoes.

Exercise E

1 Set for pairwork. Feed back orally.
2 Refer students to the table. Elicit ideas. Obviously they will only know, at most, one or two of the pieces of information here, but it is important that they realise what they are looking for in each section, e.g., *Eyewitness = a person*; *Deaths = a number*.
3 Set for individual work then pairwork checking. Play Part 2. Feed back onto an OHT or by building up the table on the board.
4 Set for pairwork. Feed back orally.

Answers

1 Students should be able to work out that the next part is about the most famous eruption – with when and where first, then why.
2 Answers depend on students.
3 Model answer:

Country	*Italy*
Date	*79 C.E.*
Place	*Pompeii*
Volcano	*Vesuvius*
Eyewitness	*Pliny*
Deaths	*3,000*
Excavated in	*1860*
Archaeologist	*Fiorelli*

4 The making of the plaster models – see Figure 1.

Exercise F

Set for individual work then pairwork checking. Play Part 3. Feed back, getting a model diagram on the board.

Answers

The diagram should look something like this:

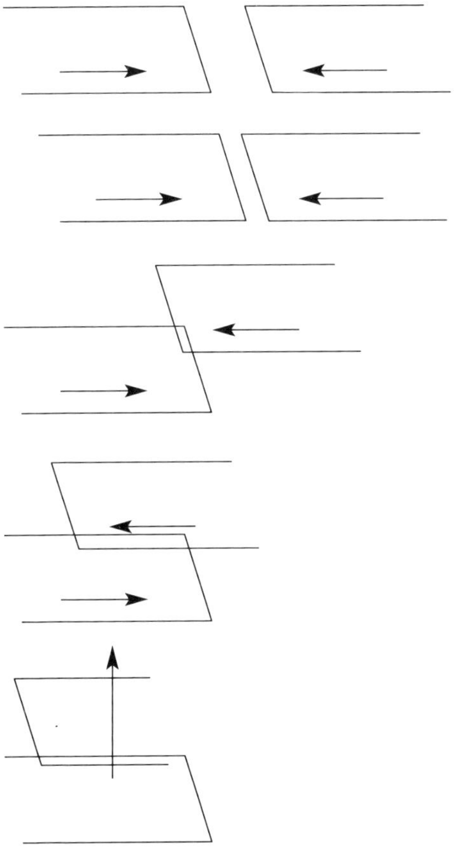

Exercise G

Set for individual work then pairwork checking. Feed back, getting a model set of notes on the board. Get students to ask you about information they missed or can't spell.

Answers

Model notes:
How form?
Most = mill. of years but some quickly

1943 Paricutin, Mexico – donkey story / ground rising up, smoke, smell
336 m high in one year
8 yrs → 25 km²
1963 Surtsey, Iceland (name of fire giant)
130 m in 6 m
4 yrs → 3 km²
170 m high

Exercise H

1 Elicit possible ideas. Students should remember that the lecturer set out to talk about the relationship between earthquakes and volcanoes, so this must come out in the end.
2 Set for pairwork. Feed back orally.

Answers

She says both earthquakes and volcanoes are caused by the movement of the continental plates.

Closure

Highlight the use of two-sided signposts in the lecture, as follows:

> ***One*** *is a dog trying to get free from its chain at the moment of death.*
> ***Another*** *is a young man trying to protect an old woman from the falling ash.*
>
> ***Most*** *volcanoes form over millions of years.*
> ***Some,*** *however, appear and grow very quickly.*
>
> ***At first,*** *there were no eruptions.*
> ***Then*** *the volcano appeared above the surface, and it began to erupt.*
>
> *Earthquakes do* ***not*** *cause volcanoes and volcanoes do* ***not*** *cause earthquakes.*
> ***Instead,*** *both earthquakes and volcanoes are caused by the movement of the continental plates.*

Lesson 1: Vocabulary

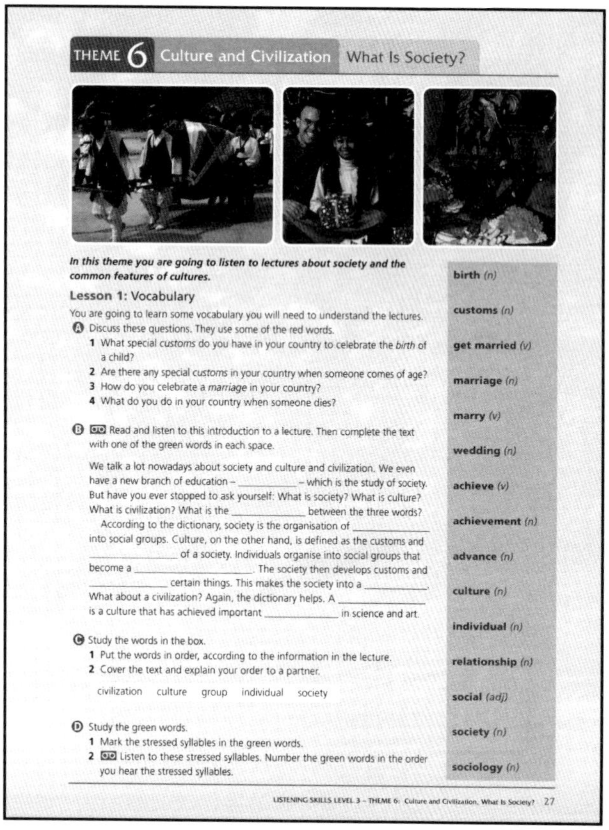

THEME 6 Culture and Civilization What Is Society?

In this theme you are going to listen to lectures about society and the common features of cultures.

Lesson 1: Vocabulary

You are going to learn some vocabulary you will need to understand the lectures.

A Discuss these questions. They use some of the red words.

1 What special *customs* do you have in your country to celebrate the *birth* of a child?
2 Are there any special *customs* in your country when someone comes of age?
3 How do you celebrate a *marriage* in your country?
4 What do you do in your country when someone dies?

B Read and listen to this introduction to a lecture. Then complete the text with one of the green words in each space.

We talk a lot nowadays about society and culture and civilization. We even have a new branch of education – __________ – which is the study of society. But have you ever stopped to ask yourself: What is society? What is culture? What is civilization? What is the __________ between the three words?
According to the dictionary, society is the organisation of __________ into social groups. Culture, on the other hand, is defined as the customs and __________ of a society. Individuals organise into social groups that become a __________. The society then develops customs and __________ certain things. This makes the society into a __________. What about a civilization? Again, the dictionary helps. A __________ is a culture that has achieved important __________ in science and art.

C Study the words in the box.

1 Put the words in order, according to the information in the lecture.
2 Cover the text and explain your order to a partner.

civilization culture group individual society

D Study the green words.

1 Mark the stressed syllables in the green words.
2 Listen to these stressed syllables. Number the green words in the order you hear the stressed syllables.

birth *(n)*
customs *(n)*
get married *(v)*
marriage *(n)*
marry *(v)*
wedding *(n)*
achieve *(v)*
achievement *(n)*
advance *(n)*
culture *(n)*
individual *(n)*
relationship *(n)*
social *(adj)*
society *(n)*
sociology *(n)*

LISTENING SKILLS LEVEL 3 – THEME 6: Culture and Civilization, What Is Society? 27

The following listening sub-skills have been covered in the course to date:

- rhetorical questions;
- abbreviations – life events;
- abbreviations – signs;
- mini-signposts;
- two-sided signposts;
- digressions;
- note-taking.

In this theme there is further practice of each of these points, in addition to new sub-skills work.

Introduction

Exploit the visual. Elicit as many related words as possible, especially the red words.

Exercise A

Set for pairwork. Feed back orally. Try to ensure that students use the additional red words in the discussion – *get married, marry, wedding*.

Exercise B

Set for individual work then pairwork checking. Feed back by saying the text and pausing for students to say each missing word in turn.

Answers

We talk a lot nowadays about society and culture and civilization. We even have a new branch of education – *sociology* – which is the study of society. But have you ever stopped to ask yourself: What is society? What is culture? What is civilization? What is the *relationship* between the three words?

According to the dictionary, society is the organisation of *individuals* into social groups. Culture, on the other hand, is defined as the customs and *achievements* of a society. Individuals organise into *social* groups that become a *society*. The society then develops customs and *achieves* certain things. This makes the society into a *culture*. What about a civilization? Again, the dictionary helps. A *civilization* is a culture that has achieved important *advances* in science and art.

Methodology note

On this occasion, the contextualising text in this lesson is the main part of the beginning of the lecture in Lesson 2. This should ensure that students are able to attack that text with confidence.

Exercise C

Define each of the following words and elicit the word in each case:

civilization	*a society that has achieved important advances in science and art*
culture	*a social group with customs and achievements*
group	*a number of people*
individual	*a person*
society	*people organised into social groups*

1 Set for individual work.
2 Set for pairwork. Feed back, building up the organisation of words on the board.

Answers

1 individuals
group
society
culture
civilization

2 Model answer:
Individuals form into *groups* that become a *society*.
A *society* develops *customs* and achieves certain things.
A *culture* that has achieved important advances in science and art becomes a *civilization*.

Exercise D

1 Set for individual work then pairwork checking.
2 Play the recording or say the stressed syllables. Feed back, getting the marked words on the board.

Answers

1	chie	a'chieve / a'chievement
2	ci	so'ciety
3	cul	'culture
4	la	re'lationship
5	ol	soci'ology
6	van	ad'vance
7	vid	indi'vidual
8	so	'social

Closure

Point out that there are many social groups in a society. Ask students what social groups they belong to. Elicit some ideas, e.g., *the college or university / a particular class in the college / university, clubs inside and outside college / university, extended family.*

Lesson 2: Listening

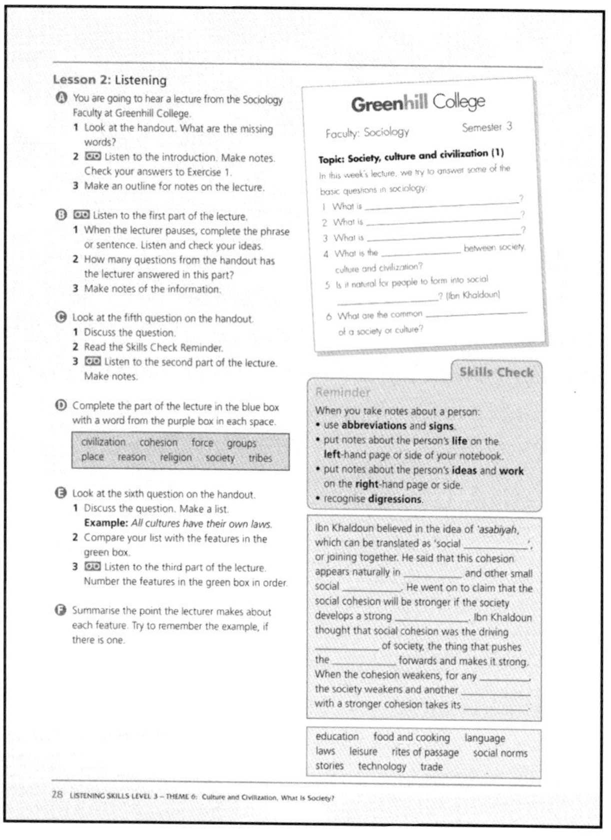

Lesson 2: Listening

A You are going to hear a lecture from the Sociology Faculty at Greenhill College.
1 Look at the handout. What are the missing words?
2 Listen to the introduction. Make notes. Check your answers to Exercise 1.
3 Make an outline for notes on the lecture.

B Listen to the first part of the lecture.
1 When the lecturer pauses, complete the phrase or sentence. Listen and check your ideas.
2 How many questions from the handout has the lecturer answered in this part?
3 Make notes of the information.

C Look at the fifth question on the handout.
1 Discuss the question.
2 Read the Skills Check Reminder.
3 Listen to the second part of the lecture. Make notes.

D Complete the part of the lecture in the blue box with a word from the purple box in each space.

civilization cohesion force groups place reason religion society tribes

E Look at the sixth question on the handout.
1 Discuss the question. Make a list.
Example: *All cultures have their own laws.*
2 Compare your list with the features in the green box.
3 Listen to the third part of the lecture. Number the features in the green box in order.

F Summarise the point the lecturer makes about each feature. Try to remember the example, if there is one.

Greenhill College
Faculty: Sociology Semester 3
Topic: Society, culture and civilization (1)
In this week's lecture, we try to answer some of the basic questions in sociology:
1 What is ______?
2 What is ______?
3 What is ______?
4 What is the ______ between society, culture and civilization?
5 Is it natural for people to form into social ______? (Ibn Khaldoun)
6 What are the common ______ of a society or culture?

Skills Check
Reminder
When you take notes about a person:
- use **abbreviations** and **signs**.
- put notes about the person's **life** on the **left**-hand page or side of your notebook.
- put notes about the person's **ideas** and **work** on the **right**-hand page or side.
- recognise **digressions**.

Ibn Khaldoun believed in the idea of *'asabiyah*, which can be translated as 'social ______', or joining together. He said that this cohesion appears naturally in ______ and other small social ______. He went on to claim that the social cohesion will be stronger if the society develops a strong ______. Ibn Khaldoun thought that social cohesion was the driving ______ of society, the thing that pushes the ______ forwards and makes it strong. When the cohesion weakens, for any ______, the society weakens and another ______ with a stronger cohesion takes its ______.

education food and cooking language laws leisure rites of passage social norms stories technology trade

28 LISTENING SKILLS LEVEL 3 – THEME 6: Culture and Civilization, What Is Society?

Introduction

Draw the following on the board, eliciting the appropriate word at each stage.

individual pin men	*individuals*
groups of pin men playing football	*(social) groups / society*
pin men round a cake and someone saying 'Happy Birthday!'	*culture*
pin men with a bicycle and a car and a beautiful building	*civilization*

Exercise A

Point out that the text in Lesson 1 is most of the introduction and first part of the lecture in this lesson. Do not let students look back at the text.

1 Refer students to the handout. Set for individual work then pairwork checking. Do not feed back.
2 Play the introduction. Feed back, building up the handout on the board.
3 Remind students that the introduction usually gives the structure of the lecture, so they should be able to make an outline now.

Answers

1 and 2

1 What is *society*?
2 What is *culture*?
3 What is *civilization*?
4 What is the *relationship* between society, culture and civilization?
5 Is it natural for people to form into social *groups*? (Ibn Khaldoun)
6 What are the common *features* of a society or culture?

3 Model outline

Society, culture and civilization (1)
1. Society
2. Culture
3. Civilization
4. Relationship (S – Cul – Civ)
5. Social groups = natural?
Ibn Khaldoun
6. Feature of soc. / cul.

Exercise B

1 Set for individual work. Play Part 1 of the lecture.
2 Quick whole-class activity.
3 Set for individual work then pairwork checking. Feed back, building up a model on the board.

Answers

1 Answers depend on students.
2 Four questions.
3 Model notes:

Society, culture and civilization (1)
1. Society
= indiv → soc. grps
2. Culture
= soc + cust / achievements
3. Civilization
= cul + imp. sc. or art
Relationship (S – Cul – Civ)
= s → cul → civ?

Exercise C

1 Set for pairwork. Feed back orally. Remind students about the social groups that they mentioned in Lesson 1.
2 Refer students to the Skills Check Reminder. Elicit some of the abbreviations and signs that they learnt in Themes 2 and 3. Check that students remember the meaning of *digression* and the way to deal with it.
3 Set for individual work then pairwork checking. Feed back, building up a model on the board.

Answers

1 Answers depend on students.
3 Model notes:

Social groups = natural?

Ibn Khaldoun = ✓

1322	b. Tun. f. = imp.	
1348	Bl. Death = killed par.	
1352	court then → Mor. / Sp.	
1375	retired. → Awlad Arif tribe (Alg.)	
- 1379	wrote Kitab al-Ibar esp. Muqaddimah = f. of soc.	social cohesion = natural + rel. = ↑ soc. coh. = driving force when soc. coh. ↓ = another society takes its place
1406	d. Cairo	

Exercise D

Set for individual work then pairwork checking. Feed back orally, pausing at the missing words.

Answers

Ibn Khaldoun believed in the idea of *'asabiyah*, which can be translated as 'social *cohesion*', or joining together. He said that this cohesion appears naturally in *tribes* and other small social *groups*. He went on to claim that the social cohesion will be stronger if the society develops a strong *religion*. Ibn Khaldoun thought that social cohesion was the driving *force* of society, the thing that pushes the *civilization* forwards and makes it strong. When the cohesion weakens, for any *reason*, the society weakens and another *society* with a stronger cohesion takes its *place*.

Exercise E

1 Do this as a whole-class activity. It is worth spending quite a long time getting students to think of things that cultures have in common, as this will help them to understand the long final section of the lecture. Help them by getting them to compare their culture with a different one. Point out that, e.g., laws are a common feature of cultures. Explain that the laws themselves are not the same, but having laws is common. Elicit at least food, customs and traditional stories.
2 Refer students to the box for the complete list. Do not explain any new words or phrases – say that these will be defined in the lecture.
3 Set for individual work then pairwork checking. Play Part 3. Feed back orally, getting the words on the board in the correct order. Deal with the new words at this stage. Play Part 3 again.

Answers

1/2 Answers depend on students.
3 The correct order is:

1 laws	6 education
2 social norms	7 leisure
3 trade	8 stories
4 technology	9 food and cooking
5 language	10 rites of passage

Exercise F

Set for pairwork. Feed back orally.

Closure

Give examples from your own culture in each of the 10 areas in Exercise F where you know things are different in the students' culture(s).

Ask students to give examples of things that are special to their culture.

Lesson 3: Learning new skills

Lesson 3: Learning new skills

A Read these sentences from the lecture (Lesson 2).

1 Think of a suitable word or words to complete each fixed phrase.

2 Listen and check your ideas.

a ______ the dictionary, society is the organisation of individuals into groups.
b Culture, on the other hand, is ______ the customs and achievements of a society.
c Incidentally, the Khalduniyah area in Tunis has hardly changed since ______.
d The death of his parents had a deep effect on Ibn Khaldoun, as ______.
e That's about a third of the population at the time. Imagine ______. 1 in 3 people died.
f The form of education ______ the society.
g People have time for leisure. In ______, they are not working every ______ of the ______.
h English people call French people 'frogs' because some French people eat frogs' legs. In ______, French people used to call English people *le rote boeuf*, or the roast beef, because they ate roast beef.
i The ______ that traditional food and methods of cooking are very important to a cultural group.

B Read these sentences from the lecture.

1 What is the important difference between Sentences A and B?

A	B
Ibn Khaldoun was born in Tunis in 1332.	Social cohesion appears naturally in small social groups.
Ibn Khaldoun's father was an important man.	Social cohesion will be stronger if the society develops a strong religion.
When Ibn Khaldoun was only 16, the Black Death killed both his parents.	Social cohesion is the driving force of society. When the cohesion weakens, for any reason, the society weakens.

2 Read Skills Check 1. Check your answers.

3 Listen to a section of the lecture again. How does the lecturer show that Sentences B are Ibn Khaldoun's opinion?

Skills Check 1

Distinguishing fact from opinion

Lecturers often give:

- **facts** about a famous person.
- the famous **person's opinions**.

It is usually quite easy to distinguish between facts and opinions.

Examples:

Facts	**Opinions**
Ibn Khaldoun was born in Tunis in 1332.	*He thought that social cohesion is the driving force of society.*

Listen for **introductory verbs**:

He / she ***thought / claimed / said / believed*** ...

But be careful. Sometimes lecturers do not use an introductory verb.

Example:

When the cohesion weakens, for any reason, the society weakens. = opinion

C Read these words from the lecture.

... *the death of his parents from the Black Death had a deep effect on Ibn Khaldoun.*

1 Is this a fact or an opinion?

2 If it is an opinion, whose opinion – Ibn Khaldoun's or the lecturer's?

3 Read Skills Check 2, then explain your answer.

Skills Check 2

Whose opinion?

Lecturers sometimes give their **own opinion** about information in the lecture. You must identify the lecturer's own opinions.

Example:

Introduction	**Opinion**
I believe / I'm sure / No doubt / Obviously,	*the death of his parents from the Black Death had a deep effect on Ibn Khaldoun.*

D Work in groups.

Listen again to the last part of the lecture in Lesson 2. After each section, give an example from your own culture.

LISTENING SKILLS LEVEL 3 – THEME 6: Culture and Civilization, What Is Society? 29

Introduction

Elicit the 10 areas that all cultures have in common. If students are struggling to remember, give the stressed syllable.

Exercise A

1 Set for individual work then pairwork checking.
2 Play the recording. Feed back, getting the fixed phrases on the board. Try to elicit the fixed phrases used in other situations.

Answers

a *According to* the dictionary, society is the organisation of individuals into groups.
b Culture, on the other hand, is *defined as* the customs and achievements of a society.
c Incidentally, the Khalduniyah area in Tunis has hardly changed since *his day.*
d The death of his parents had a deep effect on Ibn Khaldoun, as *we shall see later.*
e That's about a third of the population at the time. Imagine *that.* 1 in 3 people died.
f The form of education *depends on* the society.
g People have time for leisure. In *other words*, they are not working every *hour* of the *day*.
h English people call French people 'frogs' because some French people eat frogs' legs. In *turn*, French people used to call English people *le rote boeuf*, or 'the roast beef', because they ate roast beef.
i The *point is* that traditional food and methods of cooking are very important to a cultural group.

Fixed phrases:
according to
defined as
since his / her / their day – note, you can even say, *since my day* = when I was young
as we shall see later
imagine that
depends on
in other words
every hour of the day
in turn
the point is

Exercise B

1 Give students plenty of time to study the two sets of sentences. Do not feed back.
2 Set for individual work. Feed back.
3 Set for individual work then pairwork checking. Play the section. Elicit the introductory verbs that the lecturer uses. Elicit also the fact that sometimes there is no introductory verb, but it is still obvious that the lecturer is continuing the opinions of Ibn Khaldoun rather than giving facts. Refer students back to their notes to find some more facts in addition to the ones in Sentences A.

Answers

3 Ibn Khaldoun *believed* in the idea of *'asabiyah*, which can be translated as 'social cohesion' or joining together.
He *said* that this cohesion appears naturally in tribes and other small social groups.
He went on to *claim* that the social cohesion will be stronger if the society develops a strong religion.
Ibn Khaldoun *thought* that social cohesion is the driving force of society, the thing that pushes the civilization forwards and makes it strong.
[no introductory verb] When the cohesion weakens, for any reason, the society weakens and another society with a stronger cohesion takes its place.

Language and culture note

Note that, although the introductory verb may be in the past, the statement of belief is in the present. Point out that this is normal where a theory is still extant. Compare the following:

1. *Ibn Khaldoun believed that social cohesion appears naturally* = this is still a reasonable opinion
2. *People believed that the Earth was flat* = not a reasonable opinion anymore

Therefore, this is not traditional reported speech. Do not launch into a standard lesson about changing the verb to the past, etc.

Exercise C

Write these words on the board:

... the death of his parents from the Black Death had a deep effect on Ibn Khaldoun.

1 Elicit ideas about this sentence. Confirm or correct.
2 Refer students to Skills Check 2. Elicit ideas. Add *I believe* to the front of the sentence to show that this is the lecturer's opinion – or at least, the opinion of people other than Ibn Khaldoun himself.

Answers

1 It is a fact and an opinion – the death is a fact, the deep effect is an opinion.
2 It is the lecturer's opinion.

Exercise D

Remind students that they did this at the end of the previous lesson. Now they must do it in real time – in the same way that they might have to listen and contribute in a tutorial or seminar, as opposed to a lecture.

Put students into groups and teacher-pace the activity, i.e., play one of the points, pause the recording, allow discussion, monitor and feed back if necessary, then go on to the next point. If students cannot think of any examples, move on to the next point. Note that in some cases they may be able to give the same example as the lecturer.

Closure

Play a sort of 'Simon says', getting students to tell you whether they are hearing a fact or your opinion as follows.

Ibn Khaldoun was born in Tunis.	Fact
He was born in 1322.	Fact
I think his father was an important man.	Opinion
His parents died when he was 16.	Fact
Obviously, this had a deep effect on him.	Opinion
The Black Death came to Tunis in 1348.	Fact
I'm sure everyone was terrified of the disease.	Opinion
Khaldoun went to live with a tribe in 1375.	Fact
I believe Khaldoun wrote *Kitab al-Ibar* because of his experiences with the tribe.	Opinion

Lesson 4: Applying new skills

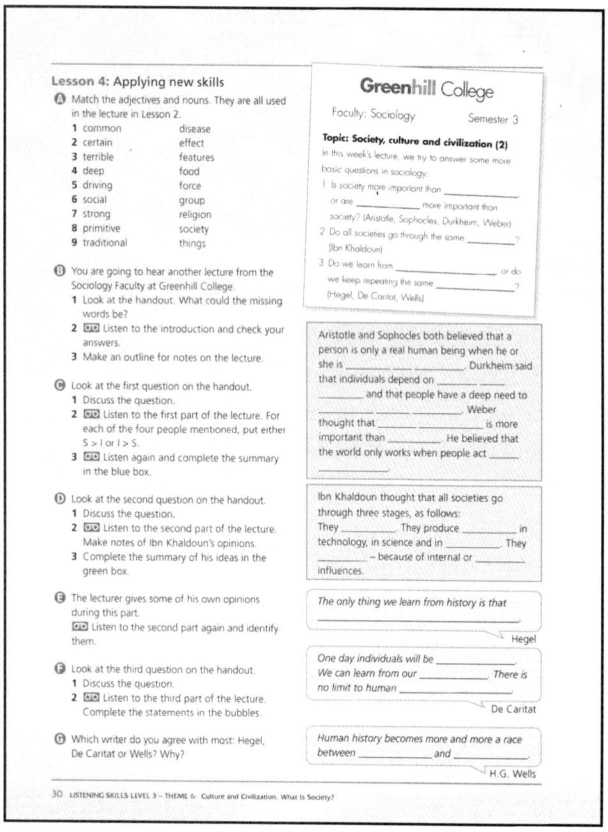

Lesson 4: Applying new skills

(A) Match the adjectives and nouns. They are all used in the lecture in Lesson 2.

1 common	disease
2 certain	effect
3 terrible	features
4 deep	food
5 driving	force
6 social	group
7 strong	religion
8 primitive	society
9 traditional	things

(B) You are going to hear another lecture from the Sociology Faculty at Greenhill College.
1 Look at the handout. What could the missing words be?
2 Listen to the introduction and check your answers.
3 Make an outline for notes on the lecture.

(C) Look at the first question on the handout.
1 Discuss the question.
2 Listen to the first part of the lecture. For each of the four people mentioned, put either S > I or I > S.
3 Listen again and complete the summary in the blue box.

(D) Look at the second question on the handout.
1 Discuss the question.
2 Listen to the second part of the lecture. Make notes of Ibn Khaldoun's opinions.
3 Complete the summary of his ideas in the green box.

(E) The lecturer gives some of his own opinions during this part.
Listen to the second part again and identify them.

(F) Look at the third question on the handout.
1 Discuss the question.
2 Listen to the third part of the lecture. Complete the statements in the bubbles.

(G) Which writer do you agree with most: Hegel, De Caritat or Wells? Why?

Greenhill College
Faculty: Sociology Semester 3
Topic: Society, culture and civilization (2)
In this week's lecture, we try to answer some more basic questions in sociology:
1 Is society more important than ____, or are ____ more important than society? (Aristotle, Sophocles, Durkheim, Weber)
2 Do all societies go through the same ____? (Ibn Khaldoun)
3 Do we learn from ____, or do we keep repeating the same ____? (Hegel, De Caritat, Wells)

Aristotle and Sophocles both believed that a person is only a real human being when he or she is ____ ____ ____. Durkheim said that individuals depend on ____ ____ ____ and that people have a deep need to ____ ____ ____. Weber thought that ____ ____ is more important than ____. He believed that the world only works when people act ____ ____.

Ibn Khaldoun thought that all societies go through three stages, as follows:
They ____. They produce ____ in technology, in science and in ____. They ____ – because of internal or ____ influences.

The only thing we learn from history is that ____.
Hegel

One day individuals will be ____. We can learn from our ____. There is no limit to human ____.
De Caritat

Human history becomes more and more a race between ____ and ____.
H.G. Wells

30 LISTENING SKILLS LEVEL 3 – THEME 6: Culture and Civilization, What Is Society?

Answers

1	common	features	6	social	group
2	certain	things	7	strong	religion
3	terrible	disease	8	primitive	society
4	deep	effect	9	traditional	food
5	driving	force			

Introduction

Give the stressed syllables of some of the key words from the lecture in Lessons 2 and 3 for students to identify the whole word, e.g.,

ac'cording	ex'change
co'hesion	'leisure
dis'ease	(rites of) 'passage
'driving (force)	tra'ditional
'educate	'weaken
ef'fect	

Exercise A

Set for individual work then pairwork checking. Feed back, getting the phrases on the board. Note that other phrases are possible, but these are the ones from the lecture and students will probably have an aural memory of them. Try to elicit the sentences that contained each of these phrases.

Exercise B

1 Set for individual work then pairwork checking. Feed back, but do not confirm or correct.
2 Play the introduction. Feed back, building up the key questions on the board.
3 Set for individual work then pairwork checking. Feed back, building up a model on the board.

Answers

2
1 Is society more important than *individuals*, or are *individuals* more important than society?
2 Do all societies go through the same *stages*? (Ibn Khaldoun)
3 Do we learn from *history*, or do we keep repeating the same *mistakes*?

3
<u>1. Indiv > soc. or soc. > ind?</u>
Aristotle
Sophocles
Durkheim
Weber
<u>2. All soc. = same stages?</u>
Ibn Khaldoun
<u>3. Learn from h.?</u>
Hegel
De Caritat
H.G. Wells.

Exercise C

1 Set for pairwork. Elicit ideas.
2 Set for individual work then pairwork checking. Show how students can complete the activity, e.g., S > I = society is more important than individuals. Play Part 1. Feed back, adding to the outline on the board.

3 Give students time to read the summary. Set for individual work then pairwork checking. Play Part 1 again. Feed back, eliciting the correct filler for each space in the summary.

Answers

1 Answers depend on students.

2

Aristotle	S > I
Sophocles	S > I
Durkheim	S > I
Weber	I > S

3 Aristotle and Sophocles both believed that a person is only a real human being when he or she is *part of society*. Durkheim said that individuals depend on *society for survival* and that people have a deep need to *belong to something*. Weber thought that *the individual* is more important than *society*. He believed that the world only works when people act *as individuals*.

Exercise D

1 Set for pairwork. Elicit ideas.

2 Set for individual work then pairwork checking. Feed back, adding to the outline on the board.

3 Refer students to the summary. Set for individual work then pairwork checking. Feed back, eliciting the correct filler for each space.

Answers

1 Answers depend on students.

2 2. All soc. = same stages?

  Ibn Khaldoun = ✓

  3 stages =

    1. grow
    2. advances
    3. die = int., e.g., leaders not strg OR ext, e.g., disease

  No progress!

3 Ibn Khaldoun thought that all societies go through three stages, as follows:

  They *grow*. They produce *advances* in technology, in science and in *art*. They *die* – because of internal or *external* influences.

Exercise E

Remind students about the ways that lecturers introduce their own opinions, i.e., *I believe / I'm sure / No doubt / Obviously*. Elicit some ideas. Play Part 2 again for students to identify the lecturer's opinions as they go.

Answers

introduction	opinion
Personally, I think	that title (father of sociology) is well-deserved.
I believe	this event (death of his parents) probably influenced his writings on this subject.
obviously,	Ibn Khaldoun believed that history endlessly repeats itself,
No doubt	he studied other civilizations and came to this rather sad conclusion.

Exercise F

1 Set for pairwork. Elicit ideas.

2 Set for individual work then pairwork checking. Play Part 3. Elicit ideas and build up the full 'quotations' on the board.

Answers

The only thing we learn from history is that *we don't learn from history.* (Hegel)

One day individuals will be *perfect*. We can learn from our *mistakes*. There is no limit to human *knowledge*. (De Caritat)

Human history becomes more and more a race between *education* and *disaster*. (H.G. Wells)

Exercise G

General discussion.

Closure

Further exploit the text. Highlight key vocabulary items and check that students can identify them from the stressed syllable.

Lesson 1: Vocabulary

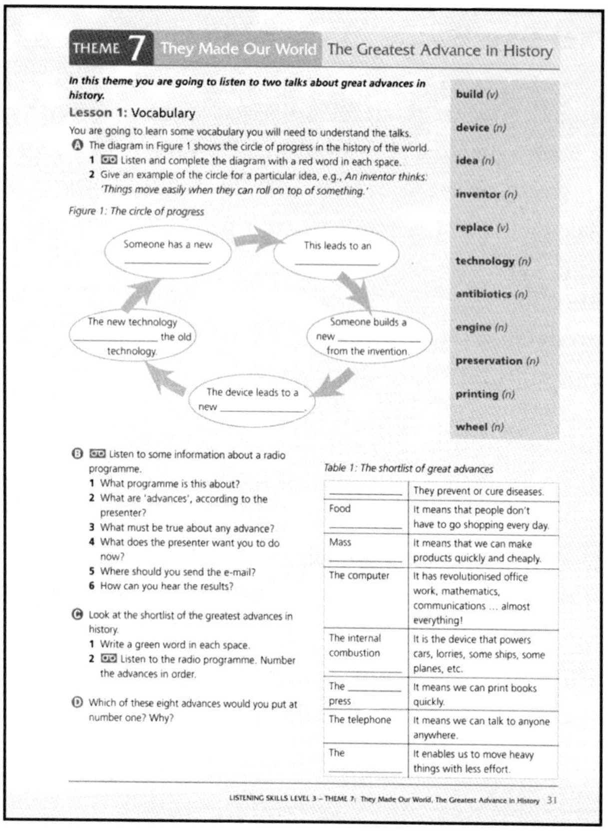

THEME 7 They Made Our World The Greatest Advance in History

In this theme you are going to listen to two talks about great advances in history.

Lesson 1: Vocabulary

You are going to learn some vocabulary you will need to understand the talks.

A The diagram in Figure 1 shows the circle of progress in the history of the world.
1 Listen and complete the diagram with a red word in each space.
2 Give an example of the circle for a particular idea, e.g., *An inventor thinks: 'Things move easily when they can roll on top of something.'*

Figure 1: The circle of progress

build *(v)*
device *(n)*
idea *(n)*
inventor *(n)*
replace *(v)*
technology *(n)*
antibiotics *(n)*
engine *(n)*
preservation *(n)*
printing *(n)*
wheel *(n)*

B Listen to some information about a radio programme.
1 What programme is this about?
2 What are 'advances', according to the presenter?
3 What must be true about any advance?
4 What does the presenter want you to do now?
5 Where should you send the e-mail?
6 How can you hear the results?

C Look at the shortlist of the greatest advances in history.
1 Write a green word in each space.
2 Listen to the radio programme. Number the advances in order.

D Which of these eight advances would you put at number one? Why?

Table 1: The shortlist of great advances

______	They prevent or cure diseases.
Food ______	It means that people don't have to go shopping every day.
Mass ______	It means that we can make products quickly and cheaply.
The computer	It has revolutionised office work, mathematics, communications … almost everything!
The internal combustion ______	It is the device that powers cars, lorries, some ships, some planes, etc.
The ______ press	It means we can print books quickly.
The telephone	It means we can talk to anyone anywhere.
The ______	It enables us to move heavy things with less effort.

LISTENING SKILLS LEVEL 3 – THEME 7: They Made Our World, The Greatest Advance in History 31

Introduction

Write the red words on the board. Ask students if they can find any connections between the words.

Methodology note

If the students did Theme 7 in Level 2, they should be able to tell you the basic connection between the words, if they remember! Otherwise, this is just a gentle lead into Exercise A.

If students are able to tell you the exact relationship, as shown in Figure 1, you could skip Exercise A altogether.

Exercise A

Refer students to the diagram. If students did the previous level, they may recognise this diagram – although it is drawn as a circle here rather than in a linear way. Give them a few moments to look at the diagram and think of possible ways to complete it with the red words.

1 Set for individual work then pairwork checking. Play the recording. Feed back, building up a model diagram on the board. Show how the pattern is a circle – a new idea in the same field will start the whole process again.
2 Elicit the example with the wheel. Elicit other examples if you think students are capable of it, e.g., the printing press instead of using people to copy manuscripts.

Answer

There is a circle of progress that is repeated again and again in history. The circle works like this.

Someone has a new *idea*. For example, an inventor sees someone dragging something heavy and thinks: 'He could move that more easily if he rolled it on a tree trunk'. This leads to a new *invention* – in this case, the wheel. Someone, perhaps the inventor, builds a new *device* from the invention – a wagon with wheels, for example, to carry goods, or a chariot for people to travel in. This device leads to a new *technology*, for example, wheeled transport. The new technology *replaces* the old technology. Suddenly, everything has wheels and people do not drag things across the ground any more. Then someone sees a horse pulling a wheeled cart and thinks: 'That cart would go much faster with an engine'.

Exercise B

Set up the idea of listening to the radio and a trailer coming on for another programme later in the day. Find out if that happens on the radio in the students' culture(s).

Set the questions for pairwork. Give students plenty of time to read the questions. Play the recording. Students do not have to write the answers, just make a few notes. Feed back orally.

Answers

Possible answers:

1 It is about *They Made Our World.*
2 They are discoveries or inventions.
3 It must be something that revolutionised the world.
4 E-mail your choice – if you haven't done it already.
5 greatest@ourworld.com
6 Listen at 5.00 today.

Exercise C

Explain the idea of a shortlist – the most popular choices.

1 Set for individual work then pairwork checking. Feed back, building up the list without the explanation on the board.
2 Set for individual work then pairwork checking. Play the recording. Feed back, adding the numbers to the items on the board. Get students to close their books and give a definition or comment on each item.

Answers

In rank order:

1 The wheel
2 The computer
3 The internal combustion engine
4 Food preservation
5 Mass production
6 The printing press
7 Antibiotics
8 The telephone

Exercise D

Set for groupwork. Feed back, eliciting ideas from each group.

Closure

Ask students to mark the stressed syllable in all the green words, except *wheel.*

Say the stressed syllable alone in random order for students to identify the word.

Answers

ad'vance
antibi'otics
'engine
preser'vation
'printing
pro'duction

Lesson 2: Listening

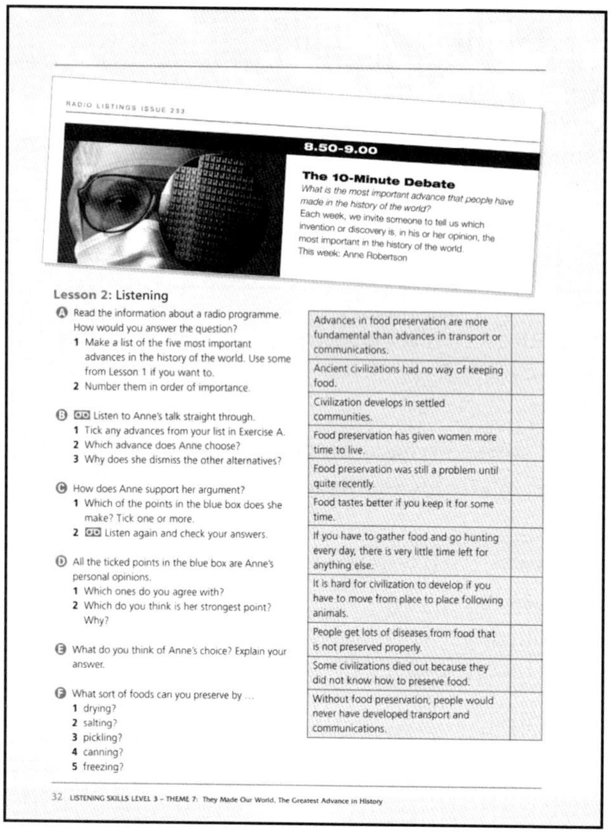

RADIO LISTINGS ISSUE 233

8.50-9.00

The 10-Minute Debate

What is the most important advance that people have made in the history of the world?

Each week, we invite someone to tell us which invention or discovery is, in his or her opinion, the most important in the history of the world.

This week: Anne Robertson

Lesson 2: Listening

A Read the information about a radio programme. How would you answer the question?
1 Make a list of the five most important advances in the history of the world. Use some from Lesson 1 if you want to.
2 Number them in order of importance.

B Listen to Anne's talk straight through.
1 Tick any advances from your list in Exercise A.
2 Which advance does Anne choose?
3 Why does she dismiss the other alternatives?

C How does Anne support her argument?
1 Which of the points in the blue box does she make? Tick one or more.
2 Listen again and check your answers.

D All the ticked points in the blue box are Anne's personal opinions.
1 Which ones do you agree with?
2 Which do you think is her strongest point? Why?

E What do you think of Anne's choice? Explain your answer.

F What sort of foods can you preserve by …
1 drying?
2 salting?
3 pickling?
4 canning?
5 freezing?

Advances in food preservation are more fundamental than advances in transport or communications.	
Ancient civilizations had no way of keeping food.	
Civilization develops in settled communities.	
Food preservation has given women more time to live.	
Food preservation was still a problem until quite recently.	
Food tastes better if you keep it for some time.	
If you have to gather food and go hunting every day, there is very little time left for anything else.	
It is hard for civilization to develop if you have to move from place to place following animals.	
People get lots of diseases from food that is not preserved properly.	
Some civilizations died out because they did not know how to preserve food.	
Without food preservation, people would never have developed transport and communications.	

32 LISTENING SKILLS LEVEL 3 – THEME 7: They Made Our World, The Greatest Advance in History

Introduction

Give the definitions / comments from Table 1 Lesson 1 and elicit the advances, students' books closed.

Exercise A

Refer students to the information. Ask checking questions.

1 Set for pairwork. Feed back orally. Deal with new words that students produce.

2 Set for pairwork. Feed back, getting the sets from different groups and then trying to make a composite set according to the rank order, i.e., if one group puts *the wheel* in top place, that's five points; if another group puts it second, that's four points, so nine points in total.

Exercise B

1 Set for individual work then pairwork checking. Explain that on this occasion you are not going to stop the recording. Point out also that on this occasion the speaker does not give as many signposts to the overall organisation of the talk, so the students will have to listen closely for changes of topic. Play the recording. Feed back, building up a list.

2 and 3 Ask these questions of the whole group and elicit ideas, building up some notes on the board. Check that students understand the word *dismiss*, in this case = not to *accept* (also new, perhaps) an argument or point of view.

Answers

1 She mentions the following:
the sail
the wheel
the internal combustion engine
writing
the printing press
the telephone
the computer

2 She chooses preserving food, including drying, salting, pickling, canning, freezing.

3 She dismisses the other points because she says food preservation gave people time to think of all the other things.

Exercise C

1 Set for pairwork. Feed back, but do not confirm or correct. Deal with new vocabulary, especially *fundamental, settled (communities), gather, hunting, diseases, die out.*

2 Set for individual work then pairwork checking. Play the recording again. Feed back, ideally onto an OHT of the table.

Answers

Advances in food preservation are more fundamental than advances in transport or communications.	✓
Ancient civilizations had no way of keeping food.	
Civilization develops in settled communities.	✓
Food preservation has given women more time to live.	✓
Food preservation was still a problem until quite recently.	✓
Food tastes better if you keep it for some time.	
If you have to gather food and go hunting every day, there is very little time left for anything else.	✓
It is hard for civilization to develop if you have to move from place to place following animals.	✓
People get lots of diseases from food that is not preserved properly.	
Some civilizations died out because they did not know how to preserve food.	
Without food preservation, people would never have developed transport and communications.	✓

Exercise D

Set for group work. Give students a structure for their points of view, e.g.,

I agree that [food preservation has given women more time to live].

Anne says, ['If you have to gather food and go hunting every day, there is very little time left for anything else.'] I don't think that's true.

I think Anne's point about [food preservation and women] is correct.

Monitor. Feed back on some of the best points made.

Exercise E

Set for pairwork. Monitor. Students may be able to make cogent arguments for or against. If they are struggling, however, quickly feed back on the best points, then move on.

Methodology note

It is important to be able to identify strong and weak points in a spoken argument. However, as this is a Listening course, we do not want to spend a lot of time developing the skill of expressing that strength or weakness. You will, therefore, have to accept simple statements like those shown in the exercise notes.

Exercise F

Do as a whole-class activity. Build up a list on the board.

Closure

Say the stressed syllable and the syllable pattern of some of the new words from this lesson. Students must identify the whole word, e.g., da da **men** da = *fundamental.*

Possible words:

settled
communities
gather
hunting
diseases
communications
develop
follow
supplies

Lesson 3: Learning new skills

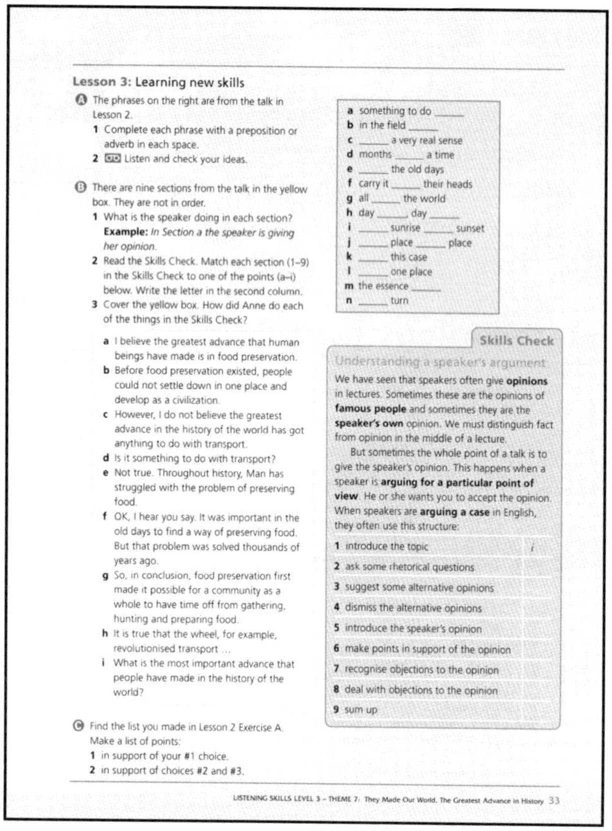

Lesson 3: Learning new skills

A The phrases on the right are from the talk in Lesson 2.

1 Complete each phrase with a preposition or adverb in each space.

2 Listen and check your ideas.

a something to do ______
b in the field ______
c ______ a very real sense
d months ______ a time
e ______ the old days
f carry it ______ their heads
g all ______ the world
h day ______, day ______
i ______ sunrise ______ sunset
j ______ place ______ place
k ______ this case
l ______ one place
m the essence ______
n ______ turn

B There are nine sections from the talk in the yellow box. They are not in order.

1 What is the speaker doing in each section?
Example: *In Section a the speaker is giving her opinion.*

2 Read the Skills Check. Match each section (1–9) in the Skills Check to one of the points (a–i) below. Write the letter in the second column.

3 Cover the yellow box. How did Anne do each of the things in the Skills Check?

a I believe the greatest advance that human beings have made is in food preservation.
b Before food preservation existed, people could not settle down in one place and develop as a civilization.
c However, I do not believe the greatest advance in the history of the world has got anything to do with transport.
d Is it something to do with transport?
e Not true. Throughout history, Man has struggled with the problem of preserving food.
f OK, I hear you say. It was important in the old days to find a way of preserving food. But that problem was solved thousands of years ago.
g So, in conclusion, food preservation first made it possible for a community as a whole to have time off from gathering, hunting and preparing food.
h It is true that the wheel, for example, revolutionised transport …
i What is the most important advance that people have made in the history of the world?

Skills Check

Understanding a speaker's argument

We have seen that speakers often give **opinions** in lectures. Sometimes these are the opinions of **famous people** and sometimes they are the **speaker's own** opinion. We must distinguish fact from opinion in the middle of a lecture.

But sometimes the whole point of a talk is to give the speaker's opinion. This happens when a speaker is **arguing for a particular point of view**. He or she wants you to accept the opinion. When speakers are **arguing a case** in English, they often use this structure:

1 introduce the topic	*i*
2 ask some rhetorical questions	
3 suggest some alternative opinions	
4 dismiss the alternative opinions	
5 introduce the speaker's opinion	
6 make points in support of the opinion	
7 recognise objections to the opinion	
8 deal with objections to the opinion	
9 sum up	

C Find the list you made in Lesson 2 Exercise A. Make a list of points:

1 in support of your #1 choice.

2 in support of choices #2 and #3.

LISTENING SKILLS LEVEL 3 – THEME 7: They Made Our World, The Greatest Advance in History 33

Introduction

Remind students of some or all of the fixed phrases / common collocations met to date, as listed below. Play games and / or get students to try to use the phrases in a context.

at first
in other words
in the circumstances
in total
it all started with
learning by experience
life and work
more or less
morning or evening
on average
on the one / other hand
past and future
primitive society
professional and social
rain or shine
right and wrong
so to sum up
social group
summer or winter
terrible disease
the rest of his / her life
thunder and lightning
to put it another way
to this day
traditional food
trial and error
warm and dry
wind and rain
all over the world
at work
cause and effect
certain things
cold and wet
common features
daytime or night-time
deep effect
driving force
for example
getting back to the point
in fact

Exercise A

1 Set for individual work then pairwork checking.

2 Play the recording. Point out that on this occasion students have to pick out the phrase from the context, from the stream of speech. Feed back, getting the whole phrases on the board.

Answers

Full sentences:

a Is it something to do with transport?

b Is it something in the field of communications?

c I accept that advances in transport and communications were very important and, in a very real sense, the advances in these fields have made the modern world that we live in.

d Sailors often got a painful and potentially fatal disease called scurvy because they did not eat fresh fruit for months at a time.

e It was important in the old days to find a way of preserving food.

f The Sumerians invented writing, which meant that information could be moved through time and space without people having to carry it in their heads.

g Johannes Gutenberg invented the printing press, which meant information could be copied and distributed all over the world quite cheaply.

h Man needs to eat food day in, day out.

i This means that most people work from sunrise to sunset gathering food or hunting.

j Before people discovered methods of preserving food, they spent all their time gathering food and hunting, often wandering from place to place following the animals that they ate.

k The problem gets worse if the animals are wild and move from place to place. In this case, you must follow them when they move.

l So it is not possible to settle down in one place.

m This is the essence of civilization.

n Civilization develops when settlements grow into towns, which in turn grow into large successful cities and then into empires.

Phrases in isolation – target items in italics:

something to do *with*	day *in*, day *out*
in the field *of*	*from* sunrise *to* sunset
in a very real sense	*from* place *to* place
months *at* a time	*In* this case
in the old days	*in* one place
carry it *in* your head	the essence *of*
all *over* the world	*in* turn

Methodology note

Throughout this course, fixed and semi-fixed phrases are highlighted and practised. The theory behind this is: if the brain can identify fixed phrases from the first two or three phonemes, it can get on with processing other parts of the sentence.

Exercise B

Remind students of the talk in Lesson 2. Point out that on this occasion there were no real signposts or pre-organisers to the talk. In other words, the speaker did not prepare the listener for the structure of the talk. Therefore, they have to be able to understand what the speaker is doing at each point of the talk.

1 Work through two or three as examples, until you are sure the students understand. With a weaker class, you might stay as a whole group for this activity. With a stronger class, set for pairwork. Elicit ideas but do not confirm or correct. Explain that this is because they will find the answers in the Skills Check.

2 Remind students that there are few signposts in Anne's talk. This is because the talk conforms to a well-known structure for this kind of text. Set for individual work then pairwork checking. Feed back, ideally using the table in Answers below.

3 As above, with a weak class, stay together as a whole group to elicit ideas. Otherwise, set for pairwork. Feed back orally.

Answers

introduce the topic	What is the most important advance that people have made in the history of the world?
ask some rhetorical questions	Is it something to do with transport?
suggest some alternative opinions	It is true that the wheel, for example, revolutionised transport and made it possible for one horse to move very heavy items over long distances.
dismiss the alternative opinions	However, I do not believe the greatest advance in the history of the world has got anything to do with transport.
introduce the speaker's opinion	I believe the greatest advance that human beings have made is in food preservation.
make points in support of the opinion	Before food preservation existed, people could not settle down in one place and develop as a civilization.
recognise objections to the opinion	OK, I hear you say. It was important in the old days to find a way of preserving food. But that problem was solved thousands of years ago.
deal with objections to the opinion	Not true. Throughout history, Man has struggled with the problem of preserving food.
sum up	So, in conclusion. Food preservation first made it possible for a community as a whole to have time off from gathering, hunting and preparing food.

Exercise C

Explain that speakers in Anne's situation consider:

a) the point they are going to make + supporting points;
b) the points that other people might make + supporting points.

They then state the possible points from other people *first* to 'get them out of the way'.

Ask if the same rhetorical style is used in the students' own culture(s). They may not know, of course!

Set for pairwork. Monitor. Feed back with ideas from a successful pair.

Conclusion

Point out that speakers also consider objections to their own points and try to deal with these, too. You therefore get this structure (build it up on the board):

- Statement of the problem / question / point for consideration.
- Alternative argument 1
- Alternative argument 2, etc.
- My argument + supporting points
- Objections to my argument
- Reactions to the objections
- Conclusion – restating my argument (and perhaps dismissing the alternatives again)

Lesson 4: Applying new skills

Lesson 4: Applying new skills

A Anne uses several fixed phrases in her talk in Lesson 2.

1 Complete this part of the talk with a suitable phrase in each space.

2 Listen again and check your ideas.

OK, I hear ______. It was important in ______ to find a way of preserving food. But that problem was solved thousands of years ago. Not true. Throughout ______, Man has struggled with the problem of preserving food. As ______, some progress was made with drying, salting and pickling thousands of years ago. But as ______ people moved away from a settled community, there were still great problems. Sailors often got a painful and potentially fatal disease called scurvy because they did not eat fresh fruit for ______. Scurvy struck the sailors on Magellan's journey around the world in 1519, for ______. The same situation was repeated all ______. Napoleon lost more men to scurvy and starvation in the war against Russia than he did in all the battles put ______. In ______, the problem for Napoleon was ______ bad ______ the French government offered a reward of 12,000 francs to the person who could solve it. The result was canning. A man called Nicholas Appert tried for years to win the prize. At ______, he had no success, but ______ he solved the problem. Finally, he put food into airtight bottles in ______ preserve it. It worked. So by the 20th century, a lot of foodstuffs could be preserved, but fresh meat and dairy products were still a problem ______ the 1950s.

B You are going to hear another talk from the radio series. Before you listen, here are some phrases and sentences from the talk. Match each one to a function.

introduce the topic	*As I see it, neither computers nor mass production make our lives better in the most important way.*
suggest alternative opinions	*Before people understood the need for clean water, decent housing and waste disposal, life for most people was short and full of pain.*
make points in support of the alternative opinions	*In my opinion, the greatest advance that human beings have made is in the conquest of infectious diseases.*
dismiss the alternative opinions	*Mass production has certainly enabled us to change the world out of all recognition.*
introduce the speaker's opinion	*Of course, you could argue that computers and mass production have made people's lives better.*
make points in support of the opinion	*Some might say it is mass production –*
recognise objections to the opinion	*What is the most important advance that people have made in the history of the world?*
deal with objections to the opinion	*If you don't have a long life free from pain, you cannot enjoy the other advances of civilization.*

C Listen to the whole talk. Check your answers to Exercise B.

D Discuss these questions.

1 What, in the speaker's opinion, is the greatest advance of all time?

2 What points does the speaker make in support of this opinion?

E Which speaker (Lesson 2 or Lesson 4) do you agree with? Or do you think the greatest advance is something else?

34 LISTENING SKILLS LEVEL 3 – THEME 7: They Made Our World, The Greatest Advance in History

Introduction

Ask students if they can remember Anne's opinion from Lesson 2 and how she supported the opinion. Ask if they agree with her and why (not).

Exercise A

Remind students about fixed phrases and how useful it is to be able to pick them out quickly from the stream of speech. Note that some of the phrases are new in this talk, and some they have met before.

1 Set for individual work then pairwork checking.
2 Set for individual work then pairwork checking. Play the recording. Feed back, ideally onto an OHT of the gapped text. Isolate the phrases and write them on the board.

Answers

OK, I hear *you say*. It was important in *the old days* to find a way of preserving food. But that problem was solved thousands of years ago. Not true. Throughout *history*, Man has struggled with the problem of preserving food. As *we have seen*, some progress was made with drying, salting and pickling thousands of years ago. But as *soon as* people moved away from a settled community, there were still great problems. Sailors often got a painful and potentially fatal disease called scurvy because they did not eat fresh fruit for *months at a time*. Scurvy struck the sailors on Magellan's journey around the world in 1519, for *example*. The same situation was repeated all *over the world*. Napoleon lost more men to scurvy and starvation in the war against Russia than he did in all the battles put *together*. In *fact*, the problem for Napoleon was *so* bad *that* the French government offered a reward of 12,000 francs to the person who could solve it. The result was canning. A man called Nicholas Appert tried for years to win the prize. At *first*, he had no success, but *gradually* he solved the problem. Finally, he put food into airtight bottles in *an attempt to* preserve it. It worked. So by the 20th century, a lot of foodstuffs could be preserved, but fresh meat and dairy products were still a problem *up to* the 1950s.

Exercise B

Remind students that talks of this nature – a speaker giving a point of view – often have a well-known structure. Elicit the structure (i.e., the points in column 1), with students' books closed. Set for pairwork. Feed back orally, but do not confirm or correct.

Exercise C

Set for individual work then pairwork checking. Play the recording all the way through. Feed back, ideally onto an OHT of the table in Answers below. Deal with new words, particularly any in the extracts in this exercise.

Answers

introduce the topic	What is the most important advance that people have made in the history of the world?
suggest alternative opinions	Some might say it is mass production –
make points in support of the alternative opinions	Mass production has certainly enabled us to change the world out of all recognition.
dismiss the alternative opinions	As I see it, neither computers nor mass production make our lives better in the most important way.
introduce the speaker's opinion	In my opinion, the greatest advance that human beings have made is in the conquest of infectious diseases.
make points in support of the opinion	Before people understood the need for clean water, decent housing and waste disposal, life for most people was short and full of pain.
recognise objections to the opinion	Of course, you could argue that computers and mass production have made people's lives better.
deal with objections to the opinion	If you don't have a long life free from pain, you cannot enjoy the other advances of civilization.

Exercise D

Set for pairwork. Feed back, building up the main point and supporting points on the board.

Answers

Possible answers:

Main point: conquest of infectious diseases = main advance in history

Supporting points:

- Life expectancy used to be very low.
- Life was full of pain.
- Without a long life free from pain, you cannot enjoy other advances.

Exercise E

Group work or general discussion.

Closure

Highlight some of the fixed phrases and common collocations from the talk, e.g.,

some might say
at the same time
at the end of
I accept that
as I see it
in my opinion
at the time of
you could argue that

Lesson 1: Vocabulary

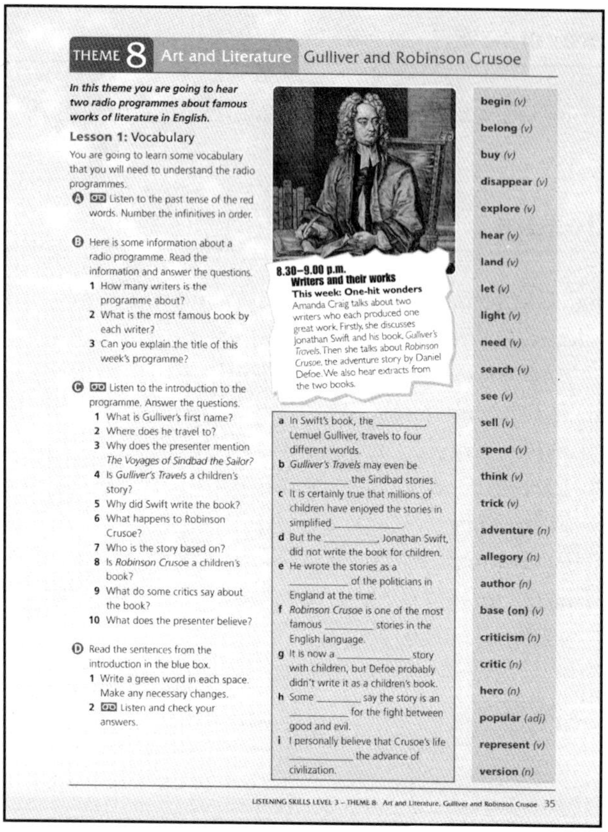
THEME 8 Art and Literature Gulliver and Robinson Crusoe

In this theme you are going to hear two radio programmes about famous works of literature in English.

Lesson 1: Vocabulary

You are going to learn some vocabulary that you will need to understand the radio programmes.

A Listen to the past tense of the red words. Number the infinitives in order.

B Here is some information about a radio programme. Read the information and answer the questions.
1 How many writers is the programme about?
2 What is the most famous book by each writer?
3 Can you explain the title of this week's programme?

C Listen to the introduction to the programme. Answer the questions.
1 What is Gulliver's first name?
2 Where does he travel to?
3 Why does the presenter mention *The Voyages of Sindbad the Sailor?*
4 Is *Gulliver's Travels* a children's story?
5 Why did Swift write the book?
6 What happens to Robinson Crusoe?
7 Who is the story based on?
8 Is *Robinson Crusoe* a children's book?
9 What do some critics say about the book?
10 What does the presenter believe?

D Read the sentences from the introduction in the blue box.
1 Write a green word in each space. Make any necessary changes.
2 Listen and check your answers.

8.30–9.00 p.m.
Writers and their works
This week: One-hit wonders
Amanda Craig talks about two writers who each produced one great work. Firstly, she discusses Jonathan Swift and his book *Gulliver's Travels*. Then she talks about *Robinson Crusoe*, the adventure story by Daniel Defoe. We also hear extracts from the two books.

a In Swift's book, the ________, Lemuel Gulliver, travels to four different worlds.
b *Gulliver's Travels* may even be ________ the Sindbad stories.
c It is certainly true that millions of children have enjoyed the stories in simplified ________.
d But the ________, Jonathan Swift, did not write the book for children.
e He wrote the stories as a ________ of the politicians in England at the time.
f *Robinson Crusoe* is one of the most famous ________ stories in the English language.
g It is now a ________ story with children, but Defoe probably didn't write it as a children's book.
h Some ________ say the story is an ________ for the fight between good and evil.
i I personally believe that Crusoe's life ________ the advance of civilization.

begin (v)
belong (v)
buy (v)
disappear (v)
explore (v)
hear (v)
land (v)
let (v)
light (v)
need (v)
search (v)
see (v)
sell (v)
spend (v)
think (v)
trick (v)
adventure (n)
allegory (n)
author (n)
base (on) (v)
criticism (n)
critic (n)
hero (n)
popular (adj)
represent (v)
version (n)

LISTENING SKILLS LEVEL 3 – THEME 8: Art and Literature, Gulliver and Robinson Crusoe 35

Introduction

If students did Level 2, they should remember all of the verbs in the red words. If not, they may know most of them from other courses. Point out that these are common verbs – used in fiction particularly, although usually in the past tense.

Exercise A

Set for individual work then pairwork checking. Play the recording or say the past tense verbs. Elicit correct infinitives, then practise giving correct past tenses.

Answers

1 let
2 see
3 light
4 need
5 begin
6 sell
7 belong
8 land
9 buy
10 disappear
11 trick
12 explore
13 hear
14 search
15 think
16 spend

Exercise B

Refer students to the information from a radio listings section of a newspaper. Make sure students know where this comes from. Set for pairwork. Feed back orally.

Answers

1 Two.
2 *Gulliver's Travels* by Swift, *Robinson Crusoe* by Defoe.
3 Each writer only wrote one book that became famous.

Language and culture note

Depending on your students, you might mention that pop groups who only have one popular record are given the title 'one-hit wonders' in slang English.

Exercise C

Give students time to read all the questions and to think of possible answers. Set for pairwork. Play the introduction to the programme. Feed back orally. Note that several of the questions are deep-end work, e.g.,

- spelling *Lemuel* and *Selkirk* pre-figures work in this theme on guessing spelling – elicit the spelling that students have in their minds and spend a few minutes on why that is right or wrong;

- explaining why Swift wrote *Gulliver's Travels* forces the students to use one of the green words before doing Exercise D.

Answers

1 Lemuel.
2 Four worlds – students might want to tell you the kinds of worlds, too.
3 Because it may be based on those stories.
4 No, although a lot of children like it.
5 As a criticism of politicians in England at the time.
6 He gets shipwrecked – like Sindbad (studied in Level 2).
7 Alexander Selkirk, or a man who spent time on a desert island.
8 He probably didn't write it as a children's story, but it is very popular with children.
9 It is an allegory of the fight between good and evil – explain that an *allegory* is a story in a kind of code: one thing means or represents something else.
10 She thinks Crusoe's life represents the advance of civilization.

Language and culture note

Allegory in Arabic could be translated as *story in code*. Use this idea of decoding a story to explain *allegory*. Many students will know some of Aesop's fables – where the code is the moral – but point out that in an allegory, everything represents something else.

Exercise D

Set for individual work then pairwork checking. Give students plenty of time to choose words before playing the recording.

Answers

a In Swift's book, the *hero*, Lemuel Gulliver, travels to four different worlds.
b 'Gulliver's Travels' may even be *based on* the Sindbad stories.
c It is certainly true that millions of children have enjoyed the stories in simplified *versions*.
d But the *author*, Jonathan Swift, did not write the book for children.
e He wrote the stories as a *criticism* of the politicians in England at the time.
f 'Robinson Crusoe' is one of the most famous *adventure* stories in the English language.
g It is now a *popular* story with children, but Defoe probably didn't write it as a children's book.
h Some *critics* say the story is an *allegory* for the fight between good and evil.
i I personally believe that Crusoe's life *represents* the advance of civilization.

Closure

Put the students into three groups. Each group must consider the problems of living in a particular strange world, as in *Gulliver's Travels*.

World 1 – a place where all the people are tiny and you are the only normal-sized person.
World 2 – a place where all the people are giants and you are the only normal-sized person.
World 3 – a place where you are the only person; all the other creatures are animals.

Ask students to consider where they would live, what they would eat, how they would travel, the advantages and the dangers of their particular situation.

Then bring the class together for each group to present its ideas to the other groups.

Lesson 2: Listening

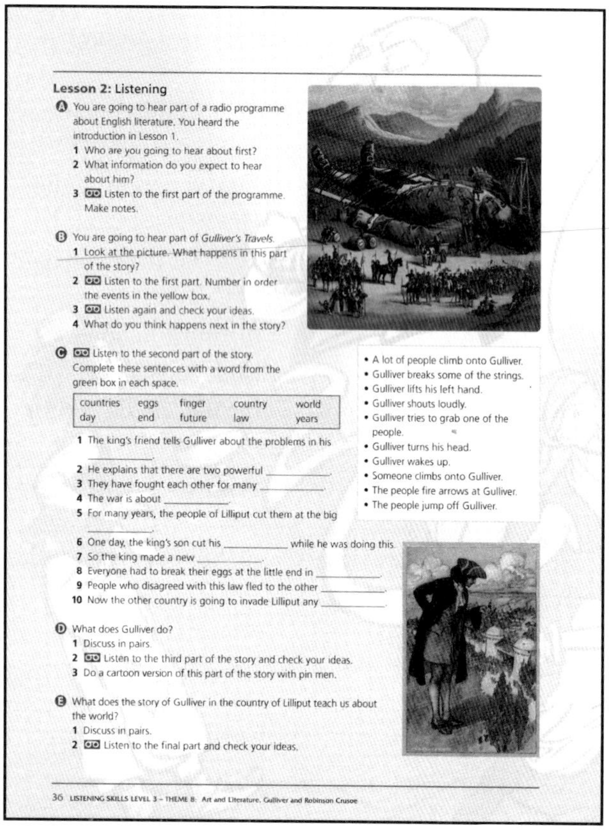

Lesson 2: Listening

A You are going to hear part of a radio programme about English literature. You heard the introduction in Lesson 1.

1 Who are you going to hear about first?
2 What information do you expect to hear about him?
3 Listen to the first part of the programme. Make notes.

B You are going to hear part of *Gulliver's Travels*.

1 Look at the picture. What happens in this part of the story?
2 Listen to the first part. Number in order the events in the yellow box.
3 Listen again and check your ideas.
4 What do you think happens next in the story?

- A lot of people climb onto Gulliver.
- Gulliver breaks some of the strings.
- Gulliver lifts his left hand.
- Gulliver shouts loudly.
- Gulliver tries to grab one of the people.
- Gulliver turns his head.
- Gulliver wakes up.
- Someone climbs onto Gulliver.
- The people fire arrows at Gulliver.
- The people jump off Gulliver.

C Listen to the second part of the story. Complete these sentences with a word from the green box in each space.

countries	eggs	finger	country	world
day	end	future	law	years

1 The king's friend tells Gulliver about the problems in his ____________.
2 He explains that there are two powerful ____________.
3 They have fought each other for many ____________.
4 The war is about ____________.
5 For many years, the people of Lilliput cut them at the big ____________.
6 One day, the king's son cut his ____________ while he was doing this.
7 So the king made a new ____________.
8 Everyone had to break their eggs at the little end in ____________.
9 People who disagreed with this law fled to the other ____________.
10 Now the other country is going to invade Lilliput any ____________.

D What does Gulliver do?

1 Discuss in pairs.
2 Listen to the third part of the story and check your ideas.
3 Do a cartoon version of this part of the story with pin men.

E What does the story of Gulliver in the country of Lilliput teach us about the world?

1 Discuss in pairs.
2 Listen to the final part and check your ideas.

36 LISTENING SKILLS LEVEL 3 – THEME 8: Art and Literature, Gulliver and Robinson Crusoe

Introduction

Dictate the green words from Lesson 1, students' books closed. Students must write down the words, trying to guess the spelling. This further pre-figures the skills work in the next lesson.

Exercise A

Remind students about the radio programme. Elicit some of the key information that they heard in Lesson 1.

1 Elicit ideas and confirm / correct.
2 Set for pairwork. Feed back orally.
3 Set for individual work then pairwork checking. Play the first part of the programme. Feed back, getting a model set of notes on the board.

Answers

1 Jonathan Swift.
2 Biographical details.
3 Model notes:

Jonathan Swift
b. Ireland 30/11/1667, s. of E. lawyer.
grew up Ire.
coll. Dublin (14–21)
1688 → sec. to Sir W. Temple (E. pol)
next 20 yrs = sec; priest = insight into politics and religion?
started writing about it
S. m. Stella Johnson c 1716?
GT = c 1712; pub. 1726
readers = recognise people / events
d 19/10/1745

Exercise B

Refer students to the picture. Elicit some ideas and some of the key vocabulary, e.g., *strings, pegs, tied, on his back*.

1 Ideally, give out the sentences on strips of paper. Set for pairwork. Play the first part of the story. Give students time to order the sentences.
2 Play the same part again. Feed back, perhaps using a large set of sentences to arrange on the board. Deal with any new vocabulary. Otherwise, write the sentences in order.
3 Elicit ideas from the students as a whole class. Point out that Gulliver must learn the little people's language, because he says *As I was told afterwards …*

Answers

1 Answers depend on students.
2 and 3 The correct order is:

1 Gulliver wakes up.
2 Someone climbs onto Gulliver.
3 A lot of people climb onto Gulliver.
4 Gulliver shouts loudly.
5 The people jump off Gulliver.
6 Gulliver breaks some of the strings.
7 Gulliver lifts his left hand.
8 Gulliver turns his head.

9 Gulliver tries to grab one of the people.
10 The people fire arrows at Gulliver.

4 Answers depend on students.

Exercise C

Give students time to look at the sentences and the words. Set for individual work then pairwork checking. Play the second part of the story. Feed back, ideally onto an OHT of the sentences.

Answers

1 The king's friend tells Gulliver about the problems in his *world*.
2 He explains that there are two powerful *countries*.
3 They have fought each other for many *years*.
4 The war is about *eggs*.
5 For many years, the people of Lilliput cut them at the big *end*.
6 One day, the king's son cut his *finger* while he was doing this.
7 So the king made a new *law*.
8 Everyone had to break up their eggs at the little end in *future*.
9 People who disagreed with this law fled to the other *country*.
10 Now the other country is going to invade Lilliput any *day*.

Exercise D

Remind students of the last line of the previous part:

I decided to end the war without bloodshed.

Elicit ideas of what this means, i.e., without anyone dying or being hurt.

1 Set for pairwork. Elicit ideas, but do not confirm or correct.
2 Set for individual work then pairwork checking. Play the final part of the story.
3 Give students plenty of time to do a cartoon version. Feed back, perhaps getting some of them to produce the cartoon version on the board.

Exercise E

1 Set for pairwork. Elicit ideas, but do not confirm or correct. Actually, you can point out that any sensible ideas are acceptable but they are now going to hear the answers of the experts.
2 Set for individual work then pairwork checking. Play the final part of this section of the programme.

Answers

Refer students to the tapescript. Deal with new vocabulary.

Closure

Ask students what they would expect to find in the story of Gulliver in the land of the giants. Encourage them to read this story in a simplified version.

Lesson 3: Learning new skills

Lesson 3: Learning new skills

A There are several proper nouns – names of people and places – in the story in Lesson 2.

1. Listen again to the proper nouns. Write the words. Guess the spelling.
2. Read Skills Check 1.
3. Listen again and check your spelling.

B Study these sentences from Lesson 2.

I felt something creeping up my arm.
Peering down, I saw a human creature …

1. Guess the meaning of each underlined word.
2. Read Skills Check 2 and check.
3. Listen to some sentences from the story. Match the dramatic verbs with the common verbs in the blue box.
4. Make a sentence about Gulliver with each of the dramatic verbs.

fled (flee)	catch
leap / plunge	jump
grab	move
creep	pull
haul / wrench / drag	run away
cry	shout

C Study these sentences from the story.

This is an immense distance for the little men …
The enemy was so terrified when they saw me …

1. Guess the meaning of each underlined word.
2. Read Skills Check 3 and check.
3. Match the extreme adjectives and the meanings in the green box.
4. Make a sentence about Gulliver with each of the extreme adjectives.

freezing	very hot
boiling	very hungry
exhausted	very wet
starving	very large
parched	very small
soaking	very thirsty / dry
enormous	very tired
tiny	very cold

Skills Check 1

Guessing the spelling of proper nouns

Speakers often do not spell proper nouns – the names of people and places. You have to guess the spelling and check it later.

Consonants are easy, but remember some consonant sounds can be spelt in different ways.

Example: /f/ = *f* or *ph*

Here are some common **vowel** patterns:

/æ/ = *a*	/ɑː/ = *a* or *ar*
/e/ = *e*	/ɜː/ = *er*
/ɪ/ = *i*	/iː/ = *ee*
/ɒ/ = *o*	/ɔː/ = *or*
/ʌ/ = *u*	/uː/ = *oo*

You cannot guess the vowel when you hear the sound schwa (/ə/). Write any vowel and check later.

Skills Check 2

Understanding dramatic language (1)

Writers of fiction often use dramatic **verbs** for more common ones.

Examples:

I felt something ~~moving~~ creeping up my arm.

~~Looking~~ Peering down, I saw a human creature …

Don't worry if the verb is not familiar to you. Just work out the meaning from the context. If you can remember the word, check its precise meaning later.

Examples:

creeping = moving very slowly
peering = looking very closely

Skills Check 3

Understanding dramatic language (2)

Writers of fiction often use extreme **adjectives** for more common ones.

Examples:

This is ~~a very big~~ an immense distance for the little men …

The enemy was so ~~very frightened~~ terrified when they saw me …

Don't worry if the adjective is not familiar to you. Just work out the meaning from the context.

LISTENING SKILLS LEVEL 3 – THEME 8: Art and Literature, Gulliver and Robinson Crusoe 37

Introduction

Elicit the main points of the story of Gulliver in the land of Lilliput.

Exercise A

Don't let students look back at Lesson 1 or their notes from Lesson 2.

1. Play the recording or say the names.
2. Set for individual work. Point out that there are also some spelling patterns for diphthongs. These include:
   /aɪ/ = *i_e* or *ai*
   /ɔː/ = *oi*
   /əʊ/ = *o_e*
3. Play the recording or say the names again. Set for pairwork checking. Feed back, getting the words on the board and dealing with the problem areas.

Answers

1. Blefuscu
2. Redresal
3. Lilliput
4. Swift
5. Dublin
6. Stella
7. Johnson
8. Jonathan
9. Spencer

Exercise B

Write the example sentences on the board:

I felt something creeping up my arm.
Peering down, I saw a human creature …

1. Set for individual work then pairwork checking.
2. Set for individual work. Feed back, making sure students understand that the dramatic verb has the same basic meaning as the more common verb.
3. Set for individual work then pairwork checking. Play the sentences. Feed back, getting the pairs of words on the board.
4. Elicit ideas from individual students.

Answers

3	fled (flee)	run away
	leap / plunge	jump
	grab	catch
	creep	move
	haul / wrench / drag	pull
	cry	shout

Exercise C

Write the example sentences on the board:

This is an immense distance for the little men …
The enemy was so terrified when they saw me …

1. Set for individual work then pairwork checking.
2. Set for individual work. Feed back, making sure students understand that the dramatic verb has the same basic meaning as the more common verb.

3 Set for individual work then pairwork checking. Feed back orally, getting the pairs of words on the board.
4 Elicit ideas from individual students.

Answers

3	freezing	very cold
	boiling	very hot
	exhausted	very tired
	starving	very hungry
	parched	very thirsty / dry
	soaking	very wet
	enormous	very large
	tiny	very small

Closure

Dictate some more names of people and places from this course or elsewhere for students to practise guessing spelling.

Lesson 4: Applying new skills

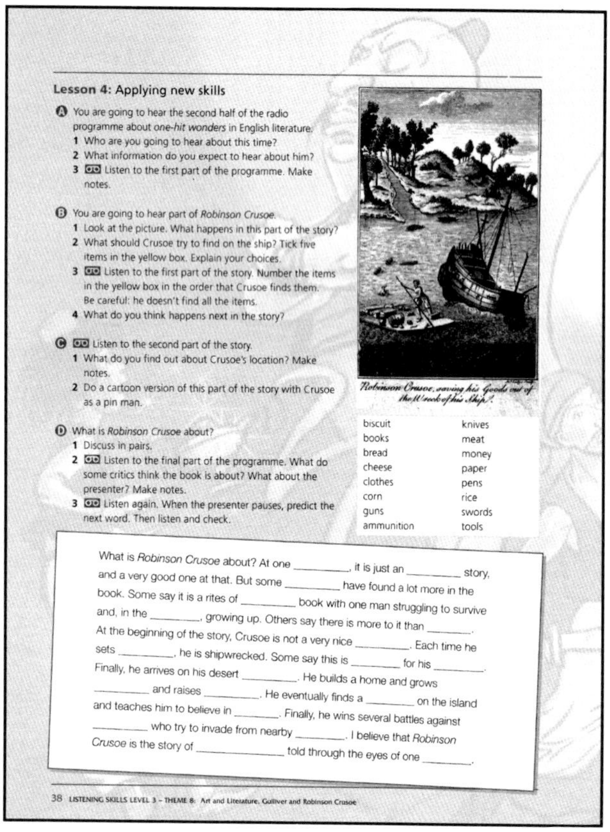

Lesson 4: Applying new skills

A You are going to hear the second half of the radio programme about *one-hit wonders* in English literature.

1. Who are you going to hear about this time?
2. What information do you expect to hear about him?
3. Listen to the first part of the programme. Make notes.

B You are going to hear part of *Robinson Crusoe*.

1. Look at the picture. What happens in this part of the story?
2. What should Crusoe try to find on the ship? Tick five items in the yellow box. Explain your choices.
3. Listen to the first part of the story. Number the items in the yellow box in the order that Crusoe finds them. Be careful: he doesn't find all the items.
4. What do you think happens next in the story?

C Listen to the second part of the story.

1. What do you find out about Crusoe's location? Make notes.
2. Do a cartoon version of this part of the story with Crusoe as a pin man.

D What is *Robinson Crusoe* about?

1. Discuss in pairs.
2. Listen to the final part of the programme. What do some critics think the book is about? What about the presenter? Make notes.
3. Listen again. When the presenter pauses, predict the next word. Then listen and check.

Robinson Crusoe, saving his Goods out of the Wreck of his Ship.

biscuit	knives
books	meat
bread	money
cheese	paper
clothes	pens
corn	rice
guns	swords
ammunition	tools

What is *Robinson Crusoe* about? At one ________, it is just an ________ story, and a very good one at that. But some ________ have found a lot more in the book. Some say it is a rites of ________ book with one man struggling to survive and, in the ________, growing up. Others say there is more to it than ________. At the beginning of the story, Crusoe is not a very nice ________. Each time he sets ________, he is shipwrecked. Some say this is ________ for his ________. Finally, he arrives on his desert ________. He builds a home and grows ________ and raises ________. He eventually finds a ________ on the island and teaches him to believe in ________. Finally, he wins several battles against ________ who try to invade from nearby ________. I believe that *Robinson Crusoe* is the story of ________ told through the eyes of one ________.

38 LISTENING SKILLS LEVEL 3 – THEME 8: Art and Literature, Gulliver and Robinson Crusoe

Introduction

Do some more work with the dramatic verbs and extreme adjectives. For example, tell the story from Lesson 2, putting normal verbs and non-extreme adjectives into the sentences and getting students to suggest changes.

OR

Simply say normal or non-extreme words and elicit the corresponding dramatic / extreme word.

Exercise A

Remind students about this prediction activity in Lesson 2.

1. Elicit that you will now hear about Daniel Defoe.
2. Elicit the sort of biographical details that you will hear. Students should have a very good idea of the content this time because of the notes they made on Jonathan Swift in Lesson 2.
3. Set for individual work then pairwork checking. Play the first part of this half of the programme.

Answers

1 Daniel Defoe.

2 Biographical details.

3 Model notes

Daniel Defoe
b. Lon. 1660 s. of James Foe = butcher / candle-maker.
disappointed = not noble? because added de = of
int. in pol. but → business
24, m. Mary Tuffley
bus + marr = not success
early 1690s = working against James II, K. of Eng. → prison.
= not take sides anymore?
after prison = wrote for both sides
started wr. fiction
many adv. stories = used other names
Rob. Cr. pub. 1719 = only classic
not make money = d. poor 1730

Exercise B

1. Refer students to the picture. Elicit ideas, but do not confirm or correct. Elicit some of the key vocabulary, e.g., *ship, rocks, shore, island, sea.*
2. Set for pairwork. Feed back orally, eliciting reasons. Clearly, there are no right or wrong answers, but this activates the schemata of 'things I need now I'm shipwrecked on a desert island'!
3. Set for individual work then pairwork checking. Play the first part of the story. Feed back, getting the items Crusoe mentions in order on the board. Feed back also on some of the dramatic verbs in this section. Remind students of the verbs and see if they worked out the common meanings – see Answers for the list. Have students discuss which of the items not mentioned by Crusoe he would need, and put them in order of usefulness.
4. Make sure students understand that Crusoe has made a raft – elicit how he did this. Then elicit

ideas. Perhaps he uses a piece of wood for a mast and finds some cloth to make a sail, or something for oars to row back to shore.

Answers

3 This is what Crusoe mentions, in order:
  1 biscuit – you could mention that this would be ship's biscuit, which was hard bread, not like modern biscuits
  2 rice
  3 cheese
  4 meat
  5 corn
  6 tools
  7 ammunition – the shot and, arguably, the powder
  8 guns
  9 swords

  These are the dramatic verbs in this section:

plunged	stuffed	slid
spied	resolved	grabbed
hauled	flung	rage

Exercise C

1 Set for individual work then pairwork checking. Play the second part of the story. Feed back, getting model notes on the board.
2 Set for pairwork. Feed back, perhaps asking students to draw their pin man version on the board.

Answers

1 Key points are:
  - it's an island – Crusoe doesn't know if there are people or wild beasts on it, or not
  - there's a hill
  - Crusoe can see all around it, so it is not very big
  - small islands in the west
  - birds on the island
  - a great (large) wood

Exercise D

1 Set for pairwork. Feed back, eliciting some ideas, but do not confirm or correct. Students may be able to remember ideas from Lesson 1.
2 Remind students that they must always recognise opinions, including the presenter's / lecturer's opinion, while they are listening. Set for individual work then pairwork checking. If you think students might guess the text is from the programme, get them to cover it. Play the final part of the programme. Feed back, getting a model set of notes on the board.
3 Give students plenty of time to read the text and think about words to fill the gaps. Set for individual work then pairwork checking. Play the final part again. Feed back orally. Deal with comprehension points.

Answers

2 (see text)
3 What is 'Robinson Crusoe' about? At one *level*, it is just an *adventure* story, and a very good one at that. But some *critics* have found a lot more in the book. Some say it is a rites of *passage* book with one man struggling to survive and, in the *process*, growing up. Others say there is more to it than *that*. At the beginning of the story, Crusoe is not a very nice *person*. Each time he sets *sail*, he is shipwrecked. Some say this is *punishment* for his *sins*. Finally, he arrives on his desert *island*. He builds a home and grows *crops* and raises *animals*. He eventually finds a *man* on the island and teaches him to believe in *God*. Finally, he wins several battles against *natives* who try to invade from nearby *islands*. I believe that 'Robinson Crusoe' is the story of *civilization* told through the eyes of one *man*.

Closure

Do some more comprehension work on the whole radio programme, perhaps using the transcript to highlight key features.

Lesson 1: Vocabulary

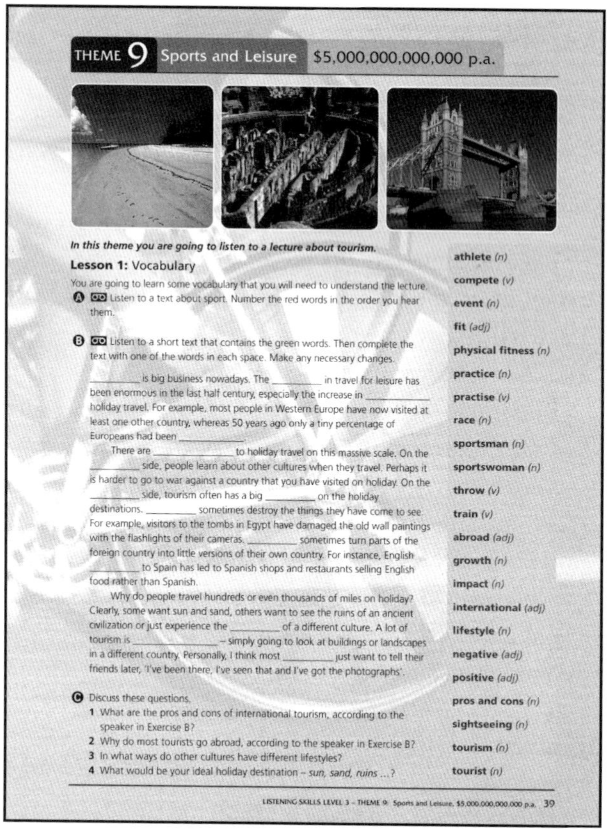

THEME 9 Sports and Leisure $5,000,000,000,000 p.a.

In this theme you are going to listen to a lecture about tourism.

Lesson 1: Vocabulary

You are going to learn some vocabulary that you will need to understand the lecture.

A Listen to a text about sport. Number the red words in the order you hear them.

B Listen to a short text that contains the green words. Then complete the text with one of the words in each space. Make any necessary changes.

__________ is big business nowadays. The __________ in travel for leisure has been enormous in the last half century, especially the increase in __________ holiday travel. For example, most people in Western Europe have now visited at least one other country, whereas 50 years ago only a tiny percentage of Europeans had been __________.

There are __________ to holiday travel on this massive scale. On the __________ side, people learn about other cultures when they travel. Perhaps it is harder to go to war against a country that you have visited on holiday. On the __________ side, tourism often has a big __________ on the holiday destinations. __________ sometimes destroy the things they have come to see. For example, visitors to the tombs in Egypt have damaged the old wall paintings with the flashlights of their cameras. __________ sometimes turn parts of the foreign country into little versions of their own country. For instance, English __________ to Spain has led to Spanish shops and restaurants selling English food rather than Spanish.

Why do people travel hundreds or even thousands of miles on holiday? Clearly, some want sun and sand, others want to see the ruins of an ancient civilization or just experience the __________ of a different culture. A lot of tourism is __________ – simply going to look at buildings or landscapes in a different country. Personally, I think most __________ just want to tell their friends later, 'I've been there, I've seen that and I've got the photographs'.

C Discuss these questions.

1 What are the pros and cons of international tourism, according to the speaker in Exercise B?
2 Why do most tourists go abroad, according to the speaker in Exercise B?
3 In what ways do other cultures have different lifestyles?
4 What would be your ideal holiday destination – *sun, sand, ruins ...*?

athlete *(n)*
compete *(v)*
event *(n)*
fit *(adj)*
physical fitness *(n)*
practice *(n)*
practise *(v)*
race *(n)*
sportsman *(n)*
sportswoman *(n)*
throw *(v)*
train *(v)*
abroad *(adj)*
growth *(n)*
impact *(n)*
international *(adj)*
lifestyle *(n)*
negative *(adj)*
positive *(adj)*
pros and cons *(n)*
sightseeing *(n)*
tourism *(n)*
tourist *(n)*

LISTENING SKILLS LEVEL 3 – THEME 9: Sports and Leisure, $5,000,000,000,000 p.a. 39

The following listening sub-skills have been covered in the course to date:

- fixed phrases;
- using abbreviations in notes;
- taking notes of stories, ideas, etc.;
- using signs in notes;
- recognising digressions;
- signposts, mini-signposts and two-sided signposts;
- leaving space in notes for missing information;
- rhetorical questions → real questions;
- distinguishing fact from opinion;
- participating in discussions;
- understanding a speaker's argument;
- guessing the spelling of proper nouns;
- understanding dramatic language.

There is further practice of most of these points in this theme, in addition to new sub-skills work.

Introduction

Write the title of the theme on the board – *Sports and Leisure*. Elicit different kinds of sport, and other leisure activities.

Make sure students recognise that leisure is free time and that there is a 'leisure industry' that provides products – like television programmes, magazines, movies – for people to occupy their leisure time with.

If students did this theme at Level 2, tell them they are going to hear a text from that theme again in Exercise A. If students didn't do this theme at Level 2, consider skipping Exercise A as it does not directly relate to anything in the lessons that follow.

Exercise A

Set for individual work then pairwork checking. Explain that the students only need to number the word or phrase on first mention. Point out that they will not hear one of the words or phrases. Play the recording. Feed back by playing the recording again, stopping after the first mention of each red word.

Answers

The correct order:

1	sportsman	8	train
2	sportswoman	9	fit
3	athlete	10	practise – it must be the verb although it sounds the same as the noun
4	race	11	compete
5	event		
6	throw		
7	physical fitness		

The students do not hear: *practice* (*n*).

The text – target items in italics:

At one time, people who did sports were called *sportsmen* or *sportswomen*. At that time, an *athlete* was a person who ran *races* or took part in *events* on the field – for example, the high jump or *throwing* the javelin. Nowadays, people use the word 'athlete' to mean any person involved in sport. The word is used to separate the playing skills from the *physical fitness* of the player. So you will often hear someone say, 'He is a great tennis player and a superb athlete'. Athletes in any sport *train* hard and are very *fit*. They usually *practise* their sport for hours each day. Top athletes love to *compete* against other top players and, of course, to beat them.

Exercise B

Exploit the visual. Elicit at least *ruins, sun* and *sand, golf course, skiing, sightseeing*. Set for individual work then pairwork checking. Play the recording. Feed back by reading the text up to each space and eliciting fillers.

Check comprehension of the text, perhaps with a 'stupid teacher' version where you keep making silly mistakes and students (books closed) try to correct you, e.g.,

> *Tourism was big business in the past. The growth in travel for leisure has been quite large in the last half century, especially the increase in national holiday travel. For example, most people in Western Europe have now visited at least ten other countries, whereas 50 years ago only tiny Europeans had been abroad.*

Answers

Tourism is big business nowadays. The *growth* in travel for leisure has been enormous in the last half century, especially the increase in *international* holiday travel. For example, most people in Western Europe have now visited at least one other country, whereas 50 years ago only a tiny percentage of Europeans had been *abroad*.

There are *pros and cons* to holiday travel on this massive scale. On the *positive* side, people learn about other cultures when they travel. Perhaps it is harder to go to war against a country that you have visited on holiday. On the *negative* side, tourism often has a big *impact* on the holiday destinations. *Tourists* sometimes destroy the things they have come to see. For example, visitors to the tombs in Egypt have damaged the old wall paintings with the flashlights of their cameras. *Tourists* sometimes turn parts of the foreign country into little versions of their own country. For instance, English *tourism* to Spain has led to Spanish shops and restaurants selling English food rather than Spanish.

Why do people travel hundreds or even thousands of miles on holiday? Clearly some want sun and sand, others want to see the ruins of an ancient civilization or just experience the *lifestyle* of a different culture. A lot of tourism is *sightseeing* – simply going to look at buildings or landscapes in a different country. Personally, I think most *tourists* just want to tell their friends later, 'I've been there, I've seen that and I've got the photographs'.

Language and culture note

Point out that *tourist / tourism* comes from the noun or verb *tour*. You can compare this word with words from the same lexical set as follows:

tour (*n*) = visits to several places, one after the other, then back to the starting point, usually for pleasure
journey = one piece of travel from A to B
trip (*n*) = short piece of travel, perhaps to one place and back

tour (*v*) = to go round and visit different places, usually for pleasure
travel (*v*) = move from place to place, often followed by the method – *We travelled by train* = there is no indication if this is for pleasure or business

Exercise C

Set for group work. Monitor and assist. Feed back with some of the interesting ideas.

Closure

Dictate the stressed syllables of the multi-syllable green words for students to identify the full word in each case, i.e.,

broad	a'broad
im	'impact
nati (i.e. /nash/	inter'national
life	'lifestyle
neg	'negative
pos	'positive
sight	'sightseeing
tour	'tourism or 'tourist

Lesson 2: Listening

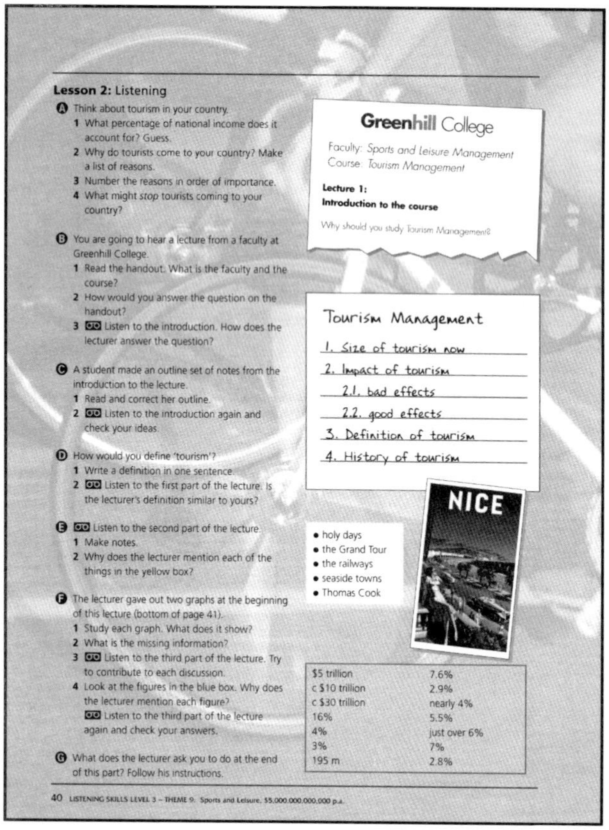

Lesson 2: Listening

A Think about tourism in your country.
1 What percentage of national income does it account for? Guess.
2 Why do tourists come to your country? Make a list of reasons.
3 Number the reasons in order of importance.
4 What might *stop* tourists coming to your country?

B You are going to hear a lecture from a faculty at Greenhill College.
1 Read the handout. What is the faculty and the course?
2 How would you answer the question on the handout?
3 Listen to the introduction. How does the lecturer answer the question?

C A student made an outline set of notes from the introduction to the lecture.
1 Read and correct her outline.
2 Listen to the introduction again and check your ideas.

D How would you define 'tourism'?
1 Write a definition in one sentence.
2 Listen to the first part of the lecture. Is the lecturer's definition similar to yours?

E Listen to the second part of the lecture.
1 Make notes.
2 Why does the lecturer mention each of the things in the yellow box?

F The lecturer gave out two graphs at the beginning of this lecture (bottom of page 41).
1 Study each graph. What does it show?
2 What is the missing information?
3 Listen to the third part of the lecture. Try to contribute to each discussion.
4 Look at the figures in the blue box. Why does the lecturer mention each figure?
Listen to the third part of the lecture again and check your answers.

G What does the lecturer ask you to do at the end of this part? Follow his instructions.

Greenhill College
Faculty: *Sports and Leisure Management*
Course: *Tourism Management*
Lecture 1:
Introduction to the course
Why should you study Tourism Management?

Tourism Management
1. Size of tourism now
2. Impact of tourism
2.1. bad effects
2.2. good effects
3. Definition of tourism
4. History of tourism

- holy days
- the Grand Tour
- the railways
- seaside towns
- Thomas Cook

NICE

$5 trillion	7.6%
c $10 trillion	2.9%
c $30 trillion	nearly 4%
16%	5.5%
4%	just over 6%
3%	7%
195 m	2.8%

40 LISTENING SKILLS LEVEL 3 – THEME 9: Sports and Leisure, $5,000,000,000,000 p.a.

Introduction

Give definitions of the green words from Lesson 1. Elicit the words.

Exercise A

Set for group work. If students are from different countries, put them into groups from the same country. Feed back, getting a list of reasons on the board for each relevant country – and a composite list of reasons that stop tourists going to a destination. Mention global epidemics like SARS, national problems like UK 'mad cow disease' and, if it is politically acceptable, mention or elicit terrorism.

Exercise B

Refer students to the handout.

1 and 2 Set for pairwork. Feed back orally. Do not confirm or correct.

3 Set for individual work then pairwork checking. Play the introduction. Feed back, getting the lecturer's reasons on the board.

Answers

1 Tourism is big business.

2 Tourism is having a huge impact on many countries and areas of the world.

Exercise C

Refer students to the outline notes. Remind them that notes like this show the anticipated structure of the lecture. In their notebooks, they should leave a lot of space under each heading and subheading for the actual notes.

1 Set for individual work then pairwork checking. Do not confirm or correct.

2 Play the introduction again. Feed back, getting a model outline on the board. Point out that the lecturer says *Before we look at …*, so these points will come before the main body of the lecture.

Answers

Tourism Management

1. *Definition of tourism*
2. *History of tourism*
3. *Size of tourism now*
4. *Impact of tourism*
   4.1. *good effects*
   4.2. *bad effects*

Exercise D

1 Set for individual work then pairwork checking. Elicit some ideas but do not confirm or correct.

2 Set for individual work then pairwork checking. Play Part 1. Feed back, getting the lecturer's first definition on the board.

Answers

A tourist is a person who travels for pleasure, goes at least 50 kilometres from his or her home and stays away at least one night.

Exercise E

Elicit the topic of the second part. Students can work it out from the model outline notes.

1. Set for individual work then pairwork checking. Do not feed back at this point.
2. Set for pairwork. Feed back onto the board.

Answers

1. Students' notes should enable them to explain the relevance of all the points in the yellow box.
2. Model answer:
   - holy days: the origins of *holiday* in English
   - the Grand Tour: very early international tourism
   - the railways: they started domestic or internal tourism
   - seaside towns: started to cater for internal tourists
   - Thomas Cook: organised the first package holiday

Language and culture note

It will not be difficult for Muslim students to appreciate that holidays were originally holy days, since the holiness of public holidays is still widely observed in the Islamic world.

Exercise F

1. Refer students to the graphs at the bottom of the facing page. Set for pairwork. Feed back orally.
2. Elicit ideas. Confirm or correct (2010 and 2020).
3. Point out that in this section the lecturer asks the audience actually to contribute. Play Part 3. When you get to key points, i.e., where students are asked to contribute, stop the recording and see if the students can contribute something relevant and perhaps even correct.
4. Refer students to the blue box with numbers and percentages. Set for pairwork. Play Part 3 again. Feed back onto the board.

Answers

1 and 2 The complete graphs:

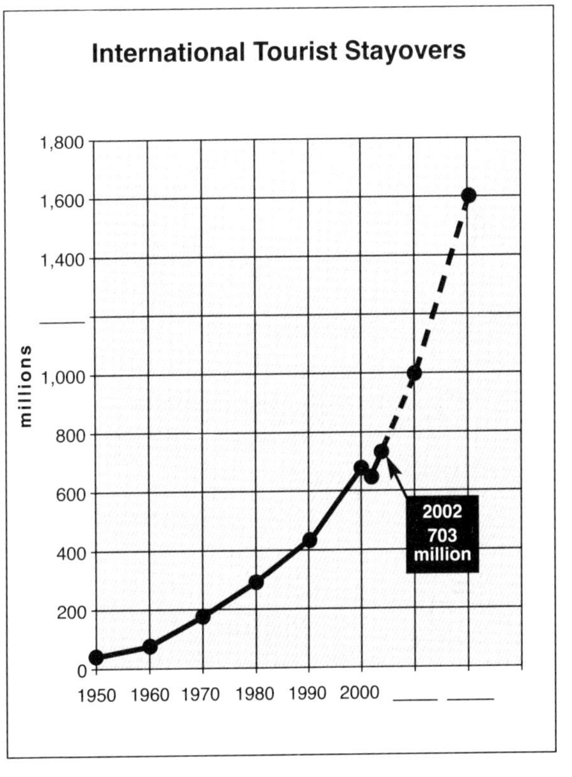

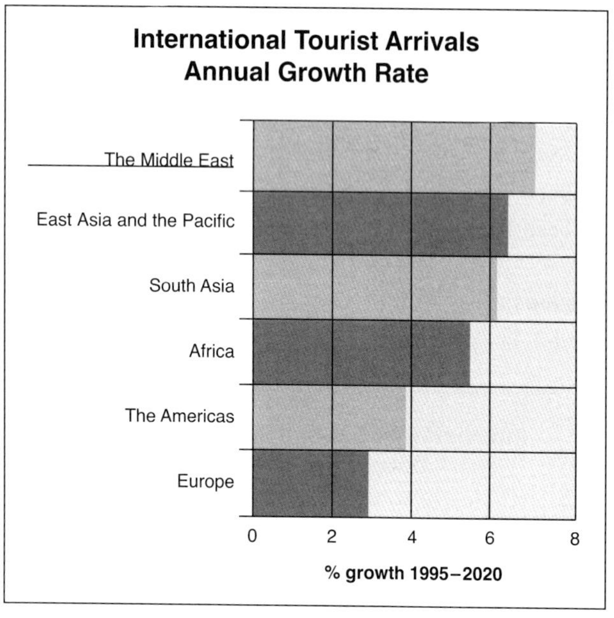

4	$5 trillion	value of tourism
	c $10 trillion	US production
	c $30 trillion	total world production
	16%	contribution of tourism to world economy
	4%	contribution of agriculture to world economy
	3%	contribution of petroleum to world economy
	195 m	the number of jobs in tourism worldwide
	7.6%	the proportion of people worldwide engaged in tourism
	2.9%	tourism growth rate in Europe
	nearly 4%	tourism growth rate in the Americas
	5.5%	tourism growth rate in Africa
	just over 6%	tourism growth rate in South Asia
	7%	tourism growth rate in the Middle East
	2.8%	growth rate in the world economy

Exercise G

Set for pairwork.

Closure

Elicit some ideas from the pairs from Exercise G. Build up a table of pros and cons of tourism on the board. Don't push students to answers they don't corporately come up with. There are plenty of ideas in Lesson 4.

Possible answers

pros	cons
increases employment	low-skill jobs
provides foreign exchange	pollution increase
supports habitation in rural areas	destroys nature
supports public transport	destroys morals, national values
protects national heritage	national heritage gets lost

Lesson 3: Learning new skills

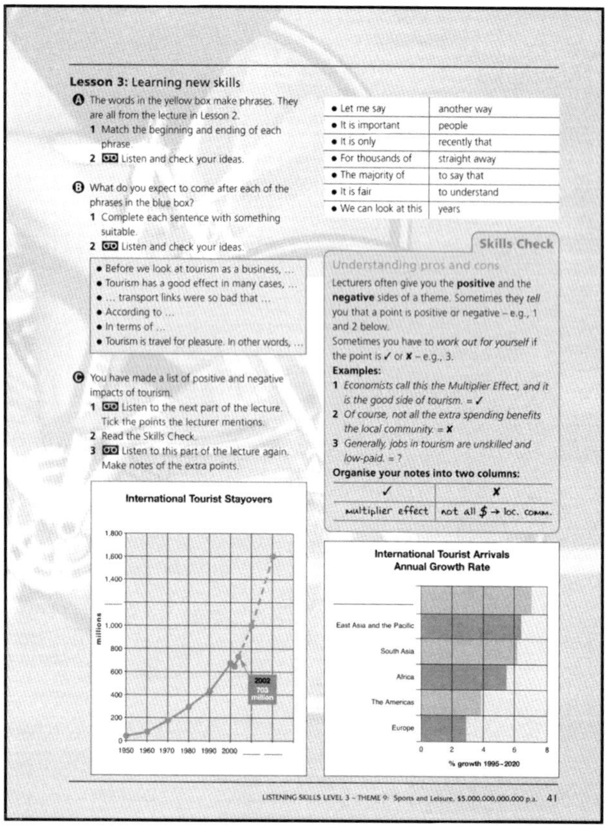
Lesson 3: Learning new skills

A The words in the yellow box make phrases. They are all from the lecture in Lesson 2.

1 Match the beginning and ending of each phrase.

2 Listen and check your ideas.

• Let me say	another way
• It is important	people
• It is only	recently that
• For thousands of	straight away
• The majority of	to say that
• It is fair	to understand
• We can look at this	years

B What do you expect to come after each of the phrases in the blue box?

1 Complete each sentence with something suitable.

2 Listen and check your ideas.

- Before we look at tourism as a business, …
- Tourism has a good effect in many cases, …
- … transport links were so bad that …
- According to …
- In terms of …
- Tourism is travel for pleasure. In other words, …

C You have made a list of positive and negative impacts of tourism.

1 Listen to the next part of the lecture. Tick the points the lecturer mentions.

2 Read the Skills Check.

3 Listen to this part of the lecture again. Make notes of the extra points.

Skills Check

Understanding pros and cons

Lecturers often give you the **positive** and the **negative** sides of a theme. Sometimes they *tell* you that a point is positive or negative – e.g., 1 and 2 below.

Sometimes you have to *work out for yourself* if the point is ✓ or ✗ – e.g., 3.

Examples:

1 *Economists call this the Multiplier Effect, and it is the good side of tourism.* = ✓

2 *Of course, not all the extra spending benefits the local community.* = ✗

3 *Generally, jobs in tourism are unskilled and low-paid.* = ?

Organise your notes into two columns:

✓	✗
multiplier effect	not all $ → loc. comm.

LISTENING SKILLS LEVEL 3 – THEME 9: Sports and Leisure, $5,000,000,000,000 p.a. 41

Introduction

1 Check that students can understand and write down very large numbers. Dictate some, e.g.,

26 million

4.5 billion

5 trillion

2 Elicit some pros of tourism and then some cons. Get students to make notes of these – they will need their notes for Exercise C below.

Exercise A

Remind students of the importance of understanding fixed and semi-fixed phrases – if you can recognise a phrase quickly, your brain can move straight on to the next piece of content.

1 Set for individual work then pairwork checking. Do not confirm or correct.

2 Play the recording. Feed back, getting the complete phrases on the board.

Answers

Let me say	straight away
It is important	to understand
It is only	recently that
For thousands of	years
The majority of	people
It is fair	to say that
We can look at this	another way

Exercise B

Remind students that phrases often help you to predict the next content. Refer students to the blue box.

1 Explain that you are looking for *actual* content, i.e., from the lecture, or *type* of content, e.g., after *According to …* you must name a source of information. Set for pairwork. Do not feed back at this point.

2 Play the recording. Elicit actual or type of content in each case.

Answers

introductory phrase	actual content	type of content
Before we look at tourism as a business, …	we need to define tourism.	something else must happen first
Tourism has a good effect in many cases, …	a bad effect in others	contrast
Even if you had time and money to travel, transport links were so bad that …	it was no pleasure to travel anyway	result
According to …	the WTO, tourism contributes about 5 trillion US dollars each year to the world economy	source – person or organisation
In terms of …	employment, the travel and tourism industry will account for 195 million jobs worldwide in 2003	field – usually an abstract noun, e.g., time, money, the economy, etc.
Tourism is travel for pleasure. In other words …	it is part of the ever-increasing leisure industry	restatement

Exercise C

Refer students to the list of pros and cons on the board. Point out that this is their list, not necessarily the lecturer's ideas.

1 Set for pairwork. Play the fourth part of the lecture. Feed back, ticking points onto the board.
2 Set for individual work then pairwork checking.
3 Play the fourth part again. Elicit ideas and build up a pros and cons table on the board. Point out that you can sometimes match up pros and cons.

✓	✗
more employment	unskilled jobs
	people leave traditional work
	people lose independence, self-respect
tourists spend money locally	not all money to local community
tourism improves facilities for everybody	tourists have priority over the locals
government gets money from taxation	not enough money sometimes to build the necessary infrastructure
	tourists destroy what they have come to see – example of coral reefs
	tourists behave badly on holiday – give locals the wrong impression of their culture

Closure

Elicit all the possible harmful effects of tourism on coral reefs:

- souvenirs of coral become popular and both locals and tourists break off pieces;
- ground-up coral is a good building material – as more buildings go up, the coral reef goes down;
- anchors of tourist boats scrape against the coral and damage it;
- extra waste products from the growing town are piped into the sea and the coral dies under the murky waters.

Lesson 4: Applying new skills

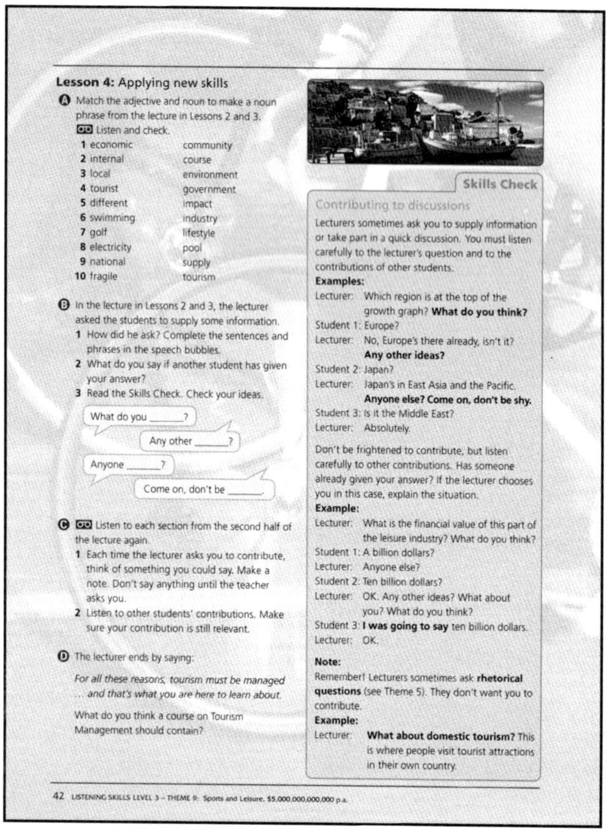

Lesson 4: Applying new skills

A Match the adjective and noun to make a noun phrase from the lecture in Lessons 2 and 3.
Listen and check.

1 economic	community
2 internal	course
3 local	environment
4 tourist	government
5 different	impact
6 swimming	industry
7 golf	lifestyle
8 electricity	pool
9 national	supply
10 fragile	tourism

B In the lecture in Lessons 2 and 3, the lecturer asked the students to supply some information.

1 How did he ask? Complete the sentences and phrases in the speech bubbles.
2 What do you say if another student has given your answer?
3 Read the Skills Check. Check your ideas.

What do you ______?
Any other ______?
Anyone ______?
Come on, don't be ______.

C Listen to each section from the second half of the lecture again.

1 Each time the lecturer asks you to contribute, think of something you could say. Make a note. Don't say anything until the teacher asks you.
2 Listen to other students' contributions. Make sure your contribution is still relevant.

D The lecturer ends by saying:

For all these reasons, tourism must be managed ... and that's what you are here to learn about.

What do you think a course on Tourism Management should contain?

Skills Check

Contributing to discussions

Lecturers sometimes ask you to supply information or take part in a quick discussion. You must listen carefully to the lecturer's question and to the contributions of other students.

Examples:

Lecturer: Which region is at the top of the growth graph? **What do you think?**
Student 1: Europe?
Lecturer: No, Europe's there already, isn't it? **Any other ideas?**
Student 2: Japan?
Lecturer: Japan's in East Asia and the Pacific. **Anyone else? Come on, don't be shy.**
Student 3: Is it the Middle East?
Lecturer: Absolutely.

Don't be frightened to contribute, but listen carefully to other contributions. Has someone already given your answer? If the lecturer chooses you in this case, explain the situation.

Example:

Lecturer: What is the financial value of this part of the leisure industry? What do you think?
Student 1: A billion dollars?
Lecturer: Anyone else?
Student 2: Ten billion dollars?
Lecturer: OK. Any other ideas? What about you? What do you think?
Student 3: **I was going to say** ten billion dollars.
Lecturer: OK.

Note:

Remember! Lecturers sometimes ask **rhetorical questions** (see Theme 5). They don't want you to contribute.

Example:

Lecturer: **What about domestic tourism?** This is where people visit tourist attractions in their own country.

42 LISTENING SKILLS LEVEL 3 – THEME 9: Sports and Leisure, $5,000,000,000,000 p.a.

Introduction

Give some of the big numbers and percentages from Lesson 2 Exercise F and see if students can remember what they refer to.

Exercise A

Remind students about collocation – particular adjectives and nouns are often found together.

Set for individual work then pairwork checking. Play the recording. Elicit the correct combinations.

Answers

1 economic	impact
2 internal	tourism
3 local	community
4 tourist	industry
5 different	lifestyle
6 swimming	pool
7 golf	course
8 electricity	supply
9 national	government
10 fragile	environment

Methodology note

What is *golf* in the expression *golf course*? Strictly speaking, it is a noun, but since it is modifying a noun, there is no reason why students shouldn't see it as an adjective. If it comes up, point out that some words in English can be nouns and adjectives.

Exercise B

Remind students about the section of the lecture where the audience contributes.

1 Set for pairwork. Do not feed back.
2 Elicit ideas. Do not feed back.
3 Set for individual work then pairwork checking. Feed back onto the board. Work through each section of the Skills Check, getting students to take the parts of the various participants.

Methodology note

With regard to the final note, point out the semiotics and paralinguistic features of lecturing. A rhetorical question looks and sounds very different from a question actually demanding a contribution – the latter will be addressed direct to the audience, with raised eyebrows, 'open' face and will have a clear questioning intonation followed by a long pause. A rhetorical question may be said, head down, in the stream of speech, and may be immediately followed by the answer.

Answers

1 What do you *think*?
Any other *ideas*?
Anyone *else*?
Come on, don't be *shy*.

2 Possible sentence: *I was going to say ...*

Exercise C

Take plenty of time to set this up. Make sure students realise that they must make notes first, not shout out. Then they contribute when they are called upon. During each pause, use the language from Exercise B to elicit contributions – don't nominate students by name on this occasion, as this is unlikely to happen in a lecture hall.

Exercise D

Set for group or whole-class discussion.

Closure

Feed back on Exercise D. Based on the lecture, it would seem that Tourism Management must address at least the following:

- how to encourage 'good' tourism, i.e., tourism that has a positive impact on the local community;
- how to reduce any negative impact on the local community, especially protection of fragile environments;
- how to pay for infrastructure;
- how to protect the local culture, its norms and values;
- how to keep tourist dollars local and prevent too much 'leakage'.

Lesson 1: Vocabulary

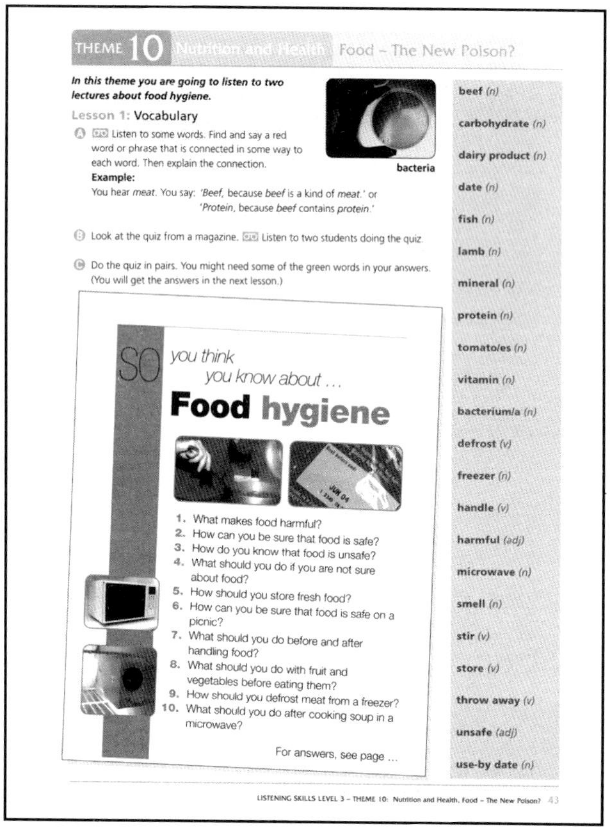
THEME 10 Nutrition and Health Food – The New Poison?

In this theme you are going to listen to two lectures about food hygiene.

Lesson 1: Vocabulary

A Listen to some words. Find and say a red word or phrase that is connected in some way to each word. Then explain the connection.

Example:

You hear *meat*. You say: '*Beef,* because *beef* is a kind of *meat*.' or '*Protein*, because *beef* contains *protein*.'

bacteria

B Look at the quiz from a magazine. Listen to two students doing the quiz.

C Do the quiz in pairs. You might need some of the green words in your answers. (You will get the answers in the next lesson.)

SO you think you know about …

Food hygiene

1. What makes food harmful?
2. How can you be sure that food is safe?
3. How do you know that food is unsafe?
4. What should you do if you are not sure about food?
5. How should you store fresh food?
6. How can you be sure that food is safe on a picnic?
7. What should you do before and after handling food?
8. What should you do with fruit and vegetables before eating them?
9. How should you defrost meat from a freezer?
10. What should you do after cooking soup in a microwave?

For answers, see page …

beef *(n)*
carbohydrate *(n)*
dairy product *(n)*
date *(n)*
fish *(n)*
lamb *(n)*
mineral *(n)*
protein *(n)*
tomato/es *(n)*
vitamin *(n)*
bacterium/a *(n)*
defrost *(v)*
freezer *(n)*
handle *(v)*
harmful *(adj)*
microwave *(n)*
smell *(n)*
stir *(v)*
store *(v)*
throw away *(v)*
unsafe *(adj)*
use-by date *(n)*

LISTENING SKILLS LEVEL 3 – THEME 10: Nutrition and Health, Food – The New Poison? 43

General note

In this course, the students have learnt how to:

- recognise a large number of fixed phrases;
- use abbreviations in notes;
- take notes of stories, ideas, etc.;
- use symbols in notes;
- leave space in notes for missing information;
- recognise digressions;
- recognise signpost language;
- recognise rhetorical questions;
- distinguish fact from opinion;
- contribute to a discussion;
- understand a speaker's argument;
- guess the spelling of proper nouns;
- understand dramatic language;
- understand pros and cons.

Most of these points are revised in this theme, but take every opportunity for revision. Be prepared to refer students back to previous themes to look again at Skills Checks and even do some of the related activities again.

Introduction

Write the subtitle of the theme on the board – *Food – the new poison?* Elicit the meaning of *poison*. Ask for ideas on the meaning of the title. Elicit the fact that you often get a stomachache if you eat bad food.

Remind students who did Level 2 about the two ways of classifying food – by type, e.g., fruit, vegetables, etc., and by nutrients, e.g., carbohydrate, protein, etc. You might like to build up the two tables from Level 2 Theme 10, as follows:

Figure 1: Classifying foods – by type

FOODS

Groups	FRUIT	VEGETABLES	MEAT	FISH	DAIRY PRODUCTS
Examples	apples	carrots	chicken	salmon	cheese
	oranges	peas	beef	hammour	milk
	melons	tomatoes	lamb	shark	butter
	dates				

Figure 2: Classifying foods – by nutrients

FOODS

Groups	CARBOHYDRATE	PROTEIN	FAT	VITAMINS	MINERALS
Foods	bread	cheese	cheese	fruit	fish
	pasta	fish	fish	vegetables	meat
	rice	meat	meat		milk
			milk		

Exercise A

Set for individual work then pairwork checking. Work through the example. Play the recording. Allow several students to contribute on each occasion. This is an opportunity to revise the language of contributing to a discussion, e.g.,

What do you think?
Any ideas?
Anyone else?

Remind students that if their choice has been taken, they can say:

I was going to say …

Answers

Possible connections:

meat	beef / lamb / protein
potatoes	carbohydrate
eggs	dairy product; protein
palm tree	date
salmon	fish; protein
sheep	lamb (the meat or the young animal)
iron	mineral
vegetable	tomato; vitamin
A, B, C, D and E	vitamin

Exercise B

Refer students to the quiz. Give them plenty of time to read the questions, but don't deal with new vocabulary at this point. Explain that the students are going to hear some information to help them with new words.

Set for individual work then pairwork checking. Play the recording. Feed back by eliciting the definitions of the new words given by Student 1 on the recording. Refer students to the illustrations to check some of the other new words from this theme.

Answers

The words Student 1 defines are:

harmful	can hurt you, harm you, make you ill
bacterium/a	tiny, living creatures that you find in the air, or in water, or in food
unsafe	the opposite of *safe*, but not as strong as *dangerous*
store	keep for some time
handle	touch with your hands; in this case, prepare and cook
defrost	'unfreeze'

Exercise C

Set for pairwork. Monitor but do not confirm or correct answers. Feed back by asking questions from the quiz at random, students' books closed, but still do not confirm or correct. The answers are given in the lecture in Lesson 2.

Closure

Say the first two or three sounds of the green words. Students try to guess the word you are going to say (e.g., *ba* = *bacterium/a*).

Methodology note

The human brain recognises words from L1 with just the first two or three phonemes. We must try to train students to do this in L2, otherwise they will be spending too long decoding incoming data and miss the next word or section of speech.

Lesson 2: Listening review (1)

Lesson 2: Listening review (1)

A Look back at the quiz in Lesson 1. Think of an answer for each question.

B In this course you have learnt to recognise signposts to help you organise your notes.
Listen to the introduction to the lecture. Complete the outline notes.

C In this course you have learnt to make notes using abbreviations and symbols.
Listen to the first part of the lecture and make notes.

Food
1 Harmful food – three factors
1.1 bacteria
1.2 ______
1.3 ______
2 Looking after food
2.1 storing
2.2 ______
2.3 use-by date

D Decide if each of the statements below is true or false.
Listen again and check your answers.
1 You cannot see bacteria without a microscope.
2 All bacteria are harmful.
3 Some bacteria can kill you.
4 Four bacteria multiply to become six.
5 Bacteria die at less than 4°C.

E In this course you have learnt to guess the spelling of proper nouns. You have also learnt to recognise digressions.
Listen to the second part of the lecture.
1 Make notes of the main points.
2 Guess the spelling of any proper nouns.
3 Do not make notes of the information in any digression.

F In this course you have learnt to recognise rhetorical questions and to contribute to discussions during a lecture.
1 Complete the rhetorical questions (blue box) from the lecture so far.
2 How does the lecturer answer each question?
3 Listen to the third part of the lecture. Recognise rhetorical questions. Contribute to the discussion when the lecturer asks you to.

When does food ______ harmful?
How can you be ______ that food is safe?
What is the correct ______ to handle food?

G Do the quiz from Lesson 1 again. Use information from the lecture to answer the questions.

44 LISTENING SKILLS LEVEL 3 – THEME 10: Nutrition and Health, Food – The New Poison?

Introduction

Explain that you are going to give definitions of the green words for students to recognise. Say the definitions in the left-hand column and perform the mimes as indicated to elicit the words in the right-hand column:

something that can hurt you, harm you, make you ill is called …	*harmful*
tiny, living creatures that you find in the air, in water or in food	*bacterium/a*
the opposite of *safe*, but not as strong as *dangerous*	*unsafe*
keep for some time	*store*
touch with your hands; in this case, prepare and cook	*handle*
'unfreeze'	*defrost*
place (household appliance) where you can keep food very cold for some time	*freezer*
place (household appliance) where you can cook food quickly	*microwave*
something you can sense with your nose [do not mime – see Language and culture note, below] – roses have a nice …	*smell*
put in the rubbish / garbage bin [mime]	*throw away*
move liquid with a spoon [mime]	*stir*
the date on food by which you must use / eat it	*use-by date*

Language and culture note

It is considered offensive by some Muslims to try deliberately to smell things. Part of the objection to dogs is their obtrusive use of the nose. Do not mime sniffing things to put across the idea of *smell* as a noun or verb.

Exercise A

Spend considerable time on this, unless this lesson is taking place only shortly after Lesson 1. You could even go through the questions again with the whole class, teasing the students when they reach consensus by saying, e.g., *Are you sure? Really? Is that your final answer?* Do not confirm or correct, but explain that they are going to get answers in the lecture.

Methodology note

It is a given of teaching listening now that we only understand spoken language fully when we are listening for a purpose. The quiz questions set up a desire to know this information, even if it was not there before. The lecture will, directly or indirectly, give answers to all the questions.

Exercise B

Remind students of the purpose of the introduction to a lecture – it usually gives you a good idea of the organisation of the lecture. Refer students to the outline notes and elicit ideas of missing words.

Set for individual work then pairwork checking. Play the introduction. Feed back, getting a model version of the outline on the board.

Answers

Model version:

<u>*Food hygiene*</u>

1 *Harmful food – three factors*
  - 1.1 *bacteria*
  - 1.2 *temp.*
  - 1.3 *time*

2 *Looking after food*
  - 2.1 *storing*
  - 2.2 *handling*
  - 2.3 *use-by date*

Exercise C

Remind students about note-taking – abbreviations and symbols. Set for individual work then pairwork checking. Play Part 1. Feed back, getting a model version on the board. Do not do any more detailed comprehension at this point – Exercise D checks that.

Answers

Model version:

1 *Harmful food – three factors*
  - 1.1 *bacteria = harmful*
  - 1.2 *temp. = 4–60°C = 'danger zone'*
  - 1.3 *time = > 2 hrs*

Exercise D

Set for pairwork. Play Part 1 again. Feed back orally. Deal with new vocabulary.

Answers

1 True – They are invisible to the naked eye.
2 False – Some are necessary.
3 True – It says they can cause death.
4 False – They become eight.
5 False – They cannot multiply, but they do not die.

Exercise E

Remind students of the common spellings of certain sounds (Theme 8 Lesson 3). Point out also that some combinations of letters make surprising sounds, e.g., *tu* in *picture*, *lecture*; *ti* in *action*, *fiction*; *ph* in *phone*.

Tell students to be ready to guess the spelling if they hear a proper noun, i.e., the name of something. Remind students about the meaning of and method for dealing with digressions. Set for individual work then pairwork checking. Play Part 2. Feed back by getting a model version on the board.

Answers

bad food ≠ smell / look funny
e.g., botulism (This is the only proper noun in this section.)
maj, food = safe BUT if in doubt, throw it out!

1. storing
   fresh f. → fridge > 4°C
   cover when not in fr.
   not > 2 hrs
   picnic = cool box + ice
   (digression about *wadi* trip)
2. handling
   wash hands before prep. AND after
   wash fr. & veg. before eating

Exercise F

Remind students about the use of rhetorical questions and invitations to contribute in lectures.

1 Set for pairwork. Feed back orally.
2 Whole-class discussion.

3 Set for individual work. Play Part 3. Pause the recording for as long as necessary to elicit contributions.

Answers

1 When does food *become* harmful?
How can you be *sure* that food is safe?
What is the correct *way* to handle food?

2 *When does food become harmful?* – Depends on three factors: there are harmful bacteria in or on the food; the food is in the temperature danger zone (between 4 and 60°C); the food is left in the danger zone for more than two hours.
How can you be sure that food is safe? – Store it correctly; handle it correctly and use it before the use-by date.
What is the correct way to handle food? – Wash your hands before starting to prepare food; wash your hands after handling food; and wash fruit and vegetables before eating them.

3 Answers depend on students.

Exercise G

Set for pairwork. Monitor.

Closure

Feed back orally on Exercise G if you feel it is necessary.

Dictate the stressed syllable of new multi-syllable words in the lecture for students to identify, e.g., *mul* (tiply).

Lesson 3: Listening review (2)

Lesson 3: **Listening review (2)**

A In this course you have learnt to recognise a lot of fixed phrases.

1. Complete each fixed phrase in the blue box with one word.
2. Listen and check your answers.
3. Choose five of the phrases. Think of a complete sentence with each phrase.

B In this course you have learnt to recognise signpost language.

1. Listen again to parts of the lecture in Lesson 2. Find a good way to continue in the yellow box.
2. Listen to the way each part continues and check your answers.

C In this course you have learnt to understand graphs in lectures. Study Figure 1, from a lecture.

1. What sentences do you expect to hear in the lecture?
   Example: *The figure for food poisoning cases in 1993 was just under 70,000.*
2. Graphs do not tell you why things happened. Suggest possible reasons for the data in Figure 1.
   Example: *Perhaps the number of cases rose in 1997 because there was a problem with meat or another food.*

Figure 1: Food poisoning cases in England and Wales

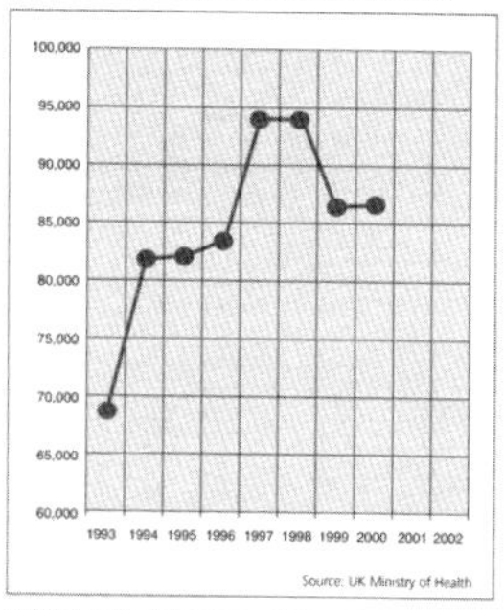

- all over the ______
- cause and ______
- for thousands of ______
- getting back to the ______
- in other ______
- it all started ______
- it is fair to ______ that
- it is important to ______
- it is only ______ that
- let me say straight ______
- on the one ______
- so to sum ______
- the majority of ______
- the rest of her ______
- to put it another ______

- Firstly, there must be harmful bacteria or microorganisms in or on the food.
- handling it correctly.
- I went on a wadi trip and the host brought the food in shopping bags. Anyway, getting back to the point.
- if in doubt, throw it out!
- Most food that we buy in a shop is safe, but we must store it correctly and handle it correctly.
- Now let's consider handling food correctly.
- one bacterium becomes two, then four, then eight, and so on.
- the freezer is a wonderful invention that enables you to keep food like meat for several months without it going bad.
- the human body needs bacteria to work properly.
- we are going to look at some facts and figures on food poisoning

LISTENING SKILLS LEVEL 3 – THEME 10: Nutrition and Health, Food – The New Poison? 45

Introduction

Remind students of the importance of fixed phrases – once they have recognised them, they can stop worrying about that bit of a lecture and prepare for the next content. Elicit some fixed phrases.

Exercise A

1. Set for pairwork. Do not feed back.
2. Play the recording. Feed back orally.
3. Set for pairwork. Elicit ideas.

Answers

all over the *world*
cause and *effect*
for thousands of *years*
getting back to the *point*
in other *words*
it all started *with*
it is fair to *say* that
it is important to *understand*
it is only *recently* that
let me say straight *away*
on the one *hand*
so to sum *up*
the majority of *people*
the rest of her *life*
to put it another *way*

Exercise B

Remind students about the importance of signpost language.

Refer students to the continuations in the yellow box. Play the recording, pausing to give students time to find a suitable continuation. Do not allow students to shout out. Allow thinking time, then elicit ideas. If you wish, repeat the exercise in 'real time' – i.e., students do shout out the continuation as soon as the lecturer pauses.

Feed back, ideally with an OHT of the answers, demonstrating how the language in column 1 helps you predict the continuation in column 2.

Answers

1	Then I'm going to talk about looking after food, which means, firstly, storing it correctly, and secondly,	handling it correctly.
2	There are basically three factors.	Firstly, there must be harmful bacteria or microorganisms in or on the food.
3	Actually, most bacteria are not harmful. In fact,	the human body needs bacteria to work properly.
4	The number of bacteria can grow very rapidly because they multiply. In other words,	one bacterium becomes two, then four, then eight and so on.

5 If you are not sure for some reason that food is safe, throw it away. In other words,	if in doubt, throw it out!
6 Finally, it means storing food correctly when you take it out of the house, for a picnic, for example. I remember once	I went on a *wadi* trip and the host brought the food in shopping bags. Anyway, getting back to the point.
7 So we've seen that we must store food correctly.	Now let's consider handling food correctly.
8 Why has food poisoning increased? Perhaps it is because people use modern household appliances wrongly in some cases. For example,	the freezer is a wonderful invention that enables you to keep food like meat for several months without it going bad.
9 So to sum up.	Most food that we buy in a shop is safe, but we must store it correctly and handle it correctly.
10 OK, in the next lecture	we are going to look at some facts and figures on food poisoning.

Exercise C

Remind students that lecturers often display graphs. If students are doing the Reading and / or Writing modules as well, they should be able to talk a great deal about graphs. Remind them about referring to information in graphs – *as you can see, just under / over*, etc.

Refer students to Figure 1. Explain that this is a graph from a lecture. Elicit what the graph shows.

1 Set for pairwork. Feed back orally. Elicit at least 10 sentences about the number of cases at various times and the movements up and down.
2 Set for pairwork. Feed back orally. Elicit some ideas for reasons behind the overall movements up and down.

Answers

1 Answers depend on students.
2 Upward movements could be the result of outbreaks of a particular kind of food poisoning, e.g., salmonella in a batch of eggs. Movement down in recent years could be the result of better food hygiene education of children and homemakers, or better regulation of restaurants and / or fast-food outlets.

Closure

Dictate the following text. Get students to complete the graph individually with the information for the missing two years, then compare in pairs.

As you can see, in 2001 the figure dropped slightly to just over 85,000, but in 2002 there was a big fall to 72,500. Perhaps this dramatic improvement is due to better food hygiene education in school, or perhaps it is due to better regulation of restaurants and fast-food shops.

Answers

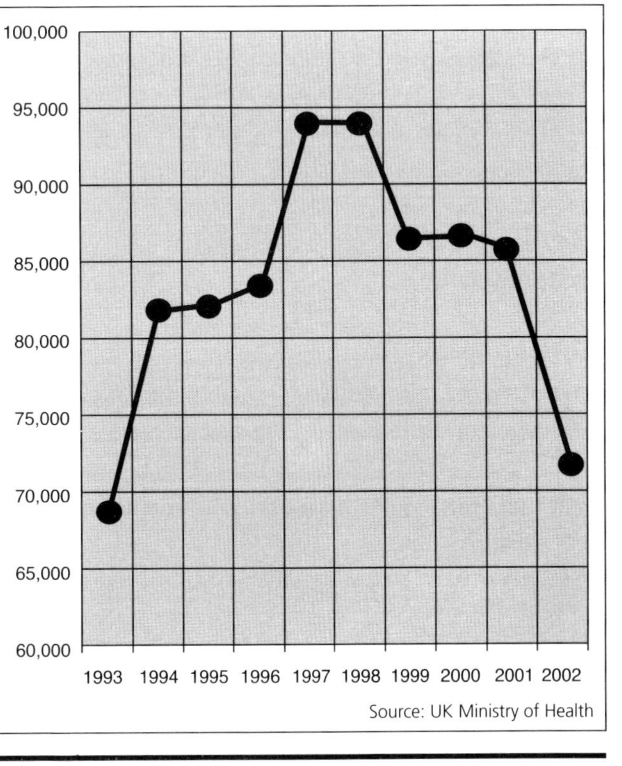

Lesson 4: Listening review (3)

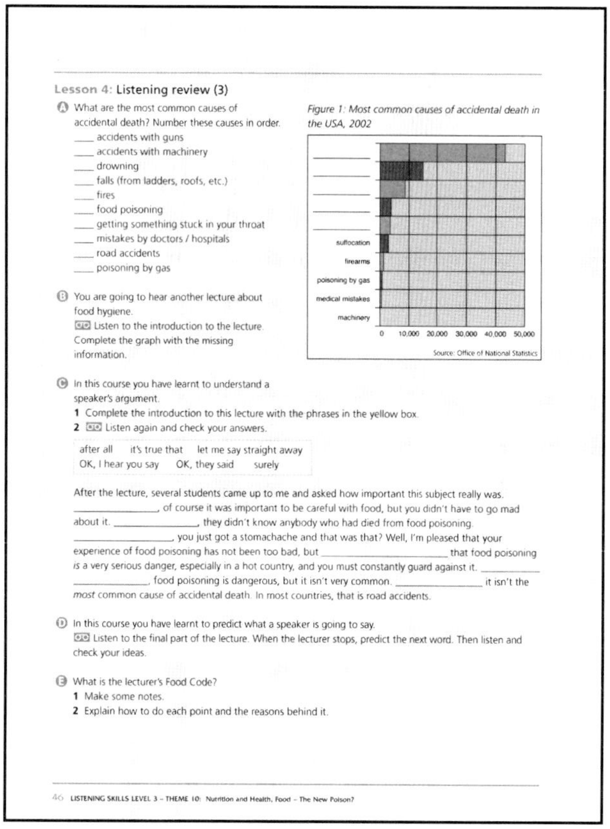

Lesson 4: Listening review (3)

A What are the most common causes of accidental death? Number these causes in order.

___ accidents with guns
___ accidents with machinery
___ drowning
___ falls (from ladders, roofs, etc.)
___ fires
___ food poisoning
___ getting something stuck in your throat
___ mistakes by doctors / hospitals
___ road accidents
___ poisoning by gas

Figure 1: Most common causes of accidental death in the USA, 2002

B You are going to hear another lecture about food hygiene.
Listen to the introduction to the lecture. Complete the graph with the missing information.

C In this course you have learnt to understand a speaker's argument.
1 Complete the introduction to this lecture with the phrases in the yellow box.
2 Listen again and check your answers.

after all   it's true that   let me say straight away
OK, I hear you say   OK, they said   surely

After the lecture, several students came up to me and asked how important this subject really was. ____________, of course it was important to be careful with food, but you didn't have to go mad about it. ____________, they didn't know anybody who had died from food poisoning. ____________, you just got a stomachache and that was that? Well, I'm pleased that your experience of food poisoning has not been too bad, but ____________ that food poisoning *is* a very serious danger, especially in a hot country, and you must constantly guard against it. ____________, food poisoning is dangerous, but it isn't very common. ____________ it isn't the *most* common cause of accidental death. In most countries, that is road accidents.

D In this course you have learnt to predict what a speaker is going to say.
Listen to the final part of the lecture. When the lecturer stops, predict the next word. Then listen and check your ideas.

E What is the lecturer's Food Code?
1 Make some notes.
2 Explain how to do each point and the reasons behind it.

46 LISTENING SKILLS LEVEL 3 – THEME 10: Nutrition and Health, Food – The New Poison?

Introduction

Ask students if they have ever had food poisoning. How did it happen – do they know? What was it like?

Ask if they think food poisoning is a serious problem, leading into …

Exercise A

Deal with the vocabulary, but do not give the different ways of referring to items as shown in the graph, i.e., *suffocation, firearms, medical mistakes*.

Set for pairwork. Feed back orally, but do not confirm or correct.

Exercise B

Refer students to the graph. Get them to associate the wording in Exercise A with the wording on the graph, as follows:

- accidents with guns – *firearms*
- getting something stuck in your throat – *suffocation*
- mistakes by doctors / hospitals – *medical mistakes*

Set for pairwork. Play the introduction. Feed back, ideally onto an OHT of the graph below. Ask if students are surprised by any of the information.

Answers

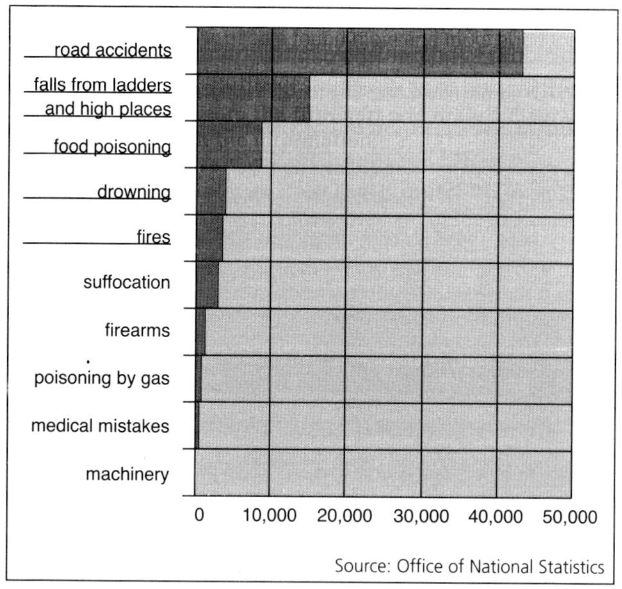

Exercise C

Remind students of the way speakers often argue a case – see Theme 7.

1. Set for individual work then pairwork checking.
2. Play the Introduction again. Feed back, ideally onto an OHT of the text below.

Answers

After the lecture, several students came up to me and asked how important this subject really was. *OK, they said*, of course it was important to be careful with food, but you didn't have to go mad about it. *After all*, they didn't know anybody who had died from food poisoning. *Surely*, you just got a stomachache and that was that? Well, I'm pleased that your experience of food poisoning has not been too bad, but *let me say straight away* that food poisoning is a very serious danger, especially in a hot country, and you must constantly guard against it. *OK, I hear you say*, food poisoning is dangerous, but it isn't very common. *It's true that* it isn't the most common cause of accidental death. In most countries, that is road accidents.

Exercise D

Remind students about this key listening skill. As before with this type of exercise, at least the first time through, do not let students shout out the answer. Wait until everyone has had a chance to think, then elicit responses from several students. If you wish, repeat the exercise in 'real time'.

Answers

OK, so food poisoning is really *serious*. You must protect yourself from food that is *unsafe*. You cannot always tell that food is *unsafe* from the way it *looks* or the way it *smells*. But there are ways to protect *yourself* from eating unsafe *food*. In the last lecture, I mentioned the most important *ones*.
But [illegible] can you remember *them*? I have devised a simple set of *rules* to help you *remember*. I call these rules the Food *Code*. You just have to remember the four *Cs*.
You must keep food *cold*.
You must keep it *clean*.
You must cook it *properly*.
You must check that it has not gone past its use-by *date*.

Methodology note

Sometimes, in exercises like this, it is impossible for students to predict accurately. That's fine, because the same understanding tension happens in real listening.

Exercise E

Set for individual work then pairwork checking. Feed back, getting a model set on the board. Elicit methods and reasons for each point orally.

Answers

1 Keep food **cold**.
  Keep it **clean**.
  Cook it properly.
  Check that it has not gone past its use-by date.
2 Answers depend on students.

Closure

Ask students if they are going to change the way they deal with food in future.

Word Lists: Thematic

THEME 1
Education,
How Do We Learn?

forget *(v)*
memorable *(adj)*
memory *(n)*
remember *(v)*

---

behave *(v)*
behaviour *(n)*
experience *(n)*
learning *(n)*
observation *(n)*
observe *(v)*
theory/ies *(n)*

THEME 2
Daily Life,
Growing Up

accept *(v)*
attitude *(n)*
behaviour *(n)*
colleague *(n)*
criticise *(v)*
neighbourhood *(n)*
occasion *(n)*
optimistic *(adj)*
trust *(v)*

---

adolescence *(n)*
adolescent *(n)*
adulthood *(n)*
baby *(n)*
conflict *(n)*
develop *(v)*
grow up *(v)*
identity *(n)*
infancy *(n)*
infant *(n)*
middle-aged *(adj)*

THEME 3
Work and Business,
Why Do People Work
Hard?

balance *(v)*
current *(adj)*
equal *(v)*
equation *(n)*
increase *(v)*
previous *(adj)*
side *(n)*

---

employee *(n)*
industrial *(adj)*
need *(n)*
produce *(v)*
production *(n)*
rest break *(n)*
team *(n)*
working hours *(n)*

THEME 4
Science and Nature,
Tornadoes and
Hurricanes

around / about
(= approx) *(prep)*
desert *(n)*
expand *(n)*
occupy *(v)*
plant *(n)*
surface *(n)*
the Earth *(n)*

---

duration *(n)*
formation *(n)*
lightning *(n)*
occur *(v)*
origin *(n)*
reach
(= max. amount) *(v)*
sandstorm *(n)*
speed *(n)*
thunder *(n)*
timing *(n)*

THEME 5
The Physical World, Natural Disasters

agriculture *(n)*
climate *(n)*
difference *(n)*
different *(adj)*
industry *(n)*
population *(n)*
similarities *(n)*
temperature *(n)*
the economy *(n)*
the same *(adj)*
trading partner *(n)*

---

damage *(n* and *v)*
death *(n)*
erupt *(v)*
fire *(n)*
natural disaster *(n)*
rock *(n)*
shake *(v)*
tidal wave *(n)*

THEME 6
Culture and Civilization, What Is Society?

birth *(n)*
customs *(n)*
get married *(v)*
marriage *(n)*
marry *(v)*
wedding *(n)*

---

achieve *(v)*
achievement *(n)*
advance *(n)*
culture *(n)*
individual *(n)*
relationship *(n)*
social *(adj)*
society *(n)*
sociology *(n)*

THEME 7
They Made Our World, The Greatest Advance in History

build *(v)*
device *(n)*
idea *(n)*
inventor *(n)*
replace *(v)*
technology *(n)*

---

antibiotics *(n)*
engine *(n)*
preservation *(n)*
printing *(n)*
wheel *(n)*

THEME 8
Art and Literature, Gulliver and Robinson Crusoe

begin *(v)*
belong *(v)*
buy *(v)*
disappear *(v)*
explore *(v)*
hear *(v)*
land *(v)*
let *(v)*
light *(v)*
need *(v)*
search *(v)*
see *(v)*
sell *(v)*
spend *(v)*
think *(v)*
trick *(v)*

---

adventure *(n)*
allegory *(n)*
author *(n)*
base (on) *(v)*
criticism *(n)*
critic *(n)*
hero *(n)*
popular *(adj)*
represent *(v)*
version *(n)*

THEME 9
Sports and Leisure, $5,000,000,000,000 p.a.

athlete *(n)*
compete *(v)*
event *(n)*
fit *(adj)*
physical fitness *(n)*
practice *(n)*
practise *(v)*
race *(n)*
sportsman *(n)*
sportswoman *(n)*
throw *(v)*
train *(v)*

---

abroad *(adj)*
growth *(n)*
impact *(n)*
international *(adj)*
lifestyle *(n)*
negative *(adj)*
positive *(adj)*
pros and cons *(n)*
sightseeing *(n)*
tourism *(n)*
tourist *(n)*

THEME 10
Nutrition and Health, Food – The New Poison?

beef *(n)*
carbohydrate *(n)*
dairy product *(n)*
date *(n)*
fish *(n)*
lamb *(n)*
mineral *(n)*
protein *(n)*
tomato/es *(n)*
vitamin *(n)*

---

bacterium/a *(n)*
defrost *(v)*
freezer *(n)*
handle *(v)*
harmful *(adj)*
microwave *(n)*
smell *(n)*
stir *(v)*
store *(v)*
throw away *(v)*
unsafe *(adj)*
use-by date *(n)*

---

abroad *(adj)*
accept *(v)*
achieve *(v)*
achievement *(n)*
adolescence *(n)*
adolescent *(n)*
adulthood *(n)*
advance *(n)*
adventure *(n)*
agriculture *(n)*
allegory *(n)*
antibiotics *(n)*
around / about (= approx) *(prep)*
athlete *(n)*
attitude *(n)*
author *(n)*
baby *(n)*
bacterium/a *(n)*
balance *(v)*
base (on) *(v)*
beef *(n)*
begin *(v)*
behave *(v)*
behaviour *(n)*
belong *(v)*
birth *(n)*
build *(v)*
buy *(v)*
carbohydrate *(n)*
climate *(n)*
colleague *(n)*
compete *(v)*
conflict *(n)*
critic *(n)*
criticise *(v)*
criticism *(n)*
culture *(n)*
current *(adj)*
customs *(n)*
dairy product *(n)*
damage *(n* and *v)*
date *(n)*
death *(n)*
defrost *(v)*
desert *(n)*
develop *(v)*
device *(n)*
difference *(n)*
different *(adj)*
disappear *(v)*
duration *(n)*
employee *(n)*
engine *(n)*
equal *(v)*
equation *(n)*
erupt *(v)*
event *(n)*
expand *(n)*
experience *(n)*
explore *(v)*
fire *(n)*
fish *(n)*
fit *(adj)*
forget *(v)*
formation *(n)*
freezer *(n)*
get married *(v)*
grow up *(v)*
growth *(n)*
handle *(v)*
harmful *(adj)*
hear *(v)*
hero *(n)*
idea *(n)*
identity *(n)*
impact *(n)*
increase *(v)*
individual *(n)*
industrial *(adj)*
industry *(n)*
infancy *(n)*
infant *(n)*
international *(adj)*
inventor *(n)*
lamb *(n)*
land *(v)*
learning *(n)*
let *(v)*
lifestyle *(n)*
light *(v)*
lightning *(n)*

marriage *(n)*
marry *(v)*
memorable *(adj)*
memory *(n)*
microwave *(n)*
middle-aged *(adj)*
mineral *(n)*
natural disaster *(n)*
need *(n* and *v)*
negative *(adj)*
neighbourhood *(n)*
observation *(n)*
observe *(v)*
occasion *(n)*
occupy *(v)*
occur *(v)*
optimistic *(adj)*
origin *(n)*
physical fitness *(n)*
plant *(n)*
popular *(adj)*
population *(n)*
positive *(adj)*
practice *(n)*
practise *(v)*
preservation *(n)*
previous *(adj)*
printing *(n)*
produce *(v)*
production *(n)*
pros and cons *(n)*
protein *(n)*
race *(n)*
reach (= max. amount) *(v)*
relationship *(n)*
remember *(v)*
replace *(v)*
represent *(v)*
rest break *(n)*
rock *(n)*
sandstorm *(n)*
search *(v)*
see *(v)*
sell *(v)*
shake *(v)*
side *(n)*
sightseeing *(n)*
similarities *(n)*
smell *(n)*
social *(adj)*
society *(n)*
sociology *(n)*
speed *(n)*
spend *(v)*
sportsman *(n)*
sportswoman *(n)*
stir *(v)*
store *(v)*
surface *(n)*
team *(n)*
technology *(n)*
temperature *(n)*
the Earth *(n)*
the economy *(n)*
the same *(n)*
theory/ies *(n)*
think *(v)*
throw *(v)*
throw away *(v)*
thunder *(n)*
tidal wave *(n)*
timing *(n)*
tomato/es *(n)*
tourism *(n)*
tourist *(n)*
trading partner *(n)*
train *(v)*
trick *(v)*
trust *(v)*
unsafe *(adj)*
use-by date *(n)*
version *(n)*
vitamin *(n)*
wedding *(n)*
wheel *(n)*
working hours *(n)*

Tapescript

Presenter: **Skills in English**
Listening: Level 3
Theme 1: Education, How Do We Learn?
Lesson 1: Vocabulary
B Listen to a short text with the green words. Then complete the text with one of the words in each space.

Voice: What is learning? Scientists define learning as a change of behaviour. But how do we learn? Nobody knows for sure, but there are many theories from psychologists and philosophers. Some say, 'People learn from experience. For example, a baby cries and his mother gives him food. He learns that certain behaviour is useful.' Other people think that we learn by observation. They say, 'We look around at the world. We observe other people. We see how they behave. We copy them.'

Presenter: **D 2 Listen and number the words you hear.**

Voice: observe
experience
behave
behaviour
learning
theory
observation

Presenter: **Lesson 2: Listening**
B 2 Listen to the introduction. Complete the outline.

Female lecturer: How do we learn? This seems like a simple question, but there is no simple answer. In the next two lectures, we are going to look at theories of learning. This week I'm going to talk about theories from the distant past. Firstly, theories from Ancient Greece. Next, theories from Islamic scholars. Finally, a very famous theory from a Russian scientist, Ivan Pavlov. Next week, I'm going to describe the work of two Americans, Skinner and Watson, in the 20th century.

Presenter: **C Listen to the first part of the lecture.**

Female lecturer: So, first, to Ancient Greece. The Greek philosopher Plato – that's P-L-A-T-O – lived from 427 BCE to about 347 BCE. He believed that learning was just memory. We have an experience. Maybe it's good. Maybe it's bad. Maybe we remember. Maybe we forget. If we remember later, that's learning by experience. For example, a child touches a fire and burns himself. He remembers next time and doesn't touch the fire.

Presenter: **D Listen to the rest of the lecture. Copy and complete Table 1.**

Female lecturer: Plato's student, Aristotle, lived from 384 BCE to 322 BCE. Aristotle is spelt A-R-I-S-T-O-T-L-E. He believed, like Plato, that we learn by doing things. But he went further. He believed that people learn when they see the cause of things, when they understand why something happens. For example, a child touches a fire and burns himself. Later he touches a match and burns himself. He sees a pattern: hot things burn you. After the child sees the pattern, he does not touch any hot things, including irons and boiling

water – things that haven't burnt him in the past. Next, the Islamic scholars. A lot of Greek learning was lost to the Western World in the 5th century AD. But Islamic philosophers and scientists translated the works of Plato and Aristotle. Scholars like Al Farabi in the 9th century AD, Ibn Sina in the 10th century and Ibn Rushd in the 12th century carried forward Aristotle's ideas. They also added theories of their own. A common theme in Islamic science is that learning comes from studying nature. Nowadays, we call this 'learning by observation'. The child observes another child touching a fire. He sees that the other child is burnt. He does not touch the fire himself. Finally, to Russia and a very important theory. In the 19th century, a Russian psychologist called Ivan Pavlov – that's P-A-V-L-O-V – started to study dogs. He was not interested in learning. He wanted to know why a dog's mouth produced saliva when it got its food. Saliva is necessary for the correct digestion of the food. But why do dogs produce saliva at the right time? First Pavlov thought it was the smell of the food. He tried an experiment. He sent a person to feed some dogs for several days. The dogs produced saliva. Then he sent the same person at the same time … but with no food. The dogs produced saliva when they saw the person. Pavlov realised that the dogs associated the person with food. Pavlov did another experiment to prove his theory. This experiment has become famous. He gave the dogs some food every few minutes. Every time the dogs started to eat the food, Pavlov rang a bell. After a short time, the dogs produced saliva when they heard the bell, even if there was no food. Pavlov continued to ring the bell but stopped giving food at the same time. Eventually, the dogs stopped producing saliva when they heard the bell.
What is the connection between Pavlov's dogs and human learning? Pavlov's experiment led to a new theory about how we learn. Scientists said that events in our environment can change the way we behave. In other words, we learn to behave in a particular way because of the way people and things behave around us. Pavlov called this process 'conditioning'. Pavlov's theory says a child can become frightened of something without having direct experience and without observing someone else having the experience. So, for example, if a mother sees her child is going to touch a fire, she shouts 'No!' She frightens the child. The child connects the fear and the fire, even though he did not get burnt himself or see anyone else getting burnt.

Presenter: **Lesson 3: Checking skills**
C 3 Listen and check your ideas.

Female lecturer: Plato's student, Aristotle, lived from 384 BCE to 322 BCE. Aristotle is spelt A-R-I-S-T-O-T-L-E. He believed, like Plato, that we learn by doing things. But he went further. He believed that people learn when they see the cause of things, when they understand why something happens. For example, a child touches a fire and burns himself. Later he touches a match and burns himself. He sees a pattern: hot things burn you. After the child sees the pattern, he does not touch any hot things, including irons and boiling water – things that haven't burnt him in the past.

Presenter: **D 2 Listen and check.**

Female lecturer: He gave a dog some meat powder every few minutes. Every time the dog licked the powder, Pavlov rang a bell. After a short time, the dog salivated when it heard the bell, without getting the food. He reversed the experiment. He rang a bell but didn't give the dog any food. After a short time, the dog stopped salivating when it heard the bell.

Presenter: **E 2 Listen and check.**

Female : lecturer What is the connection between Pavlov's dogs and human learning? Pavlov's experiment led to a new theory about how we learn. Scientists said that events in our environment can change the way we behave. Pavlov called this process 'conditioning'. Pavlov's theory says a child can become frightened of something without having direct experience and without observing someone else having the experience.

Presenter: **Lesson 4: Applying skills**
B 2 Listen to the introduction. Make outline notes for the lecture.

Female lecturer: This is the second of two lectures on the topic: How do we learn? Last week, we talked about a number of theories through history. Firstly, we heard about the theories of Plato and Aristotle in Ancient Greece. Then we learnt about the theories of the Islamic scholars Al-Farabi, Ibn Sina and Ibn Rushd in the Arab World. Finally, I talked about the psychologist, Pavlov, and his famous experiment in 19th-century Russia. We learnt that philosophers believe we learn by remembering, or by understanding why, or by observing or through conditioning.
This week, we are going to look at some theories from the 20th century. Firstly, I am going to talk about the theory of an American called Watson. Then, I will describe the theory of another American called Skinner. His ideas had a big effect on the way people started to teach foreign languages.

Presenter: **C Listen to the first part of the lecture. What is the main point of this part?**

Female lecturer: John Watson accepted the ideas of Pavlov. He believed that you could extend them to human beings. He believed that experiences in people's lives changed their behaviour. He said this was much more important than any natural behaviour that people inherited from their parents.
Watson conducted a famous experiment in 1919 and 1920. He used a baby called Albert in his experiment. He gave baby Albert a white rat. Albert tried to touch the rat. Watson made a loud noise just behind the baby's ear. Albert started to cry. Every time he tried to touch the rat, Watson made a loud noise and frightened the baby. Every time, the baby started to cry. Soon, Albert cried when the rat appeared. In fact, he cried when he saw anything that looked like a rat – a furry toy or a fur coat. Watson's experiment proved that conditioning worked in people as well as animals.

Presenter: **D Listen to the second part of the lecture. Connect the pictures and explain the main ideas in this part.**

Female lecturer: Watson's work was important. However, the work of another American, B.F. Skinner, was much more important in the history of education. Skinner

worked in a laboratory in the 1940s. He also knew about the work of Pavlov. Pavlov showed that a new stimulus, like a bell ringing, can make an animal produce *existing* behaviour, like salivating for food. Skinner thought, 'Can I teach animals to learn *new* behaviour through conditioning?'
First, he did experiments with rats. He taught rats to get through very complicated mazes to find food. They had to push buttons and move levers to open doors. At the end of the maze, they found food. Then Skinner did something amazing. He taught pigeons to play table tennis. How did he do this? He watched the pigeons very closely. Every time they did something like push a table tennis ball with their beaks, he gave them some food. Finally, he conditioned the pigeons to play table tennis to get food.

Presenter: **E Listen to the third part of the lecture. Number these events in order.**

Female lecturer: Skinner worked with animals, not people, but he believed that his results could apply to people as well. In particular, he said that conditioning pigeons to play table tennis was like conditioning children to speak their own language. For example, a baby makes a sound when his mother comes in the room. The mother thinks the sound is like the word 'Mummy'. She repeats it. This happens hundreds of times. Finally, the child says 'Mummy' when his mother comes into the room.

Presenter: **Theme 2: Daily Life, Growing Up**
Lesson 1: Vocabulary
B Listen to a short text with the green words. Then complete the text with one of the words in each space. Make any necessary changes.

Voice: Do you sometimes ask yourself: 'Who am I?' If you do, you are normal. Indeed, psychologists say that we ask ourselves this question throughout our lives. The meaning of the question changes as we grow up. Babies ask, 'Who am I? Is this hand part of me, or part of you?' Infants ask, 'Who am I? My parents choose my clothes, my food, my school, my bedtime.' Adolescents ask, 'Who am I? A nice person or a nasty one?' Middle-aged adults ask, 'Who am I? What have I done with my life?'
We ask the question because, according to Erik Erikson (see Lesson 4), at every age there is an identity crisis – a conflict or battle between who we are and who we would like to be. At every age we find different answers, because, according to Piaget (see Lesson 2), our brains develop in a predictable way through infancy and adolescence to adulthood.

Presenter: **C 2 Listen and check your ideas.**

Voice:
1 birth
2 infancy
3 childhood
4 adolescence
5 adulthood
6 middle age
7 death

Presenter: **Lesson 2: Listening**
B Listen to the introduction. Make a set of outline notes for this week's lecture.

Male lecturer: In these two lectures, we are going to look at two theories of child development. Firstly, this week, I'm going to look at Jean Piaget. That's ET at the end because he was a French speaker. Next week, I'll talk about the life and work of Erik Erikson.
OK, so this week, I'm going to talk about Piaget's life and how he developed his ideas. Then I'm going to explain to you Piaget's four stages of child development.

Presenter: **D 1 Listen to the first part of the lecture.**

Male : lecturer Jean Piaget was born in Switzerland on August 9, 1896. When he was 11 years old, he wrote a scientific essay about a small bird. This was the start of a long career of research and writing that included more than 60 books and hundreds of articles.
After birds, he became interested in shellfish. He published many articles on the subject while he was still at school.
After he left school, he studied natural sciences at the University of Neuchâtel – that's N-E-U-C-H-A-T-E-L. He got his PhD and then left Switzerland to work in a school in France. This was the beginning of his work with children, which continued for the rest of his life. He developed a test for intelligence in five- to eight-year olds, and he became interested in the way that brains develop, or what he called 'the biological explanation of knowledge'. He discovered that children at a certain age could solve problems that children at an earlier age could never solve. He decided to find out more.
In 1921, he returned to Switzerland to become director of studies at an institute in Geneva. He got married two years later, and the couple had three children. This was important in his professional as well as his social life. He studied the development of the three children closely, from infancy to adulthood. During the next 40 years, he held a succession of important posts in universities and research institutes. He died in Geneva on September 16, 1980.

Presenter: **D 3 Listen again. Put the notes on Piaget's life, work and ideas together.**
[REPEAT OF LESSON 2 EXERCISE D1]

Presenter: **E Listen to the second part of the lecture.**

Male lecturer: For the whole of his adult life, Piaget kept asking the same question: 'How does knowledge grow?' He had the idea, which was unusual at the time, of actually talking to children and finding out their ideas. For example, there is one story about a conversation with a five-year-old girl. He asked her: 'What makes the wind?'
The child replied: 'The trees.'
'How do you know?'
'I saw them waving their arms.'
'How does that make the wind?'
'Like this. Only they are bigger. And there are lots of trees.'
'What makes the wind on the ocean?'
'It blows there from the land. No. It's the waves ...'
Piaget said, 'Children only really understand things that they invent themselves. If we try to teach them something too quickly, we stop them reinventing it themselves.'
In another experiment, Piaget told lots of children the same story. He said, 'Imagine that one boy is washing up after dinner and he breaks two cups. Imagine that another boy asks his mother, 'Can I have some chocolate?' and the mother says, 'No'. Then this boy tries to get the chocolate and he breaks a cup. Which child is naughtier?' Young children always answered,

'The first child, because he broke two cups. The other child only broke one cup.' Older children said, 'The second child, because he was doing something naughty when he broke the cup. The first child was trying to be helpful.' This shows that ideas of right and wrong change as children grow up.
Piaget decided, after many years, that knowledge grows in a predictable way, from simple ideas to more complex ones. He concluded that the brain of an infant is different from the brain of a child, and different from the brain of an adolescent or an adult.
Piaget's work has influenced people all over the world in many fields, including psychology, sociology and education. His theories of child development are still the basis of most thinking in this area.
So what did Piaget actually discover? He found that there are four major stages of development, although each of these stages has many subdivisions.

Presenter: **F Listen to the third part of the lecture.**

Male lecturer: The first stage lasts from birth up to about 18 months or two years. He called this stage the sensorimotor stage, that's S-E-N-S-O-R-I-M-O-T-O-R. Babies do not know how things will react, and so they are always experimenting – shaking things, putting things in their mouths, throwing. They are learning by experience. We sometimes call this kind of learning trial and error.
The second stage lasts from 18 to 24 months to 7 years. Piaget called this stage pre-operational. Pre means before, so this is before operational thought. In this stage, children learn to speak. They can pretend and they can understand past and future. However, they cannot understand cause-and-effect. In other words, they cannot understand 'if I do this, this will happen'.
The third stage is from 7 to 12 years. Piaget called this the stage of concrete operational thought. Concrete, spelt C-O-N-C-R-E-T-E, in this case, means real, not abstract. At this stage, children can understand that real things stay the same, even if you move them around. For example, a litre of water is a litre of water in a small bottle or a big bottle.
The final stage of child development happens after about 12 years old. Piaget called this the stage of formal operational thought. Formal in this case means not real, but abstract. At this stage, children can understand algebra – for example, a + b = c, and they can understand hypotheses and abstract ideas like fairness and justice.
So, to sum up, Piaget believed that all children go through these four stages more or less at the same age. Although some people today criticise his ideas, he is still widely regarded as the greatest developmental psychologist of the 20th century. Einstein called his discovery of developmental stages 'so simple that only a genius could have thought of it.'
OK. Next week, Erik Erikson and some more ideas on child development.

Presenter: **Lesson 3: Learning new skills**
B 3 Listen and check your ideas.

Voice:
a cause and effect
b in other words
c learning by experience
d life and work
e more or less
f past and future
g professional and social
h right and wrong
i so to sum up
j trial and error
k all over the world
l the rest of his life

Presenter: **Lesson 4: Applying new skills**
A 2 Listen and check your ideas.

Voice:
a career
b research
c explanation
d knowledge
e infancy
f adulthood
g professional
h social
i experience
j effect
k algebra
l react
m error
n trial
o theory

Presenter: **B You are going to hear the second lecture about child development. Listen to the introduction. Make a set of outline notes.**

Male lecturer: Last week, we talked about the work of Jean Piaget on child development. This week, we are going to look at the life and work of another famous person in this field, Erik Erikson – that's E-R-I-K E-R-I-K-S-O-N. First I'm going to tell you a little about his life, because it is possible that his life influenced his work. Then I'm going to describe his theories of child development.

Presenter: **C Listen to the first part of the lecture.**

Male lecturer: Erikson was born in Germany on June 15th, 1902. There is no record of the name of his real father. In 1905, when Erik was three, his mother married Erik's doctor, Theodor Homberger – that's H-O-M-B-E-R-G-E-R. So he grew up as Erik Homberger.
Erikson left school in about 1920. He became an artist and then a teacher. Then he studied child psychology in Austria. During this time he got married. He and his wife emigrated to the United States in 1933. He taught at Yale and Harvard, on the East Coast. In 1939, he moved to California, on the West Coast, to teach at the university at Berkeley. He began to study groups of Native American children. He studied the way they developed the values of their parents.
Also in 1939, Erik Homberger became an American citizen and changed his family name to Erikson. There is an interesting story about this. Erik never knew his real father, but at some point he became aware that his real name was not Homberger. His mother refused to give him any information about his real father. For some reason, Erikson started to believe that he was the son of a royal prince from Denmark. Is that why he gave himself a Danish family name? And did this confusion about his own identity lead to Erik's interest in identity in children?
Erikson moved back to the East Coast of the United States in 1950 and continued working and teaching there until he retired in 1970. He died on May 12th, 1994.

Presenter: **D Listen to the second part of the lecture.**

Male lecturer: Erikson published his first book in 1950. It was called *Childhood and Society*. The book is still widely read in the field of psychoanalysis. In this book, Erikson developed his theory of the identity crisis. This is the idea that a child must find its own identity as it moves through various stages of development. It is clear that Erikson did not find his full identity. Even the simplest personal questions seemed to cause a problem for him. There are many stories about this. For example, if someone asked Erikson 'How are you?' he often turned to his wife and said, 'Well, Joan. How are we?' But perhaps the most surprising story is about Erikson and food. If someone gave Erikson some food that he wasn't expecting, he sometimes turned to his wife and asked, 'Do I want this, Joan?'

Presenter: **E Listen to the third part of the lecture. Copy and complete the table of Erikson's stages of development.**

Male lecturer: What about his work and ideas? Erikson identified eight stages of development, through childhood and adult life. We are only going to look at the first five stages, because these lectures are about child development, not adult development. At each stage, Erikson said that there is a conflict, a battle, a war, with a good result and a bad result.

The first stage lasts for the first one or two years of life. It is the stage of trust versus mistrust. An infant learns to trust his or her parents and adults in general – or learns that adults are not to be trusted. Trust versus mistrust.

The second stage is from about two years to about four years. It is the stage of self-confidence versus shame. A young child learns to be confident in his ability to do things by himself – or he learns to be ashamed of his failure to do things. Unfortunately for parents, the confident child is also developing willpower, and often refuses to obey. This is difficult for the parents but is part of the child's social development. So the second stage is self-confidence versus shame.

The third stage is from about four to entry into school at five or six. It is the stage of initiative versus guilt. Perhaps those words are new to you. Initiative is spelt I-N-I-T-I-A-T-I-V-E, and it means doing something yourself, without being told to do it. Guilt – G-U-I-L-T – means feeling bad about something you have done wrong. At this stage, the child learns to take initiative, to cooperate with other children, to lead and to follow. The child also learns to imagine and to pretend. This is the wonderful period of make-believe. So, initiative is the good result. Or the child feels guilty and refuses to take part in games, does not play with other children and does not develop play skills or imagination. So this stage is initiative versus guilt.

The fourth stage occurs during the early years of schooling. It is the stage of structured play versus inferiority. Structured play means playing team games with other children. Inferiority – I-N-F-E-R-I-O-R-I-T-Y – means feeling that you are not as good as other children. The child learns to play structured games that involve teamwork. The child also learns self-discipline and manages his or her own homework. A child who has come through stages 1, 2 and 3 successfully will have little difficulty with this stage – he will trust adults and work with initiative. However, the child who has had problems at earlier stages will fail at this stage, too. He will mistrust adults and not take charge of his own life. He will feel shame, guilt and inferiority.

The fifth stage is the stage of adolescence, from 13 or 14 to about 20. It is the stage of identity – of knowing who you are – versus diffusion – that's D-I-F-F-U-S-I-O-N – as Erikson calls it – not knowing who you are. The successful adolescent learns self-confidence rather than self-consciousness, which means being embarrassed about the way you look, the way you speak, the way you dress, etc.

Erikson believed that there are three more stages that occur in adulthood. As we are talking about child development, I am not going to discuss those here. Erikson's theory is that a child needs to learn to socialise – to become part of the society he or she lives in. The job of a parent and a teacher is to help the child to move from being helpless and centred on him or herself, to being a part of society, but also to be an independent thinker.

Presenter: **F These statements are true or probably true. Listen to the lecture again and find evidence.** [REPEAT OF LESSON 4 EXERCISES B, C, D AND E]

Presenter: **Theme 3: Work and Business, Why Do People Work Hard?**

Lesson 1: Vocabulary

A 3 Listen and check your answers.

Voice: We often use equations in business. For example, the price of something in a shop usually equals the cost to make it plus some profit for the company. We can write this as an equation: cost + profit = price. Both sides of an equation must be the same. In other words, they must balance. So if the cost is $20 and the profit is $2, the price must be $22. What happens if the cost increases? We can use our equation to make sure the profit stays the same. If the previous cost was $20 and the current cost is $22, then the new price must be $24.

Presenter: **B 3 Listen and check your answers.**

Voice: Equation 1: salary per hour x working hours per week = total salary per week
Example: $10 x 48 hours = $480

Equation 2: working hours per day - rest breaks = total working hours per day
Example: 8 hours - 1.5 hours = 6.5 hours

Equation 3: managers + workers = employees
Example: 5 managers + 100 workers = 105 employees

Presenter: **C 2 Listen to each sentence. What form of the word do you hear? What does the word mean in this situation?**

Voice:

a This is Mr Jones. He is the production manager.
b Good morning, Mr. Jones. What do you actually produce here?
c This is the industrial part of the city. All the factories are here.
d The workers have started to work as a team. They are producing a lot more now.
e We all have a number of needs. We need food and drink and love, for example.

Presenter: **D 2 Listen and check your ideas.**

Voice: balance

current
equal
equation
increase
previous
employee
industrial
produce
production
working

Presenter: **Lesson 2: Listening**
C Listen to the introduction.

Female lecturer: This week and next week, I am going to talk about ideas in the field of Industrial Psychology. We know what psychology means – it is the study of how the brain works, of how people think. So what is Industrial Psychology? It is the study of the way people think about work and the effects of working conditions on productivity. Productivity is the amount of work that a person does in one time period, say one day. So for example, if one worker makes five items in one day and another worker makes six items, the second worker has a higher productivity than the first worker.
This week, I'm going to talk about the experiment that started Industrial Psychology and the conclusions that the researcher, Elton Mayo, reached about the results. Next week, I'm going to describe the theories of two writers in this field, Maslow and Herzberg.

Presenter: **D 2 Listen to the first part of the lecture. Follow the suggestions in the Skills Check Reminder.**

Female lecturer: It all started with a series of experiments at a factory in Chicago in the USA. The factory was called the Hawthorne Works. The experiments were carried out by Elton Mayo. He was an Australian, born on the 26th December, 1880. He moved to the UK in 1901, and then, in 1923, he went to the USA to teach at the University of Pennsylvania. Later, he became a professor at Harvard Business School. He became interested in the effect of working conditions on productivity. He decided to conduct some experiments. There was nothing very original about the experiments themselves but the results form the basis of Industrial Psychology to this day.
Between 1924 and 1927, Mayo conducted experiments at the Hawthorne Works. He wondered if the level of light in the factory affected the productivity of the workers. He experimented with the lighting levels for three years, but he found no change in productivity.
Mayo then decided to look at the effect of tiredness on productivity. He wondered if productivity increased if you gave workers regular rest breaks or if you reduced the length of the working day. I don't know if you have ever been into a factory. I remember once I had to visit a factory. It was incredibly noisy and, of course, noise all day makes you tired. So it was a reasonable assumption that factory workers would be tired.
So, anyway, getting back to the point … between 1927 and 1932, Mayo conducted another experiment with a group of six girls in the Hawthorne Works. During those five years, Mayo and his researchers observed the girls at work and made changes to their rest breaks and their working hours. After each change, a researcher talked to the girls about the changes and listened to any complaints they had.

Presenter: **E Listen to the second part of the lecture, which gives details of the experiment.**

Female lecturer: Before the experiment started, the girls worked a 48 hour week. They had no rest periods during the day. They did not have a specific target for productivity, but on average, each girl produced 2,400 items a week.
Mayo introduced five-minute rest breaks, one in the morning and one in the afternoon. Productivity went up.
Mayo lengthened the rest breaks to ten minutes each. Productivity went up sharply.
Mayo introduced another four rest breaks, but the girls complained that their work rhythm was broken, and productivity went down slightly. These extra rest breaks were removed and productivity went up again.
The girls were allowed to leave at 4.30 p.m. instead of 5.00 p.m. Productivity went up.
Then they were allowed to leave at 4.00 p.m. They were now working one hour a day less in total, but productivity did not go down.
Mayo concluded that tiredness did have an effect on productivity. He believed, at this point, that a shorter working day and regular rest breaks were the key to increasing productivity.

Presenter: **F Listen to the third part. Each time the lecturer stops, answer her question.**

Female lecturer: Before he closed the experiment, however, he decided to do one final thing. It is the thing that any good researcher would do in the circumstances. What did he decide to do? [PAUSE] He took all the changes away, but continued to observe the girls and talk to them. The girls went back to the same conditions as before the experiment started – a 48-hour week, no rest breaks. What happened? [PAUSE] Productivity went up again. In fact, at this point, the girls reached an all-time record of over 3,000 items per week. How can the results be explained? [PAUSE]

Presenter: **G Listen to the fourth part. What is the Hawthorne effect?**

Female lecturer: Mayo concluded that this is what happened: during the experiments, the six girls became a team. They realised that the management was interested in their work and listened to their complaints. They also realised that the amount of work they did – their productivity – was noticed. Mayo decided that productivity is affected by the amount that a worker is involved in the production process. Before the experiment started, nobody talked to the girls about their work. They felt they were just part of the factory machine. They did not feel valued. They did their work, but they did not do anything extra. When Mayo's researchers started to talk to them about their work, they felt that someone was noticing them as people. They felt valued. They did their work better because now they were putting extra effort into it.
This discovery – that workers need to feel valued as people – is so important in the field of Industrial Psychology that it has a name, taken from the factory. When workers increase productivity because managers value their work, it is called the Hawthorne Effect.
One other point came out of the experiment. Mayo noticed that, although all the girls were making the same item, they each had their own particular way of doing it. To put it another way, they each had a

personal way to make a boring job a little bit more interesting. Mayo realised that people need to organise their own work in a way that will be interesting to them. There's a funny story about this. A man was visiting a factory where they make jam tarts. You know, they are little pieces of pastry with some jam on them. And he spoke to one of the girls who was operating a machine. He said, 'What do you do?' And she said, 'I push this button and the strawberry jam comes out of here.' And he said, 'But doesn't that get boring?' And she said, 'No. When I get bored, I push that button instead and make some tarts with *raspberry* jam.' Where was I? Oh, yes. Mayo wrote about the results of the Hawthorne experiments in a book published in 1933. It was called *The Human Problems of an Industrial Civilization*. He went on to write two other books, in 1939 and 1947. He died on 1st September, 1949.
So we have heard about Elton Mayo and the Hawthorne Effect, the discovery that really started the idea of Industrial Psychology – or the way that people think about work.
Next week, I'm going to talk about two people and their theories about Industrial Psychology.

Presenter: **Lesson 3: Learning new skills**
A 2 Listen and check your ideas.

Voice:
it all started with
to this day
in fact
in the circumstances
in other words
getting back to the point
on average
in total
at work
for example
to put it another way

Presenter: **D 4 Listen to this part of the lecture again.**

Female lecturer: Mayo then decided to look at the effect of tiredness on productivity. He wondered if productivity increased if you gave workers regular rest breaks or if you reduced the length of the working day. I don't know if you have ever been into a factory. I remember once I had to visit a factory. It was incredibly noisy and, of course, noise all day makes you tired. So it was a reasonable assumption that factory workers would be tired.
So, anyway, getting back to the point …

Presenter: **6 Listen to this part of the lecture again.**

Female lecturer: One other point came out of the experiment. Mayo noticed that, although all the girls were making the same item, they each had their own particular way of doing it. To put it another way, they each had a personal way to make a boring job a little bit more interesting. Mayo realised that people need to organise their own work in a way that will be interesting to them. There's a funny story about this. A man was visiting a factory where they make jam tarts. You know, they are little pieces of pastry with some jam on them. And he spoke to one of the girls who was operating a machine. He said, 'What do you do?' And she said, 'I push this button and the strawberry jam comes out of here.' And he said, 'But doesn't that get boring?' And she said, 'No. When I get bored, I push that button instead and make some tarts with *raspberry* jam.' Where was I? Oh, yes.

Presenter: **Lesson 4: Applying new skills**
B Listen to the introduction.

Female lecturer: Last week, I talked about the start of Industrial Psychology, which is the study of how people think about work. I described the experiments of Elton Mayo at the Hawthorne Works, and the Hawthorne Effect, which says that people work better when they feel valued.
This week, two more writers in the field of Industrial Psychology. But before that, I'm going to mention the thing they have in common: motivation. In the end, Industrial Psychology is all about motivation at work. What motivates people to work hard – or not to work hard?
OK, so first, motivation. What is it? One definition is: *a way of satisfying needs through action and behaviour*. In other words, we need something, like money or food, and we try to get it. We are motivated by our needs. Researchers have discovered that different things motivate different people. Some people are motivated by very strange things. I remember once I met a boy who collected train numbers. Yes, that's right. The numbers of trains. Trains all look the same in Britain, but each one has an identification number. This boy travelled to railway stations and stood for hours writing down the train numbers in a notebook. If I said to most boys, 'Go and write down train numbers,' they would be very bored. But this boy was motivated to do it for fun. Sorry. Where was I? Oh yes. Motivation. Different things motivate different people, so managers must understand the theories of motivation to get the best out of their employees.

Presenter: **D Listen to the first part of the lecture. Make notes on the life of Maslow.**

Female lecturer: Right. So, let's look at some of the theories. Firstly, we have Abraham Maslow, spelt M-A-S-L-O-W. Maslow was born on April 1, 1908, in New York. He was one of seven children born to uneducated Russian parents. His mother and father pushed him very hard to succeed. He went to university in New York for some time and studied law. While he was still a student, he got married and moved to Wisconsin to continue his studies at the university there. He switched from law to psychology and got his BA in 1930, his MA in 1931 and his PhD three years later. He went back to New York to work as a teacher at a college. He wrote several books, including *Motivation and Personality* in 1943. In this book, he described his most famous theory – the hierarchy of needs. Maslow retired to California in his early 60s, and died there on June 8th, 1970.

Presenter: **F Listen to the second part of the lecture. Check your answers to Exercise E.**

Female lecturer: As I just said, Maslow is best known for his Hierachy of Needs. A hierarchy is a list of things in some sort of order – for example, important things at the top and less important things at the bottom. Maslow believed that inside every human being there are five needs. We can put them into a pyramid. Look at Figure 1 on your handout. At the base of the pyramid are the physiological needs – the needs for food, drink and a place to sleep. At the next level there are the safety needs. Above safety needs are social needs. These include the need for love and friendship. Next there is the need for esteem. People need to develop self-respect and to feel that other

people respect them, too. At the top of the pyramid is an even more complicated idea. Maslow called it Self-Actualisation. Put simply, this means achieving everything that you are capable of achieving. Not many people reach that level. This is why he has drawn the hierarchy as a pyramid.
Maslow's key point about the hierarchy is this: a person is not motivated by higher level needs until the lower level needs have been satisfied. In other words, a person is not motivated by concerns for safety if he is hungry or thirsty. But once that need for food and drink is satisfied, it no longer motivates. Now, a person can only be motivated by greater safety in his life. And so on.

Presenter: **G Listen to the third part of the lecture. Make notes on the life of Herzberg.**

Female lecturer: OK. So that's Abraham Maslow. The second writer I want to talk about today is Frederick Herzberg, that's H-E-R-Z-B-E-R-G. Herzberg was a psychologist. He was born on April 18th, 1923, in the United States. His parents were poor, like Maslow's, and, like Maslow's, they were immigrants, from Lithuania, which in the 1920s was part of Russia. Herzberg did very well at school and, when he was 16, he won a place at college. While he was there, he got married, in 1944. He got his BS in 1946, his MS in Industrial Psychology in 1949 and his PhD the following year. He worked as a manager of a research laboratory from 1951 to 1957, and then became a professor of psychology at a university in Ohio. Herzberg wrote several books, including *Motivation to Work* in 1959. In this book, he described his famous theory of satisfiers and dissatisfiers. He died on January 19th, 2000.

Presenter: **H 1 Look at Figure 1 again. Listen to the fourth part. Label each item in the figure either Hygiene factor (H) or Motivator (M).**

Female lecturer: Herzberg knew about the work of Maslow, of course, but he developed a theory with a very important difference. Let's compare Herzberg's ideas with Maslow's. Look at Figure 1 again. Herzberg said Maslow's lower-level needs – physiological and safety – are not motivators. He called them 'hygiene' factors. Hygiene means keeping things clean. We teach children hygiene when we say, 'Wash your hands before you eat a meal. Clean your teeth after your meal.' Hygiene helps to prevent disease. In the same way, Herzberg said, a good salary and a safe place to work are just hygiene factors. They prevent workers being dissatisfied, but they don't motivate them. According to Herzberg, the motivators are the higher-level needs of Maslow's hierarchy – esteem and self-actualisation. These are the things that make people work harder.

Presenter: **I Listen to the fifth part.**

Female lecturer: What does Herzberg's theory mean for managers? It means they must make sure all the hygiene factors are in place, but they must also make sure that employees are valued as people. There's quite a good story about this. A man sees three people working on a building site. He says to the first man, 'What are you doing?' The man says, 'I don't know. I just work here.' He asks the second man. He says, 'I'm cutting these stones so they are perfectly straight, and then I'm putting them on top of each other to make a perfect wall.' And he says to the third man, 'What are you doing?' And the third man says, 'I'm helping to build this mosque.' What does that story tell us? The first man is not motivated to work hard. The second man is working hard, perhaps, but for his own satisfaction. He doesn't see how his work fits into the whole job. The third man knows how important his job is. He is motivated because he sees the value of his work.
OK. We've run out of time. More next week …

Presenter: **Theme 4: Science and Nature, Tornadoes and Hurricanes**
Lesson 1: Vocabulary
A 2 Listen and check your answers.

Voice: The Sahara Desert occupies a third of the African continent.
In fact, it occupies around eight per cent of the land area of the Earth.
In total, it is about eight million square kilometres.
It is expanding at the rate of about one kilometre a month.
But the Sahara is not just sand. In fact, there are about 1,000 different types of plant.

Presenter: **B 2 Listen and check your ideas.**

Voice: The *haboob* is a turning sandstorm or duststorm. Its name comes from the Arabic word for strong wind. It can reach up to two kilometres wide and one kilometre high. It travels across the land at speeds of between 50 and 80 kilometres per hour. A *haboob* can last from one hour up to three hours. The *haboob* occurs mainly in the Sahara, but can also appear in the southwestern states of the United States. How does a *haboob* form? Air falls from thunderclouds in their final stage. When the falling air hits the ground, it picks up huge amounts of sand or dust. The wall of sand moves forward with the thunderclouds.

Presenter: **Lesson 2: Listening**
D Listen to the first part of the talk.

Roger Dawkins: Today I'm going to talk about tornadoes. Firstly, I'm going to define a tornado. Secondly, I'm going to talk about the origins of the word. Then I'll tell you about the size, speed and duration of tornadoes. Next, I'll explain where they occur and when. After that, I'll describe two scales for measuring tornadoes. Finally, I'm going to talk about three theories that try to explain why tornadoes form.

Presenter: **E Listen to the second part of the talk.**

Roger Dawkins: So, first, what is a tornado? A tornado is a column of wind which is turning violently. The name comes from a Spanish word meaning 'thunderstorm'. The average tornado is 100 metres across – that's about the length of a football field – and it turns at 500 kilometres per hour – that's about four times as fast as the speed limit on a motorway. However, the magnitude and turning speed can vary enormously. Tornadoes *can* reach one kilometre across – that's 10 football pitches – and can turn at 800 kilometres per hour – that's the speed of a commercial aeroplane. By the way, don't confuse the *turning* speed with the *travelling* speed, that is the speed across the ground. Tornadoes travel quickly, but not at 500 kilometres an hour. They move across the land at about 50 kilometres an hour, although they can go two or three times that speed. I don't know if you saw that film of people trying to outrun a tornado in their car. They were filming a tornado in the distance when, suddenly, they realised that it was coming in their direction. It was very frightening, because the tornado caught up with them, even though they were driving very fast, but they kept filming out of the back of the vehicle, right up to the moment when they crashed the car. Nobody was hurt, thankfully.

Anyway, where was I? Oh, yes, size and speed can vary enormously. Similarly, the duration of tornadoes covers a wide range. Most only last a few minutes, but some go on for up to two hours.

Lastly, the distance they travel. Again, there's a big range – from about seven kilometres to over 200. Incidentally, some tornadoes can cause some very strange effects. Tornadoes do not contain rain, but things can fall out of the sky after a tornado. For example, a recent story comes from the town of Villa Angel Flores in Mexico. At 11 p.m. on June 2nd, 1997, small creatures began to fall on the town. They were toads – a kind of frog. The explanation came eventually. A tornado picked up the toads from a lake and dropped them several kilometres away on the town. So, if you hear an English person say, 'It's raining cats and dogs', he or she might be telling the truth! Actually, that's got nothing to do with tornadoes. Cats and dogs used to sleep on the roofs of houses, and when the roofs got very wet from heavy rain, they fell off ... so people said, 'It's raining cats and dogs.'

OK, so tornadoes are columns of turning wind. Now let's see where they happen. Well, turning winds occur all over the world, but tornadoes are the most violent kind, and the destructive ones occur mostly in the United States. In fact, most of them happen in just one part of the United States, in an area of the central plains called Tornado Alley. The US experiences more than 500 tornadoes every year. There are also tornadoes in Western Europe, India, China, Japan and Australia.

OK. We've heard that tornadoes occur in many parts of the world. But when do they occur? Summer or winter? Daytime or night-time? Morning or evening? Tornadoes can occur at any time of the day, in any month of the year. In the United States, however, three-quarters of tornadoes arise from March to July, with the majority in May.

Now let's consider how we can measure tornadoes. We can measure tornadoes on two main scales, the Fujita scale – that's F-U-J-I-T-A – and the Torro scale – T-O-R-R-O. Both scales classify the speed and destructive power of the tornado. The Fujita scale goes from 0 to 5, whereas the Torro scale runs from 0 to 12. On the Torro scale, one is mild; the wind will blow down small trees and blow off the tops of chimneys. Twelve is a super-tornado; the wind will move cars over 100 metres and even steel-reinforced buildings will be seriously damaged.

Presenter: **G 2 Listen to the third part of the talk.**

Roger Dawkins: So now we know what tornadoes are and where they occur. We also know how to measure them. But how do tornadoes form? There are three theories about this.

The first theory is the main one. It's called the Rising Air Theory. This theory says that tornadoes happen when a long column of quickly rising air stretches up from the ground. It often goes to a thundercloud. This can happen when the ground gets very hot and a bubble of air starts rising.

Now let's consider the second theory. The second theory is called the Downward Spiral Theory. This suggests that the tornado develops in a downward direction from a thunderstorm cloud to the ground. Finally, the third theory. This is the Electrical Storm Theory. I'm going to tell you a story to explain this theory. One day, in the middle of a storm, a farmer looked up into the heart of a tornado. What could he see? The farmer said the middle of the tornado was constantly lit by lightning flashes. So the Electrical Storm Theory says that lightning is the cause of tornadoes.

So, to sum up, we don't really know the exact cause of tornadoes. It could be rising air, a downward spiral or lightning.

That's all for this week. In next week's programme, we'll look at another violent turning wind – the hurricane.

Presenter: **Lesson 4: Applying new skills**
A 3 Listen and check your ideas.

Voice:
tornado
kilometres
violent
incidentally
electrical
develop
classify
damaged
seriously
destructive
vary
effects

Presenter: **C Listen to the first part of the talk.**

Roger Dawkins: Welcome to *Violent Nature*. Last week, I talked about tornadoes. This week, I'm going to talk about another powerful turning wind – the hurricane. Firstly, I'm going to explain what a hurricane is and tell you the origins of the name. Secondly, I'm going to tell you where and when they occur. Next, I'll describe some ways of measuring hurricanes. Finally, I'm going to talk about two theories that try to explain how hurricanes form.

Presenter: **D Listen to the second part of the talk.**

Roger Dawkins: So, first, what is a hurricane? Well, it's a turning wind, like a tornado, but there are two main differences between hurricanes and tornadoes. Firstly, hurricanes only start over water, whereas tornadoes only start over land. Secondly, hurricanes are huge rainstorms, whereas tornadoes don't have any rain in them.

I suppose you could add a third difference. Hurricanes are much more destructive than tornadoes. In fact, hurricanes are the most destructive form of weather in the world. A hurricane that hit the American city of Galveston in 1900 is still considered to be the worst natural disaster in US history. More than 37,000 people died and 3,600 buildings were completely destroyed.

Now there is more protection for people and buildings against hurricanes, but Hurricane Andrew, which hit the US in 1993, still killed 26 people and caused over 25 billion dollars worth of damage.

By the way, perhaps you have noticed that hurricanes always have the names of people – like Andrew. This practice started in Australia in the early 1900s. An Australian called Clement Wragge introduced the idea. It is said that he gave each hurricane the name of a person that he didn't like. Nowadays, a committee decides on the list of names for hurricanes. You can find the list of names for the next few years on www.fema.gov/kids/hunames.htm. That's www dot f-e-m-a dot g-o-v forward slash kids forward slash h-u-n-a-m-e-s dot h-t-m.

Anyway, the name *hurricane* itself comes from Mayan – M-A-Y-A-N – the language of the tribes who lived in Mexico hundreds of years ago. Hurakan, spelt H-U-R-A-K-A-N was a god who breathed on the oceans and made dry land. Later, Indians who lived in the Caribbean used the name Hurican – H-U-R-I-C-A-N – as the name of an evil god, and many years later the University of Miami adopted the name, with a change in spelling, for any strong turning storm, that forms over warm water with winds above 119 kilometres an hour.

OK, so hurricanes, like tornadoes, are turning storms. Now, let's see where they happen. Well, as I said just now, hurricanes form over warm water, so we don't get hurricanes in the Antarctic Ocean. In fact, the temperature of the air above the water must be more than 27 degrees centigrade, so the majority of hurricanes form in the tropics. In fact, there are six main areas, including the Western Atlantic, the Eastern Pacific and the South Indian oceans. Incidentally, you can see where the current hurricanes are all over the world if you go to www.solar.ifa.hawaii.edu. That's w-w-w dot s-o-l-a-r dot i-f-a dot hawaii dot e-d-u.

OK. So we've seen that hurricanes occur in many parts of the world. But when do they happen? Is there a hurricane season, in the same way as there is a tornado season? Well, the answer is 'yes and no'. Hurricanes generally happen in the summer, but the length of the hurricane season varies in each hurricane area. For example, the Atlantic hurricane season officially starts on June 1 and ends on November 30, but most tropical storms and hurricanes form between August 15 and October 15. By contrast, hurricanes occur year-round in the western North Pacific, while in the North Indian Ocean, there are two peaks of activity, in May and November.

Now let's consider how we can measure hurricanes. The most commonly used scale is the Saffir-Simpson scale. The scale runs from 1 to 5, with a Level 1 hurricane having winds of 119 to 153 kilometres per hour. This level causes minimal damage, mainly to trees and bushes. Level 5, on the other hand, has wind speeds of up to 270 kilometres an hour and causes catastrophic damage to buildings and great loss of life. By the way, don't be confused by the numbers on the Saffir-Simpson scale. A Level 5 hurricane is not five times as violent as a Level 1 hurricane. It's not even 50 times as violent. It is 500 times as violent.

Presenter: **G Listen to the talk again. Check your answers to the questions in Exercise F.**
[REPEAT OF LESSON 4, EXERCISE D]

Presenter: **H Listen to the final part of the talk. Draw a diagram showing the formation of hurricanes according to each theory.**

Roger Dawkins: So now we know what hurricanes are and where they occur. We also know how to measure them. But how do hurricanes form? There are two theories about this.

The first theory is the main one. It's called the Convection Theory. Convection, which is spelt C-O-N-V-E-C-T-I-O-N, means air moving upwards. Air starts to turn slowly over a tropical ocean. Hot air inside rises. More air is sucked in at the bottom and that air rises, too. The air on the outside starts to turn more quickly. This process continues and grows until a hurricane is formed. The hurricane continues to grow until it moves over land or over cooler water.

Now let's consider the second theory. It is called the Electromagnetic Theory. Some scientists believe that hurricanes occur when the Earth gets closer to the sun. This happens from June to November every year. According to this theory, the sun has an influence on part of the Earth's atmosphere, which causes areas of low pressure. These areas produce clouds and electrical storms. The electrical activity starts a turning wind and, eventually, a hurricane forms.

So, to sum up, most people believe that hurricanes form when more and more air is sucked up in organised convection, but some people believe electrical activity is the cause.

That's all for this week. Next week, we are going to look at some more forces of nature – not weather this time, but movements that start inside the Earth itself.

Presenter: **Theme 5: The Physical World, Natural Disasters**
Lesson 1: Vocabulary
B Listen and look at the pictures. Copy the green words and phrases into one or both columns.

Voice: There are many similarities between earthquakes and volcanoes. Both can cause natural disasters. When an earthquake occurs in a town or city, the earth shakes violently, and this can cause a lot of damage to buildings. This often leads to many deaths. In a similar way, when a volcano erupts near a town or city, the hot rocks and ash can damage buildings and kill people. Both kinds of event can also cause tidal waves. In fact, tidal waves after earthquakes or volcanic eruptions often cause more damage than the original event.

There are also some differences between earthquakes and volcanoes. Earthquakes usually only last for a few seconds or minutes, whereas volcanoes can erupt for days or even months. With a volcano, fire often shoots high into the air, while earthquakes are not usually linked with fire from underground. Of course, damaged buildings often catch fire after an earthquake.

Presenter: **Lesson 2: Listening**
A Listen to the introduction. What exactly are you going to hear about in this lecture?

Female lecturer: There are two natural disasters that have killed millions of people in the history of the Earth. One shakes the ground, the other explodes and sends rocks and fire out of the ground. We call the first one an earthquake. We call the second one a volcano. For centuries, people believed there was a relationship between earthquakes and volcanoes. Do earthquakes cause volcanoes? Do volcanoes cause earthquakes? Or does something else cause both of them? This week, we are going to look at earthquakes, next week we will look at volcanoes, and by the end of the two lectures you should be able to answer the question: *What is the relationship between these two terrible natural disasters?*

So this week we are going to hear about early theories of the cause of earthquakes, and then we are going to hear about a famous earthquake that led to scientific research in Europe. We are then going to hear how the real cause of earthquakes was finally discovered.

Presenter: **C Listen to the first part of the lecture.**

Female lecturer: Thousands of years ago, people believed that there were huge animals that lived underground. Some people thought they were snakes, others believed they were turtles. Some even said they were giant spiders. According to these people, the animals sometimes got angry and when they did, the earth shook. Aristotle, the famous Greek philosopher of the 4th century B.C.E., did not believe in giant underground animals. His explanation was almost as strange, though. He thought there were huge winds under the earth that sometimes caused the ground to shake. In fact, the Greek word for 'shaking' is *seismos* – S-E-I-S-M-O-S. Eventually, therefore, the science of earthquakes became known as *seismology*.

Presenter: **D Listen to the second part of the lecture.**

Female lecturer: The earliest recorded earthquake was in 1177 B.C.E. in China, but scientists in Europe were not interested in earthquakes until around 1750 C.E. At that time, earthquakes started to shake England. This was very unusual, and the English scientists of the day became interested in them. These small earthquakes were warnings of a much bigger earthquake. On Sunday November 1st, 1755, a huge earthquake hit the city of Lisbon, in Portugal. The earthquake, and the tidal wave that followed it, flattened the city and killed around 70,000 people. There were eyewitness accounts of the terrible scenes. One wrote:
We began to hear a rumbling noise, like that of carriages, which increased to such a degree as to equal the noise of the loudest cannon; and immediately we felt the first shock, which was succeeded by a second and a third; on which, as on the fourth, I saw several light flames of fire issuing from the sides of the mountains, resembling that which may be observed on the kindling of coal. . . . I observed from one of the hills called the Fojo that there issued a great quantity of smoke, very thick, but not very black which still increased with the fourth shock, and after continued to issue in a greater or less degree. Just as we heard the underground rumblings, we observed it would burst forth at the Fojo; for the quantity of smoke was always proportional to the underground noise.
Anyway, after the Lisbon earthquake, scientists in Europe realised that earthquakes could be very dangerous, and they began to record the times and locations of earthquakes. They also began to work on ways of measuring earthquakes. As communications between countries got better, scientists in Europe began to collect observations from places as far away as South America and Japan. In the early 19th century, scientists suspected that there was something about the geology or type of rock in particular places that led to earthquakes.

Presenter: **E 2 Listen to the third part and check your ideas.**

Female ecturer: In the 1850s, the first true seismologist appeared, a man called Robert Mallet, and in 1880 the first instrument for measuring earthquakes was invented, by a man called John Milne, while he was working in Japan. He called it a seismograph.
In the United States, a man called Gilbert studied the rocks after an earthquake and decided that the lines he found in the rocks came before the earthquake, not after it. These lines were called faults. Similarly, a man called Reid studied fault lines in rocks after the 1906 San Francisco earthquake. He concluded that pressure builds up along a fault line and is eventually released as an earthquake.

Presenter: **F 2 Listen to the fourth part and check your ideas.**

Female lecturer: What is a fault line? How does it occur? If you look at a map showing the main earthquake areas, you can see immediately that earthquakes are more common in some places than others. Why is this? In the 1920s, a German meteorologist and astronomer named Alfred Wegener proposed a startling theory. He said the continents were not fixed in their position on the globe. Instead, they were moving around on huge plates. In some places, the plates come together. This is where earthquakes happen. At first, other scientists laughed at his ideas, but gradually, people found more and more evidence for his plate theory.

Presenter: **G Listen to the fifth part and draw a diagram from the information.**

Female lecturer: We now know that Reid's conclusion about earthquakes and fault lines is correct. The main cause of earthquakes is the movement of the rocks along fault lines where two continental plates meet. One plate is trying to move north, for example. The other plate is trying to move south. Friction between the rocks on each plate prevents this from happening. Pressure builds up, until finally, the rocks slide against each other. We call this an earthquake. There are more than 100 earthquakes a day. Incidentally, if you want to see the location of current earthquakes, go to www.gps.caltech.edu and follow the links to earthquakes and records of the day.
How do the plates move? Actually, the solid rock that we see on the surface of the Earth is lying on a layer of very soft rock. The plates can slide on this soft rock. Very, very slowly, but they can slide.
So, in a strange way, Aristotle was almost right about earthquakes. There are no winds under the ground to move the rocks around, but there is a kind of river that is moving all the time – a river of soft rock.

Presenter: **Lesson 3: Learning new skills**
A 3 Listen and check your ideas.

Voice:
- a Some people thought they were snakes, others believed they were turtles. Some even said they were giant spiders.
- b Aristotle thought there were huge winds under the earth that sometimes caused the ground to shake.
- c After the Lisbon earthquake, scientists in Europe realised that earthquakes could be very dangerous.
- d In the early 19th century, scientists suspected that there was something about the geology in particular places that led to earthquakes.
- e Gilbert decided that fault lines in rocks came *before* the earthquake, not after it.

f Reid concluded that pressure builds up along a fault line and is eventually released as an earthquake.
g Wegener proposed a startling theory.

Presenter: **C 1 Listen to the first signposts from the lecture in Lesson 2. Can you remember how the lecturer continues in each case?**

Female lecturer:
1 One plate is trying to move north, for example.
2 Some people thought there were snakes underground.
3 The continents were not fixed in their position on the globe.
4 At first, other scientists laughed at Wegener's ideas, ...

Presenter: **2 Listen and check your ideas.**

Female lecturer:
1 One plate is trying to move north, for example. The other plate is trying to move south.
2 Some people thought there were snakes underground. Other people believed there were turtles.
3 The continents were not fixed in their position on the globe. Instead, they were moving around on huge plates.
4 At first, other scientists laughed at Wegener's ideas, but gradually people found more and more evidence for his plate theory.

Presenter: **3 Listen to some more first signposts. What will come next?**

Voice:
1 On the one hand, I want to go out this evening.
2 One parent wants his son to be a doctor.
3 Some people like meat.
4 I did not wait for the person to call me.
5 At first, nobody believed him, ...

Presenter: **Lesson 4: Applying new skills**
A 3 Listen and check your ideas.

Voice:
natural
disaster
explodes
earthquake
volcano
observations
communications
geology
eventually
evidence
concluded
meteorologist

Presenter: **C Listen to the introduction.**

Female lecturer: Last week we looked at earthquakes and we saw that they are caused by the movement of the continental plates. This week, we are going to look at another natural disaster, volcanoes. We are going to consider a number of questions. What is the origin of the name? When and where was the most famous volcanic eruption? Why is it famous? How do volcanoes appear? How long do they take to form? And finally, what is the relationship between earthquakes and volcanoes?

Presenter: **D Listen to the first part of the lecture.**

Female lecturer: The word 'volcano' comes from the name of a small island in the Mediterranean Sea. Hundreds of years ago, people living in the area noticed fire coming out of the mountain on the island. They believed that the mountain was the chimney of a blacksmith's shop owned by a man called Vulcan. A blacksmith is a person who works with hot metal to make shoes for horses and metal objects like swords. According to legend, Vulcan the blacksmith made weapons for Mars, the Roman god of war. So, some people believed volcanoes were the flames from underground fires. Others thought there was fire under the whole of the Earth. Aristotle, as we have heard, said there were winds rushing around under the Earth. These winds caused earthquakes and, when they broke through the Earth, they caused volcanoes.

Presenter: **E 3 Listen to the second part and check or complete the table.**

Female lecturer: What is the most famous volcanic eruption? Well, you have probably heard of it. It occurred in Italy in 79 C.E. On that day, the volcano Vesuvius erupted. It destroyed several places, including the city of Pompeii. But why is the eruption so famous? Firstly, the event was described by Pliny the Younger in two letters. In his eyewitness account he wrote:
The cloud was rising from Vesuvius. I can best describe its shape by likening it to a pine tree. It rose into the sky on a very long 'trunk' from which spread some 'branches.' Some parts of the cloud were white; other parts were dark with dirt and ash .... Meanwhile, broad sheets of flame were lighting up many parts of Vesuvius; their light and brightness were the more vivid for the darkness of the night. The buildings were being rocked by a series of strong tremors, and appeared to have come loose from their foundations and to be sliding this way and that. Outside, however, there was danger from the rocks that were coming down ...
As the column of ash rose over 30 kilometres, and over 3,000 people died, Pliny watched and wrote his account of the eruption.
However, Pliny's eyewitness account was not enough to ensure that Pompeii went down in history. In fact, the story of the eruption was completely forgotten over the years, and Pompeii lay buried under metres of ash. Then, the city was rediscovered. A small amount of excavation happened in the early 1800s, then, in 1860, an archaeologist called Giuseppe Fiorelli – that's F-I-O-R-E-L-L-I, became director of the excavations. Fiorelli realised that the bodies under the ash had completely disappeared but had left empty spaces. He poured plaster into the empty spaces, then dug away the ash. We can still see the result of his work today. One is a dog trying to get free from its chain at the moment of death. Another is a young man trying to protect an old woman from the falling ash.
Incidentally, the eruption of Vesuvius is certainly not the earliest recorded volcanic eruption. Before the time of written language, someone painted a picture on the wall of a house in Catal Hayuk in modern-day Turkey. It shows a volcano erupting. Archaeologists have dated the painting to about 6200 BCE.

Presenter: **F Listen to the third part of the lecture. Draw a diagram to show the modern theory of volcano formation.**

Female lecturer: Anyway, where was I? Oh, yes. How do volcanoes appear? As we heard last week, scientists believe that there is a layer of soft rock under the hard rock at the surface of the Earth. The hard rock is moving around on the soft rock on huge continental plates. When the pressure builds at the meeting point of two plates, earthquakes occur. However, sometimes, when two plates meet, one plate is forced under the other plate. The plates rub together and friction turns the rock to a liquid called magma, spelt M-A-G-M-A. The plates continue to move and the pressure increases. Finally, the magma is forced to the surface and erupts out of the ground as a volcano.

Presenter: **G Listen to the fourth part of the lecture. Make notes of the important information.**

Female lecturer: How long does it take volcanoes to form? Most volcanoes form over millions of years. Some, however, appear and grow very quickly. I don't know if you have heard about the volcano that appeared in Mexico in 1943. A farmer in a place called Paricutin looked out of his window one day and saw that his donkey was standing on a small hill. This was strange, because the night before he tied the donkey to a tree in a flat field. He went and untied the donkey before the rope strangled him. Then he watched in amazement as the hill grew and grew. Another farmer, Domini Pulido explained how the eruptions started:

In the afternoon I heard a noise, like thunder during a rainstorm. At 4 p.m., I noticed that a small hole had opened in the ground. Then the ground raised itself two metres high, and a kind of smoke or fine dust – grey, like ashes – began to rise up.

Immediately more smoke began to rise, with a hiss or whistle, loud and continuous, and there was a smell of sulphur. I then became greatly frightened.

Anyway, the volcano at Paricutin grew to a height of 336 metres in the next year and began erupting the day after it first appeared. Eruptions continued for eight years and lava spread over an area of 25 square kilometres. By the way, lava is the name we give to the magma or liquid rock when it flows out of the volcano.

So, the volcano at Paricutin grew in just eight years. Similarly, a volcano grew in the sea near Iceland in just four years. In fact, the volcano grew 130 metres from the seabed to the surface in just six months, from May to November 1963. At first, there were no eruptions. Then the volcano appeared above the surface, and it began to erupt. The lava eventually created a new island of three square kilometres and 170 metres at its highest point. Local people called the volcanic island Surtsey, after a fire giant in Icelandic stories.

Presenter: **H 2 Listen and check your ideas.**

Female lecturer: OK. So to sum up. Do earthquakes cause volcanoes? Do volcanoes cause earthquakes? No. Earthquakes do not cause volcanoes and volcanoes do not cause earthquakes. Instead, both earthquakes and volcanoes are caused by the movement of the continental plates. Incidentally, there are more than 1,500 active volcanoes in the world at the moment. You can see the latest information about eruptions if you go to http://volcano.und.nodak.edu – that's h-t-t-p://v-o-l-c-a-n-o dot u-n-d dot n-o-d-a-k dot e-d-u – and follow the links to current eruptions. OK. Next week, we are going to talk about other natural disasters, like tidal waves and floods, and find out the cause of each.

Presenter: **Theme 6: Culture and Civilization, What Is Society?**

Lesson 1: Vocabulary

B Read and listen to this introduction to a lecture. Then complete the text with one of the green words in each space.

Male lecturer: We talk a lot nowadays about society and culture and civilization. We even have a new branch of education – sociology – which is the study of society. But have you ever stopped to ask yourself: What is society? What is culture? What is civilization? What is the relationship between the three words? According to the dictionary, society is the organisation of individuals into social groups. Culture, on the other hand, is defined as the customs and achievements of a society. Individuals organise into social groups that become a society. The society then develops customs and achieves certain things. This makes the society into a culture. What about a civilization? Again, the dictionary helps. A civilization is a culture that has achieved important advances in science and art.

Presenter: **D 2 Listen to these stressed syllables. Number the green words in the order you hear the stressed syllables.**

Voice :
1 chie
2 ci
3 cul
4 la
5 ol
6 van
7 vid
8 so

Presenter: **Lesson 2: Listening**

A 2 Listen to the introduction. Make notes. Check your answers to Exercise 1.

Male lecturer: We talk a lot nowadays about society and culture and civilization. We even have a new branch of education – sociology – which is the study of society. But have you ever stopped to ask yourself: What is society? What is culture? What is civilization? What is the relationship between the three words? In this talk, I am going to consider these questions and several other questions that are related to them. Is it natural for people to form into social groups? Is society more important than individuals, or are individuals more important than society? What are the common features of a society? Next week, we will look at some other points about society and culture.

Presenter: **B Listen to the first part of the lecture.**

Male lecturer: So, first, what is society and what is [PAUSE] culture? According to the [PAUSE] dictionary, society is the organisation of individuals into [PAUSE] groups. Culture, on the other [PAUSE] hand, is defined as the customs and achievements of a [PAUSE] society. Individuals organise into social [PAUSE] groups that become a society. The society then develops customs and achieves certain [PAUSE] things. This makes the society into a [PAUSE] culture. What about a [PAUSE] civilization? Again, the dictionary [PAUSE] helps. A civilization is a culture that has achieved important [PAUSE] advances in science and [PAUSE] art. So the relationship is – society forms a [PAUSE] culture that, sometimes, becomes a [PAUSE] civilization.

Presenter: **C 3 Listen to the second part of the lecture. Make notes.**

Male lecturer: The next question is: Is it natural for people to form into social groups? Many people believe that it is. The great Arab scholar, Ibn Khaldoun, wrote extensively about society in his book *Muqaddimah*. Ibn Khaldoun was born in Tunis in 1332. Incidentally, the Khalduniyah area in Tunis has hardly changed since his day, and one can still see the house in which, according to tradition, he was born. Anyway, Ibn Khaldoun's father was an important man, but in 1348, when Ibn Khaldoun was only 16, a terrible disease called the Black Death came to Tunis and killed both his parents. I don't know if you know that the Black Death was one of the biggest dangers of the 14th century. It killed over 25 million people in Europe in just five years. Anyway, where was I? Oh, yes. The death of his parents had a deep effect on Ibn Khaldoun, as we shall see later. When he was only 20, Ibn Khaldoun served at the court in Tunis and then went abroad to Morocco and Spain to represent his country. Finally, in 1375, he retired from politics and went to live with the tribe of Awlad 'Arif, in present-day Algeria. For the next four years, he concentrated on writing his *Universal History, Kitab al-Ibar,* of which the massive introduction, the *Muqaddimah*, is the most important section. In fact, his writings are so important that some people called him the father of sociology. Ibn Khaldoun believed in the idea of *'asabiyah*, which can be translated as 'social cohesion' or joining together. He said that this cohesion appears naturally in tribes and other small social groups. He went on to claim that the social cohesion will be stronger if the society develops a strong religion. Ibn Khaldoun thought that social cohesion is the driving force of society, the thing that pushes the civilization forwards and makes it strong. When the cohesion weakens, for any reason, the society weakens and another society with a stronger cohesion takes its place. Ibn Khaldoun died in Cairo in 1406.

Presenter: **E 3 Listen to the third part of the lecture. Number the features in the green box in order.**

Male lecturer: But what exactly is a society or a culture? How can we recognise a cultural group?

If we bring together the ideas of various sociologists, we can identify at least 10 features that societies have in common.

1 There are particular laws. For example, in the UK you are not allowed to marry until you are 16 years old, and only then with your parents' consent.
2 There are particular standards – things that people normally do. These are called 'social norms'. *Norm* comes from the word *normal*. Again, in the UK, people usually give up their seats to disabled people on a bus or train. This is a social norm.
3 People in the society trade with each other. In other words, they buy and sell things or, in a primitive society, they exchange things. For example, in old farming societies, one person might make bread and exchange it with another person for vegetables, whereas in more sophisticated societies, people form companies and the companies trade with each other.
4 People use technology to change the natural world. At its simplest, the society makes tools to help cultivate crops. In a more advanced example, scientists may make rain by spraying the clouds with chemicals.
5 People know the correct language to use in different situations. For example, in many cultures there is, on the one hand, an informal variety of the language for social contact, and on the other a formal variety of the language for business. In some countries, two completely different languages are used for social and business contact. I don't know if you know that in Finland a person will socialise in Finnish but conduct business in English.
6 People educate their children. The form of education depends on the society. Perhaps the men educate the young boys and the women educate the young girls, or perhaps the society has a formal system of schooling, from primary through secondary to college or university.
7 People have time for leisure. In other words, they are not working every hour of the day. They may spend the time on sports or on producing artistic work, but they are not struggling to survive from day to day.
8 There are traditional stories, superstitions, folk tales, songs and myths. For example, the Greeks had *Aesop's Fables*, or stories, the Arab World had *The Thousand and One Nights*.
9 There is traditional food and methods of cooking. This is so important that societies are sometimes named from their food. English people call French people 'frogs' because some French people eat frogs' legs. In turn, French people used to call English people *le rote boeuf*, or the roast beef, because they ate roast beef. Anyway, the point is that traditional food and methods of cooking are very important to a cultural group.
10 The society marks 'rites of passage' in particular ways. Rites of passage are the special events of people's lives – birth, coming of age, marriage and death. People are often shocked by the rites of passage in a different culture. Did you know that there was a tradition at one time in India that the widow of a dead man must burn herself on his funeral fire? Many people outside the culture found this shocking, and the British tried to stop it when they ruled India.

Presenter: **Lesson 3: Learning new skills**

A 2 Listen and check your ideas.

Voice:

a According to the dictionary, society is the organisation of individuals into groups.
b Culture, on the other hand, is defined as the customs and achievements of a society.
c Incidentally, the Khalduniyah area in Tunis has hardly changed since his day.
d The death of his parents had a deep effect on Ibn Khaldoun, as we shall see later.
e That's about a third of the population at the time. Imagine that. One in three people died.
f The form of education depends on the society.
g People have time for leisure. In other words, they are not working every hour of the day.
h English people call French people 'frogs' because some French people eat frogs' legs. In turn, French people used to call English people *le rote boeuf*, or the roast beef, because they ate roast beef.
i The point is that traditional food and methods of cooking are very important to a cultural group.

Presenter: **B 3 Listen to a section of the lecture again. How does the lecturer show that Sentences B are Ibn Khaldoun's opinion?**
[REPEAT OF LESSON 2 EXERCISE C3]

Presenter: **D Listen again to the last part of the lecture in Lesson 2. After each section, give an example from your own culture.**
[REPEAT OF LESSON 2 EXERCISE E3]

Presenter: **Lesson 4: Applying new skills**
B 2 Listen to the introduction and check your answers.

Male lecturer: Last week, I talked about society and culture. I listed the common features of societies or cultural groups. Today, I want to look at some more questions about society and look at the answers that various sociologists have come up with throughout history. These are the questions we are going to consider today.
Is society more important than individuals, or are individuals more important than society? Do all societies go through the same stages? Do we learn from history, or do we keep repeating the same mistakes?

Presenter: **C 2 Listen to the first part of the lecture.**

Male lecturer: OK. First question. Is society more important than individuals, or are individuals more important than society? This is one of the really big questions of sociology! In Ancient Greece, in the third and fourth centuries BCE, the philosophers Aristotle and Sophocles wrote about this question. They both believed that a person is only a real human being when he or she is part of society. Two thousand years later, in the late 19th century, the French sociologist Emile Durkheim agreed. He said that individuals depend on society for survival. Durkheim stated that people have a deep need to belong to something. Society helps them to fulfil that need. However, the German sociologist Max Weber, who was writing at the same time, did not agree with Durkheim. Instead, he thought that the individual is more important than society. He believed that the world only works when people act as individuals.
So, to sum up, we have two opposite views about individuals and society. Some philosophers and sociologists believe that individuals need society; some think that society needs individuals.

Presenter: **C 3 Listen again and complete the summary in the blue box.**
[REPEAT OF EXERCISE C2]

Presenter: **D 2 Listen to the second part of the lecture. Make notes of Ibn Khaldoun's opinions.**

Male lecturer: Our second question is this: Do all societies go through the same stages? Do you remember last time we talked about Ibn Khaldoun? He is the father of sociology, according to some people. Personally, I think that title is well-deserved. Anyway, he believed that all societies went through the same stages. His studies into the nature of society and social change led to the development of a new science, which he called *'ilm al-'umran*, or the science of culture. He said all societies go through three stages. In the first stage they grow, in the second stage they produce advances in technology, in science and in art. In the final stage, they die. Sometimes they die because of internal influences – for example, the leaders of the society are not strong enough to hold the society together. Sometimes they die because of external influences, like a terrible disease. If you remember, Ibn Khaldoun's parents were killed by the Black Death, and I believe this event probably influenced his writings on this subject.
So, obviously, Ibn Khaldoun believed that history endlessly repeats itself, with societies in different times and different geographic locations showing the same changes in response to external events, such as the Black Death or foreign invasion, or internal developments, such as inventions or discoveries. No doubt he studied other civilizations and came to this rather sad conclusion. To put it another way, Ibn Khaldoun did not see any evidence of progress in individual cultures, except in the first stage, when they grow from a primitive to a civilized society.

Presenter: **E Listen to the second part again and identify them.**
[REPEAT OF EXERCISE D2]

Presenter: **F Listen to the third part of the lecture. Complete the statements in the bubbles.**

Male lecturer: So Ibn Khaldoun did not see any evidence of progress in individual cultures. Down the years, other thinkers have agreed with Ibn Khaldoun. The German philosopher Hegel, writing in the 18th century, said: 'The only thing we learn from history is that we *don't* learn from history.' He believed that we endlessly repeat the same mistakes. When society is faced with the same problem, according to Hegel, it reacts in the same way, even if that is not the best way to react. There is no actual improvement.
Many famous people throughout history have agreed with Ibn Khaldoun and Hegel. But one man, Marie-Jean de Caritat, did not agree. De Caritat was born in 1743 in France. He became a leading French philosopher and a strong supporter of education for everybody. He believed, quite simply, that mankind can continually improve and eventually become perfect. He imagined a future age in which there will be equality between nations and equality between people. He foresaw a future in which the individual will be perfect – morally, physically and intellectually. He was not just a dreamer. He accepted that people make mistakes and real progress is not easy for a culture. However, he believed that human beings can learn from their failures. He believed that there is no limit to human knowledge. He thought there is no end to human compassion for people who are ill or poor. He even claimed that human life can go on forever. He saw education for everybody as the key to this infinite improvement.
Two hundred years later, the British writer H.G. Wells saw the role of education in society in a rather more dramatic way. He said, 'Human history becomes more and more a race between education and disaster.' Wells believed in education. He obviously believed that there was a chance for education to save the world. But he was not sure that it would actually do so. What do you think? Do societies repeat the mistakes of earlier societies, or do we learn from history? Can education save us from ourselves?

Presenter: **Theme 7: They Made Our World, The Greatest Advance in History**
Lesson 1: Vocabulary
A 1 Listen and complete the diagram with a red word in each space.

Voice: There is a circle of progress that is repeated again and again in history. The circle works like this. Someone has a new idea. For example, an inventor sees someone dragging something heavy and thinks: 'He could move that more easily if he rolled it on a tree trunk.' This leads to a new invention – in this case, the wheel. Someone, perhaps the inventor, builds a new device from the invention – a wagon with wheels, for example, to carry goods, or a chariot for people to travel in. This device leads to a new technology, for example, wheeled transport. The new technology replaces the old technology. Suddenly, everything has wheels and people do not drag things across the ground any more. Then someone sees a horse pulling a wheeled cart and thinks: 'That cart would go much faster with an engine.'

Presenter: **B Listen to some information about a radio programme.**

Radio presenter: Last month on *They Made Our World*, we asked you to e-mail us with your list of the greatest advances of all time. We said it could be an invention or a discovery, but it must be something that revolutionised the world – something that changed the way we live or do something.
The response has been enormous – thousands of you have sent in your ideas already. But if you haven't e-mailed us yet, there is still time. Send your choice now to greatest at ourworld dotcom. Do it now and listen in at five o'clock today to find out the result. That's the greatest advance in the history of the world on *They Made Our World* on Channel 45 at five o'clock today.

Presenter: **C 2 Listen to the radio programme. Number the advances in order.**

Radio presenter: Welcome to They Made Our World. This week, we have the winner of our search to find the greatest advance in the history of the world. As you know, the response to our request for e-mails has been enormous, but we have a clear winner. I'm going to give you the top eight in reverse order. In other words, I'll give you number eight first, then number seven and so on, until we get to number one, our winner.
So, in eighth place we have … the telephone. I thought that would be higher, but there you are.
In seventh place, antibiotics. I never thought of those at all.
Sixth we have the printing press.
At number five we have mass production – I'm really surprised at that one.
Coming in at number four … food preservation. Apparently, you all think the world is a much better place for frozen chips and canned beans.
So now we have the top three. At number three, the internal combustion engine. You think it is important, but not as important as … at number two, the computer. I really thought that would be number one, but in fact, the top spot goes to the greatest advance in history … the wheel.
So there you have it. The wheel, the computer, the internal combustion engine, food preservation, mass production, the printing press, antibiotics and the telephone.

Presenter: **Lesson 2: Listening**
B Listen to Anne's talk straight through.

Female voice: What is the most important advance that people have made in the history of the world? Is it something to do with transport – the ability to move people and goods quickly around the world? Certainly, the Ancient World changed when the first Egyptian raised a piece of cloth as a sail and started to travel down the Nile. It is true that the wheel, for example, revolutionised transport and made it possible for one horse to move very heavy items over long distances. The invention of the internal combustion engine in the 19th century led to the conquest of the land, the sea and the air in the next 100 years. However, I do not believe the greatest advance in the history of the world has got anything to do with transport.
Is it something from the field of communications – the ability to send information quickly around the world? The Sumerians invented writing, which meant that information could be moved through time and space without people having to carry it in their heads. Johannes Gutenberg invented the printing press, which meant information could be copied and distributed all over the world quite cheaply. Telephones and then computers have led to the Communications Age, where everyone can talk or write to everyone else in the world instantly for a tiny amount of money. However, there is an advance that is much more important in the history of the world than anything from the field of communications.
I accept that advances in transport and communications were very important and, in a very real sense, the advances in these fields have made the modern world that we live in. But I believe there is a much more fundamental advance than either of these. I believe the greatest advance that human beings have made is in the area of food preservation. Let me explain. Man needs to eat food day in, day out. Early civilizations grew up near local sources of food. They needed large quantities of edible plants – fruit trees or nut trees, or bushes with berries. They needed herds of wild animals that they could kill and eat. However, there was a big problem with these natural supplies of food. On the one hand, in the correct season, usually the summer and autumn, the food was plentiful. But on the other hand, for large parts of the year, usually the winter months, there was little or no food. Why couldn't they store the food? Because, of course, most food goes bad very quickly if you just put it in a big storeroom.
For early societies, this was a serious problem. If you cannot store food, you must gather food every day, or at least every week. You must also kill animals regularly. This means that most people work from sunrise to sunset gathering food or hunting. There is very little time left for anything else – very little time for all the things we think of when we say civilization – science, the arts, industry, technology, leisure. The problem gets worse if the animals are wild and move from place to place. In this case, you must follow them when they move. So it is not possible to settle down in one place. And this is the essence of civilization. Civilization develops when settlements grow into towns, which in turn grow into large successful cities and then into empires. With food preservation comes civilization. The Ancient Egyptians knew how to dry fruit and corn to preserve it. The Inuit knew how to dry meat, and the Greeks and

Romans salted food to keep it longer. The inhabitants of the Indus Valley pickled food to preserve it.
So this is what I believe. Before people discovered methods of preserving food, they spent all their time gathering food and hunting, often wandering from place to place following the animals they ate. Before food preservation existed, people could not settle down in one place and develop as a civilization. So food preservation is more important than anything to do with transport or communications or any other part of the modern world. Without food preservation, people would never have developed transport and communications anyway, because they would not have had the time or the settled communities to do it in.
OK, I hear you say. It was important in the old days to find a way of preserving food. But that problem was solved thousands of years ago. Not true. Throughout history, Man has struggled with the problem of preserving food. As we have seen, some progress was made with drying, salting and pickling thousands of years ago. But as soon as people moved away from a settled community, there were still great problems. Sailors often got a painful and potentially fatal disease called scurvy because they did not eat fresh fruit for months at a time. Scurvy struck the sailors on Magellan's journey around the world in 1519, for example. The same situation was repeated all over the world. Napoleon lost more men to scurvy and starvation in the war against Russia than he did in all the battles put together. In fact, the problem for Napoleon was so bad that the French government offered a reward of 12,000 francs to the person who could solve it. The result was … canning. A man called Nicholas Appert tried for years to win the prize. At first, he had no success, but gradually he solved the problem. Finally, he put food into airtight containers in an attempt to preserve it. It worked.
So, by the 20th century, a lot of foodstuffs could be preserved, but fresh meat and dairy products were still a problem up to the 1950s. I remember my grandmother kept her meat in a small box called a meat safe. It was open to the air, but protected from flies by a mesh on the front. She kept her bottles of milk in the kitchen sink, floating in cold water. Of course, she had to use the milk the same day and the meat within two days, or it was bad. Nowadays, we can go to the supermarket once a week, buy fresh meat and dairy products and keep them in a freezer or a fridge. We can prepare a meal in a few moments and know that it is safe to eat. And what can we do with all the time we save? We can live.
So, in conclusion, food preservation first made it possible for a community as a whole to have time off from gathering, hunting and preparing food. With this time, civilizations invented the wheel and writing, the telephone and the computer. Without this time, no other inventions would have happened. More recently, food preservation has freed the housewife from the daily grind of food shopping and cooking. It is truly the greatest advance of all time.

Presenter: **C 2 Listen again and check your answers.**
[REPEAT OF LESSON 2 EXERCISE B]

Presenter: **Lesson 3: Learning new skills**
A 2 Listen and check your ideas.

Female voice:
a Is it something to do with transport?
b Is it something in the field of communications?
c I accept that advances in transport and communications were very important and, in a very real sense, the advances in these fields have made the modern world that we live in.
d Sailors often got a painful and potentially fatal disease called scurvy because they did not eat fresh fruit for months at a time.
e It was important in the old days to find a way of preserving food.
f The Sumerians invented writing, which meant that information could be moved through time and space without people having to carry it in their heads.
g Johannes Gutenberg invented the printing press, which meant information could be copied and distributed all over the world quite cheaply.
h Man needs to eat food day in, day out.
i This means that most people work from sunrise to sunset gathering food or hunting.
j Before people discovered methods of preserving food, they spent all their time gathering food and hunting, often wandering from place to place following the animals that they ate.
k The problem gets worse if the animals are wild and move from place to place. In this case, you must follow them when they move.
l So it is not possible to settle down in one place.
m This is the essence of civilization.
n Civilization develops when settlements grow into towns, which in turn grow into large successful cities and then into empires.

Presenter: **Lesson 4: Applying new skills**
A 2 Listen again and check your ideas.

Female voice: OK, I hear you say. It was important in the old days to find a way of preserving food. But that problem was solved thousands of years ago. Not true. Throughout history, Man has struggled with the problem of preserving food. As we have seen, some progress was made with drying, salting and pickling thousands of years ago. But as soon as people moved away from a settled community, there were still great problems. Sailors often got a painful and potentially fatal disease called scurvy because they did not eat fresh fruit for months at a time. Scurvy struck the sailors on Magellan's journey around the world in 1519, for example. The same situation was repeated all over the world. Napoleon lost more men to scurvy and starvation in the war against Russia than he did in all the battles put together. In fact, the problem for Napoleon was so bad that the French government offered a reward of 12,000 francs to the person who could solve it. The result was canning. A man called Nicholas Appert tried for years to win the prize. At first, he had no success, but gradually he solved the problem. Finally, he put food into airtight bottles in an attempt to preserve it. It worked. So by the 20th century, a lot of foodstuffs could be preserved, but fresh meat and dairy products were still a problem up to the 1950s.

Presenter: **C Listen to the whole talk. Check your answers to Exercise B.**

Male voice: What is the most important advance that people have made in the history of the world? Some might say it is mass production – the way that factories can produce huge quantities of goods nowadays with the help of machines, whereas in the past people had to make each item by hand. One definition of a civilization is a culture that changes the world in a clear way. Mass production has certainly enabled us to change the world out of all recognition. Most people (in the developed world at least) have a car, a television, a telephone and hundreds of other mass-produced items, things they could not have afforded if they were handmade. However, I think the greatest advance in the history of the world is more fundamental than material goods, like televisions and CD players.

What about computers? They are certainly a major part of nearly every area of modern-day life. With computers, we can calculate at an incredible speed and store and retrieve vast amounts of information. We can use them to play very sophisticated games or to store and reproduce hundreds of hours of music. Word-processing through computers has speeded up writing to an incredible extent. When I was young, I worked in an office, and we were expected to type up 10 perfect letters a day. Now we expect an office assistant to produce 50 or 60 letters a day, and then e-mail them to thousands of people at the same time, if necessary. But the invention of the modern computer comes at the end of a long trail of civilization. I believe the greatest advance comes a little earlier in our history.

I accept that mass production and computers have changed our world out of all recognition. Even my own grandfather would not understand most of the things I use in my everyday life, or the ways I use computers for work and pleasure. Computers make our lives more efficient, mass production gives us more things to own and enjoy. But, as I see it, neither computers nor mass production make our lives better in the most important way. In my opinion, the greatest advance that human beings have made is in the conquest of infectious diseases.

We have succeeded in conquering water-borne diseases like typhoid and cholera through better public health. Before people understood the need for clean water, decent housing and waste disposal, life for most people was short and full of pain. At the time of the Roman Empire, life expectancy in the civilized world was just 24 years. The Black Death in the 14th century killed a third of the population of the civilized world. Things had hardly improved by the start of the 20th century. In 1900, worldwide life expectancy was still only about 30 years. However, by 1985 it was about 62 years. This improvement is mainly due to better public health systems, but it is also due to the discovery of antibiotics and other powerful medicinal drugs.

Of course, you could argue that computers and mass production have made people's lives better. What is the point of having a long life if it is endless, hard, boring work?

I accept that this is true, but which is more important? To have a better life when you are well, or not to get an infectious disease in the first place? I maintain that first we had to give people lives free of pain and the fear of fatal illness. Then they could begin to enjoy their lives.

So, to sum up. I believe that the greatest advance in the history of the world is in the conquest of infectious diseases, through better public health and the discovery of powerful medicinal drugs to fight disease when it does occur. If you don't have a long life free from pain, you cannot enjoy the other advances of civilization.

Presenter: **Theme 8: Art and Literature, Gulliver and Robinson Crusoe**

Lesson 1: Vocabulary

A Listen to the past tense of the red words. Number the infinitives in order.

Voice:

1 let
2 saw
3 lit
4 needed
5 began
6 sold
7 belonged
8 landed
9 bought
10 disappeared
11 tricked
12 explored
13 heard
14 searched
15 thought
16 spent

Presenter: **C Listen to the introduction to the programme. Answer the questions.**

Female presenter: *Gulliver's Travels* is one of the most famous books in English literature. In Swift's book, the hero, Lemuel Gulliver, travels to four different worlds. In one world, the people are very small, in another they are giants, and in a third, the country is ruled by horses. Most people today think of *Gulliver's Travels* as a children's story, like *The Voyages of Sindbad the Sailor*. In fact, *Gulliver's Travels* may even be based on the Sindbad stories. It is certainly true that millions of children have enjoyed the stories in simplified versions. But the author, Jonathan Swift, did not write the book for children. He wrote the stories as a criticism of the politicians in England, in particular, at the time of the war between Britain and France. *Robinson Crusoe* is one of the most famous adventure stories in the English language. The hero, Crusoe, is shipwrecked on a desert island and lives there for 28 years before being rescued. The story, written by Daniel Defoe, is based on the true story of Alexander Selkirk, who spent three years on the uninhabited desert island of Juan Fernandez. It is now a popular story with children, but Defoe probably didn't write it as a children's book. Some critics say the story is an allegory for the fight between good and evil. I personally believe that Crusoe's life represents the advance of civilization from primitive society to modern life – at least, modern life in the 17th century.

Presenter: **D 2 Listen and check your answers.**

Female presenter:

a In Swift's book, the hero, Lemuel Gulliver, travels to four different worlds.
b *Gulliver's Travels* may even be based on the Sindbad stories.
c It is certainly true that millions of children have enjoyed the stories in simplified versions.
d But the author, Jonathan Swift, did not write the book for children.
e He wrote the stories as a criticism of the politicians in England at the time.
f *Robinson Crusoe* is one of the most famous adventure stories in the English language.
g It is now a popular story with children, but Defoe probably didn't write it as a children's book.

h Some critics say the story is an allegory for the fight between good and evil.

i I personally believe that Crusoe's life represents the advance of civilization.

Presenter: **Lesson 2: Listening**

A 3 Listen to the first part of the programme. Make notes.

Female presenter: Jonathan Swift was born in Ireland on November 30th, 1667, the son of an English lawyer. He grew up in Ireland and attended college in Dublin from the age of 14 to 21. When he left in 1688, he became the secretary to Sir William Temple, an English politician. During the next 20 years, he worked as a secretary and as a priest in various situations. Clearly, this work gave him an insight into the worlds of politics and religion, and he started writing about these subjects. Incidentally, some people say that Swift married a woman called Stella Johnson around 1716. Others maintain that there is no proof of this. It is believed that Swift started *Gulliver's Travels* in about 1712, but he did not publish it until 1726. Apparently, readers of the day could recognise real people and events in the fictional characters and events in the book.
Swift wrote several other books, but nothing as important as *Gulliver's Travels*. He died on 19 October, 1745, aged 78.

Presenter: **B 2 Listen to the first part. Number in order the events in the yellow box.**

Female presenter: Let's hear part of the first story. Gulliver's ship is wrecked in a storm and he wakes up in the strange world of Lilliput.

Male reader: *When I awoke, it was just daylight. I tried to get up, but I was not able to move. I had fallen asleep on my back and I found that my arms and legs were strongly fastened on each side to the ground; and my hair, which was long and thick, was tied down in the same way. I felt other thin ropes across my body, from my chest to my thighs. I could only look upwards; the sun began to grow hot, and the light hurt my eyes. I heard a strange noise near me; but as I lay tied on the ground, I could not see anything except the sky. After a little while, I felt something creeping up my left leg, then over my stomach and onto my chest and up almost to my chin. Peering down, I saw a human creature no more than 15 centimetres high. He had a bow and arrow in his hands. Shortly, I felt more and more of the creatures until there were at least forty of them on my body. I was so surprised that I cried loudly and they all ran back in fear. Some of them, I was told afterwards, were hurt leaping to the ground.*
After a little while, I started struggling and managed to break the strings and wrench out the pegs which held my left arm to the ground. I dragged my head up, although the strings in my hair hurt me a lot. I was just able to turn my head about five centimetres. But the creatures fled a second time, before I could grab any of them. Suddenly I heard one of them cry aloud "TOLGO PHONAC" and in an instant I felt more than a hundred arrows like needles pierce my left hand.

Presenter: **B 3 Listen again and check your ideas.**
[REPEAT OF EXERCISE B2]

Presenter: **C Listen to the second part of the story.**

Female presenter: Eventually, Gulliver makes friends with the little people of Lilliput and learns their language. Then he finds out about the problems of the strange world.

Male reader: *One day, the king of Lilliput sent his friend, Reldresal, to see me. I put him on my hand so I could see him and hear him.*
'I have come' he said, 'to tell you about the problems in Lilliput. In our world there are two powerful countries. One is Lilliput, the other is called Blefescu. These two countries have fought a war for many, many years. It is all about eggs.'
'Eggs?' I cried. 'How can a war be about eggs?'
'It began as follows,' he replied. 'We always used to break eggs open at the big end before we ate them. Then one day the king's son cut his finger doing this, so his father decided that, in future, everybody should break open their eggs at the little end. Many people disagreed with this law and fled from Lilliput. They went to the other great country, Blefuscu. Now the Big-endian exiles are so important in Blefuscu that the country has declared war on Lilliput. They are going to invade us any day.'
I was troubled. On the one hand, I did not think it was right that I should intervene in their war, but, on the other, the people of Lilliput had been so kind to me. I decided to end the war without bloodshed.

Presenter: **D 2 Listen to the third part of the story and check your ideas.**

Female presenter: Gulliver tells the king about his plans and then sets out to end the war.

Male reader: *The country of Blefuscu is an island situated to the north-east of Lilliput, from which it is separated only by a channel eight hundred metres wide. Of course, this is an immense distance for the little men, but nothing to me, for I am a prodigious swimmer. The whole fleet of Blefuscu lay at anchor in the main harbour, ready for the invasion of Lilliput. I made a strong cable and attached fifty hooks to it. Then I plunged into the sea, holding my cable with the hooks. I arrived at the fleet in less than half an hour. The enemy was so terrified when they saw me, that they leaped out of their ships, and swam to shore. I then took my cable, and, fastening a hook to the hole at the front of each ship, I began to pull the ships out of the harbour. While I was doing this, the enemy fired several thousand arrows, many of which stuck in my hands and face. They hurt me a lot but they could not seriously wound me. My only worry was my eyes and I had the sudden thought to put on my spectacles. When the people of Blefuscu saw their whole fleet moving away from the harbour, they set up such a scream of grief and despair as it is almost impossible to describe or imagine.*

Presenter: **E 2 Listen to the final part and check your ideas.**

Female presenter: What is *Gulliver's Travels* about? It seems at first to be a fantasy, with strange worlds and impossible creatures. Perhaps we could call it the first work of science fiction. But it is far more than that. It is an allegory of English politics of Swift's day. Perhaps it is an allegory of all societies in any age. Gulliver learns, in the land of the little people, that people argue and go to war over stupid things. In the second land, the giants live together without fighting, but Gulliver is tiny in that land. Does Swift mean humans are too small to understand? In the final land, Gulliver sees that humans can never learn to live together peacefully. It is a sad and bitter view of the world, from a man who was sad and bitter at the end of his life.

Presenter: **Lesson 3: Learning new skills**
A 1 Listen again to the proper nouns. Write the words. Guess the spelling.

Voice:
1 Blefuscu
2 Redresal
3 Lilliput
4 Swift
5 Dublin
6 Stella
7 Johnson
8 Jonathan
9 Spencer

Presenter: **A 3 Listen again and check your spelling.**
[REPEAT OF EXERCISE A1]

Presenter: **B 3 Listen to some sentences from the story. Match the dramatic verbs with the common verbs in the blue box.**

Male reader:
1 After a little while, I felt something creeping up my left leg, then over my stomach and onto my chest and up almost to my chin.
2 Peering down, I saw a human creature no more than 15 centimetres high. He had a bow and arrow in his hands.
3 I was so surprised that I cried loudly and they all ran back in fear.
4 Some of them, I was told afterwards, were hurt leaping to the ground.
5 After a little while, I started struggling and managed to break the strings and wrench out the pegs which held my left arm to the ground.
6 I dragged my head up, although the strings in my hair hurt me a lot. I was just able to turn my head about five centimetres.
7 But the creatures fled a second time, before I could grab any of them.
8 I made a strong cable and attached fifty hooks to it. Then I plunged into the sea, holding my cable with the hooks.

Presenter: **Lesson 4: Applying new skills**
A 3 Listen to the first part of the programme. Make notes.

Female presenter: Daniel Defoe was born in London in 1660. His father, James Foe, was a butcher and candle-maker. It seems that the young Daniel was disappointed that he did not come from a noble family. Perhaps this is why he added *De* to his surname. *De* is French for *of*, and noblemen used it after their first names to say which lands they owned. Daniel Foe became Daniel of Foe overnight.
As a young man, Daniel was interested in politics, but eventually he went into business. When he was 24, he married Mary Tuffley. But neither Defoe's business nor his marriage was successful. By the early 1690s, he was involved in politics again, working secretly against James II, the king of England. He was caught and sent to prison. It may be that he decided in prison not to take sides any more. Certainly when he came out, he wrote for both sides of the political argument. Late in his life, he took up writing fiction and produced a large number of adventure stories, although he did not publish all of them under his own name. His books were popular at the time, but only *Robinson Crusoe*, published in 1719, has become a classic work of English literature. Incidentally, Defoe did not make much money from his writing and, in fact, died a poor man in 1730.

Presenter: **B 3 Listen to the first part of the story. Number the items in the yellow box in the order that Crusoe finds them. Be careful! He doesn't find all the items.**

Female presenter: Defoe's character, Robinson Crusoe, has many adventures before he is shipwrecked on his desert island. But most people only remember this part of the story …

Male reader: *When I woke up it was broad daylight, the weather was clear, and the storm had abated, so that the sea did not rage and swell as before: I was surprised to see that the ship was still afloat, stuck on a rock about two kilometres from the shore.*
I resolved, if possible, to get to the ship, so I plunged into the water. But when I got there, I could see no way to get on board. I swam round twice, and the second time I spied a small piece of a rope, and by the help of that, hauled myself up into the forecastle of the ship; I found that she was holed, and had a great deal of water in her, but the stern was lifted up and everything in that part was dry. First I went to the bread-room and stuffed my pockets with biscuit, and ate it as I did other things, for I had no time to lose. Then I realised that I needed a boat to help me carry things back to the shore. We had several spare yard arms, and two or three large pieces of wood. I resolved to work with these, so I flung as many of them over board as I could manage for their weight, tying each one with a rope so it did not drift away; when this was done I slid down the ship's side, and pulling them to me, I tied four of them together at both ends as well as I could, in the form of a raft, and laying two or three short pieces of plank upon them cross-ways, I found I could walk upon it very well. What should I load it with? And how can I preserve it from the sea? I first got three of the seamen's chests, which I had broken open and emptied, and lowered them down upon my raft; the first of these I filled with bread, rice, three Dutch cheeses, five pieces of dried goat's meat, and a little corn. Next, I searched for and found tools to work with on shore. What about ammunition and guns? There were two very good rifles in the great Cabin, and two pistols, these I grabbed first, with some powder-horns, and a small bag of shot, and two old rusty swords; and now I thought myself pretty well freighted, and began to think how I should get to shore with them, having no sail, oar, or rudder…

Presenter: **C Listen to the second part of the story.**

Female presenter: Crusoe gets back to the shore eventually, but his problems are not over …

Male reader: *My next job was to view the country, and look for a proper place for my habitation, and where to stow my goods to secure them from whatever might happen; I had no idea where I was, whether on the mainland or on an island, whether inhabited or uninhabited, whether in danger from wild beasts or not. There was a hill no more than half a kilometre from me, which rose up very steep and high. I took*

out one of the rifles, and one of the pistols, and thus armed I struggled up to the top of that hill. I arrived after much difficulty and, to my despair, saw my fate. I was on an island surrounded on every side by the sea, with no more land to be seen except two islands, smaller even than this one, which lay about five kilometres to the West.
I found also that the island was barren, and, as far as I could see, uninhabited, except presumably by wild beasts, although I could not see any. I did see a huge number of birds and when I shot at one which I saw sitting upon a tree on the side of a great wood, I believe it was the first gun that had been fired there since the Creation of the World.

Presenter: **D 2 Listen to the final part of the programme. What do some critics think the book is about? What about the presenter? Make notes.**

Female presenter: What is *Robinson Crusoe* about? At one level, it is just an adventure story, and a very good one at that. But some critics have found a lot more in the book. Some say it is a rites of passage book with one man struggling to survive and, in the process, growing up. Others say there is more to it than that. At the beginning of the story, Crusoe is not a very nice person. Each time he sets sail, he is shipwrecked. Some say this is punishment for his sins. Finally, he arrives on his desert island. He builds a home and grows crops and raises animals. He eventually finds a man on the island and teaches him to believe in God. Finally, he wins several battles against natives who try to invade from nearby islands. I believe that *Robinson Crusoe* is the story of civilization told through the eyes of one man.

Presenter: **D 3 Listen again. When the presenter pauses, predict the next word. Then listen and check.**

Female presenter: What is *Robinson Crusoe* about? At one [PAUSE] level, it is just an [PAUSE] adventure story, and a very good one at that. But some [PAUSE] critics have found a lot more in the book. Some say it is a rites of [PAUSE] passage book with one man struggling to survive and, in the [PAUSE] process, growing up. Others say there is more to it than [PAUSE] that. At the beginning of the story, Crusoe is not a very nice [PAUSE] person. Each time he sets [PAUSE] sail, he is shipwrecked. Some say this is [PAUSE] punishment for his [PAUSE] sins. Finally, he arrives on his desert [PAUSE] island. He builds a home and grows [PAUSE] crops and raises [PAUSE] animals. He eventually finds a [PAUSE] man on the island and teaches him to believe in [PAUSE] God. Finally, he wins several battles against [PAUSE] natives who try to invade from nearby [PAUSE] islands. I believe that *Robinson Crusoe* is the story of [PAUSE] civilization told through the eyes of one [PAUSE] man.

Presenter: **Theme 9: Sports and Leisure, Five Trillion Dollars per Annum**
Lesson 1: Vocabulary
A Listen to a text about sport. Number the red words in the order you hear them.

Female voice: At one time, people who did sports were called sportsmen or sportswomen. At that time, an athlete was a person who ran races or took part in events on the field – for example, the high jump or throwing the javelin. Nowadays, people use the word 'athlete' to mean any person involved in sport. The word is used to separate the playing skills from the physical fitness of the player. So you will often hear someone say, 'He is a great tennis player and a superb athlete'. Athletes in any sport train hard and are very fit. They usually practise their sport for hours each day. Top athletes love to compete against other top players and, of course, to beat them.

Presenter: **B Listen to a short text that contains the green words. Then complete the text with one of the words in each space. Make any necessary changes.**

Male voice: Tourism is big business nowadays. The growth in travel for leisure has been enormous in the last half century, especially the increase in international holiday travel. For example, most people in Western Europe have now visited at least one other country, whereas 50 years ago only a tiny percentage of Europeans had been abroad.
There are pros and cons to holiday travel on this massive scale. On the positive side, people learn about other cultures when they travel. Perhaps it is harder to go to war against a country that you have visited on holiday. On the negative side, tourism often has a big impact on the holiday destinations. Tourists sometimes destroy the things they have come to see. For example, visitors to the tombs in Egypt have damaged the old wall paintings with the flashlights of their cameras. Tourists sometimes turn parts of the foreign country into little versions of their own country. For instance, English tourism to Spain has led to Spanish shops and restaurants selling English food rather than Spanish.
Why do people travel hundreds or even thousands of miles on holiday? Clearly, some want sun and sand, others want to see the ruins of an ancient civilization or just experience the lifestyle of a different culture. A lot of tourism is *sightseeing* – simply going to look at buildings or landscapes in a different country. Personally, I think most tourists just want to tell their friends later, 'I've been there, I've seen that and I've got the photographs'.

Presenter: **Lesson 2: Listening**
B 3 Listen to the introduction. How does the lecturer answer the question?

Male lecturer: Welcome to the Faculty of Sports and Leisure Management. You are here today because you have chosen to study Tourism Management. Let me say straight away that I think you have made an excellent choice, for two reasons. Firstly, tourism is big business nowadays – we'll hear just how big in a few minutes. Secondly, it is important to study tourism because it is having a huge impact on many countries and areas of the world – a good effect in many cases, a bad effect in others. It is important to understand the impact of tourism because then we can begin to manage it correctly. So Tourism Management is an important and growing part of the massive global leisure industry. Before we look at tourism as a business and its impact on the world, however, we need to define the word. What exactly is 'tourism'? It is also useful to see how tourism started and how it has grown in recent years.

Presenter: **C Listen to the introduction again and check your ideas.**
[REPEAT OF EXERCISE B3]

Presenter: **D 2 Listen to the first part of the lecture. Is the lecturer's definition similar to yours?**

Male lecturer: One definition says that a tourist is a person who travels for pleasure, goes at least 50 kilometres from his or her home and stays away at least one night. Even this definition has been challenged. What about domestic tourism? This is where people visit tourist attractions in their own country and even their own town or local area and do not stay overnight. Perhaps there is only one key point about tourism – it is travel for pleasure. In other words, it is part of the ever-increasing leisure industry.

Presenter: **E Listen to the second part of the lecture.**

Male lecturer: International tourism on any scale is only about 50 years old. For people to travel for pleasure, they need time, money and good transport links. It is only recently that these three commodities have come together for a large number of people in large parts of the world.
For thousands of years, most people hardly had leisure time at all. They worked, ate and slept. There were occasional holidays – the word 'holiday' in English comes, in fact, from 'holy day', so holidays were originally days for prayer and religious celebration. But even on these holy days or holidays, the majority of people had no money to spend on leisure activities. For the few wealthy people with time and money, transport links were so bad that it was no pleasure to travel anyway. Some people did make the effort, of course. Rich people from Britain and the States did the Grand Tour, visiting Rome and Athens and other locations from ancient history. Domestic tourism became more popular in England after the arrival of the railways in the 1840s. By the way, we distinguish between international tourism, where people go to another country on holiday, and domestic or internal tourism, where people stay in their own country. Seaside towns, in particular, started to cater for tourists in the summer. The first package holiday, which included transport by train, hotel rooms and food, was, apparently, organised by Thomas Cook in 1861. He arranged for a group of working men to go to Paris for six days. The package cost around two pounds per person.

Presenter: **F 3 Listen to the third part of the lecture. Try to contribute to each discussion.**

Male lecturer: So some ordinary people were travelling abroad on holiday by the end of the 19th century. But it is fair to say that there was very little international tourism until the 1950s. Indeed, the World Tourism Organisation, or WTO, estimates that in 1950 there were only 25 million international stayovers per annum worldwide. This may seem large until we compare it with more recent figures. I've given you a handout with a graph that shows the growth in world tourism over the last 50 years and an estimate for future growth. Can you find it? ... What was the figure for total tourist stayovers in 1980?

Man 1: Two hundred.

Male lecturer: Two hundred what?

Man 1: Million.

Male lecturer: No, it's a bit more than that.

Man 2: Three hundred million.

Male lecturer: Yes, it's about 300 million, or perhaps a little less. What has it reached by 1990?

Woman 1: Just over four hundred million.

Male lecturer: Absolutely. And by 2002, the number had reached ...?

Various: Seven hundred and three million.

Male lecturer: That's right. Actually, there's a slight dip in 2001. Why is that, do you think?

Man: SARS?

Male lecturer: No, that was later.

Man: September 11th.

Male lecturer: Yes. International terrorism can have a big effect on international tourism. For example, recently a very small country has been badly affected ...

Man: America.

Male lecturer: No, I'm thinking of a small country that has seen a big decline in tourism because of terrorism ...

Woman: Bali.

Male lecturer: Exactly. Anyway, back to the graph. The WTO has done an estimate of growth in international tourism in the next 15 years. When does it think the figure will reach one billion?

Man: Two hundred and ten.

Man 2: Two thousand and ten.

Male lecturer: Yes, we can say two thousand and ten or twenty ten. The WTO estimates that the number will reach one billion in 2010 and 1.6 billion by 2020. And, of course, for every *international* stayover there are probably at least ten domestic stayovers. Domestic or internal tourism is also rising rapidly around the world.
What is the financial value of this part of the leisure industry? I always ask my students this question at the start of the course, so what do you think?

Man: A billion dollars?

Male lecturer: Anyone else?

Man 2: Ten billion dollars?

Male lecturer: OK. Any other ideas? What about you? What do you think?

Woman: I was going to say ten billion dollars.

Male lecturer: OK. Well, actually, it is much, much more. According to the WTO, tourism contributes about five trillion US dollars each year to the world economy. That's a five and 12 noughts. That's about half the total annual production of the USA and about a sixth of the total annual production of the whole world.
We can look at this huge figure another way. Tourism contributes about 16 per cent of the total world economy. How does tourism compare with other sectors? Well, agriculture contributes about four per cent to the world economy – so the industry that produces all the food in the world is about a quarter the size of tourism. What about petroleum? The industry that gives us most of our energy worldwide contributes about three per cent to the world economy, so tourism is five times bigger than the petroleum industry. In terms of employment, the World Travel and Tourism Council, or WTTC, estimates that, in 2003, the Travel & Tourism Industry will account for 195 million jobs worldwide, which is 7.6 per cent of total employment.
Growth in this sector is also impressive. I've given you a block graph on this. As you can see, in Europe, tourism is growing annually at 2.9 per cent, while in the Americas it is nearly four per cent. What about in Africa? ... Anybody?

Man: Five per cent.

Male lecturer: Well, it's a bit more than five per cent, isn't it?

Man 2: 5.5 per cent?

Male lecturer: Yes, that's right. What's the figure for South Asia?

Woman: Just over six per cent.

Male lecturer: Right. But which region is at the top of the growth graph? What do you think?

Man: Europe?

Male lecturer: No, Europe's there already, isn't it? Any other ideas?

Man: Japan?

Male lecturer: Japan's in East Asia and the Pacific. Anyone else? … Come on, don't be shy.

Woman: Is it the Middle East?

Male lecturer: Absolutely. It's the Middle East, with an amazing seven per cent annual growth rate in tourism. This is at a time when the world economy is only growing at about 2.8 per cent and many sectors are actually declining.
Now, I'd like you to work with the people near you for a few minutes. Think about this question. What are the pros and cons of tourism – the positive impacts and the negative impacts? Can you discuss that for a few minutes?

Presenter: **F 4 Listen to the third part of the lecture again and check your answers.**
[REPEAT OF EXERCISE F3]

Presenter: **Lesson 3: Learning new skills**
A 2 Listen and check your ideas.

Male lecturer: Let me say straight away
It is important to understand
It is only recently that
For thousands of years
The majority of people
It is fair to say that
We can look at this another way

Presenter: **B 2 Listen and check your ideas.**

Male lecturer: Before we look at tourism as a business, we need to define tourism.
Tourism has a good effect in many cases, a bad effect in others.
Even if you had time and money to travel, transport links were so bad that it was no pleasure to travel anyway.
According to the WTO, tourism contributes about five trillion US dollars each year to the world economy
In terms of employment, the travel and tourism industry will account for 195 million jobs worldwide in 2003.
Tourism is travel for pleasure. In other words, it is part of the ever-increasing leisure industry.

Presenter: **C 1 Listen to the next part of the lecture. Tick the points the lecturer mentions.**

Male lecturer: So tourism is big business. But what is the economic and social impact on a particular location? Let's imagine a small, sleepy fishing village, surrounded by rich farmland, miles from the nearest airport. There is not much employment in the village, but it has good weather and a nice sandy beach. People start to hear about the village and begin to visit it. Perhaps they are internal tourists. They stay in the one hotel in the village. The hotel has to employ more staff to look after the extra guests. The staff have more money to spend in the local community, which becomes more prosperous. As more tourists come, the hotel expands and the spiral begins to rise. Economists call this the Multiplier Effect, and it is the good side of tourism, the side that all national tourist boards try to encourage.
Of course, not all the extra spending benefits the local community. The hotel might import a lot of the food to meet the demands of the tourists, rather than purchasing it from the local farmers and fishermen. Economists call this leakage. And what about the jobs in the hotel and other parts of the tourist industry? Generally, jobs in tourism are unskilled and low-paid. There is demand for maids, waiters, cleaners, etc. As it gets bigger, the hotel might bring in people from outside the village, from another country even, because they are cheaper. Again, there is leakage from the local community.
There may be another negative impact of employment creation in tourism. People may leave the local production and extraction industries, like farming and fishing, to work in service industries – in the hotel itself and in restaurants and other tourist attractions that spring up. Eventually, some of the traditional sources of employment may die out altogether. The old fishing village surrounded by rich farmland may become a new tourist town with no room for fishing boats and nobody to work the fields.
Finally, there may be a social impact of the new jobs. Fishermen and farmers are very independent. They manage their own lives. If they become gardeners or cleaners, they may develop a different view of themselves. They may lose their self-respect.
There is another issue relating to different lifestyles. Tourists often do not have the same lifestyle as the locals. They demand different facilities, in many cases, including swimming pools and golf courses. Sometimes, facilities get better for everybody, including the local community. But often, tourists have priority over locals for the supply of water and electricity, and this can cause resentment and even do damage to other parts of the local economy.
Tourists spend money in the local community, and some of that will go back to the government in the form of tax, so the national government will benefit from local tourism. But this is not a complete gain either. Some of the taxation money must be spent on building the infrastructure for the new tourist industry. The old route to the fishing village is slow and the road is bumpy. The government has to build a new road from the airport, which, of course, has been expanded and updated. All of this costs money. In some cases, the cost of the infrastructure can be higher than the income from tourism. There is another effect of infrastructure – some of it is built on the beautiful land that the tourists came to see. This is the terrible irony of some tourism. Tourists may actually destroy the things they came to see and enjoy. A lot of tourism is sightseeing, but what if the sights are damaged by the tourists who have come to see them? A small, quiet, beautiful fishing village can become a noisy, busy, ugly tourist town.
The effect can be even worse where the environment is particularly fragile. Many tropical resorts, for example, are popular because of the coral under the sea very close to the shore. The rise of tourism in such an area can destroy the coral in just a few years.

Firstly, souvenirs of coral become popular and both locals and tourists break off pieces. Secondly, ground up coral is a good building material. As more buildings go up, the coral reef goes down. Thirdly, the anchors of tourist boats scrape against the coral and damage it. Finally, the extra waste products from the growing town are piped into the sea and the coral dies under the murky waters.
What about the social impact on the original community? Tourism often divides local communities. Many in the community, usually the young, want the tourists to come, and like the changes that tourism brings. But others resent the way their community is changed by the tourists. I said at the beginning that the one certain thing about tourism is that it is travel for pleasure. When people go on holiday, they want to enjoy themselves, and this may mean that they behave differently from the way they normally do at home. They may also not understand or not care about the local values of the area they are visiting. The attitude of tourists can, therefore, have negative effects. Firstly, the local people start to resent the tourists. Secondly, they may see the tourists as representatives of the culture they come from. Travel, they say, broadens the mind, but travellers can set the minds of local people against them, with their rudeness and bad behaviour. Tourism may even contribute to terrorism, with resentment turning into hatred.
For all these reasons, tourism must be managed … and that's what you are here to learn about.

Presenter: **C 3 Listen to this part of the lecture again. Make notes of the extra points.**
[REPEAT OF EXERCISE C1]

Presenter: **Lesson 4: Applying new skills**
A Listen and check.
Voice 1: 1 economic impact
Voice 2: 2 internal tourism
Voice 1: 3 local community
Voice 2: 4 tourist industry
Voice 1: 5 different lifestyle
Voice 2: 6 swimming pool
Voice 1: 7 golf course
Voice 2: 8 electricity supply
Voice 1: 9 national government
Voice 2: 10 fragile environment

Presenter: **C Listen to each section from the second half of the lecture again.**
Lecturer: So tourism is big business. But what is the economic and social impact on a particular location? Let's imagine a small, sleepy fishing village, surrounded by rich farm land, miles from the nearest airport. There is not much employment in the village, but it has good weather and a nice sandy beach. People start to hear about the village and begin to visit it. Perhaps they are internal tourists. They stay in the one hotel in the village. The hotel has to employ more staff to look after the extra guests. What happens to the local community? Any ideas?
Of course, not all the extra spending benefits the local community. The hotel might import a lot of the food to meet the demands of the tourists, rather than purchasing it from the local farmers and fishermen. Economists call this leakage. And what about the jobs in the hotel and other parts of the tourist industry? Generally, jobs in tourism are unskilled and low-paid. There is demand for maids, waiters, cleaners, etc. As it gets bigger, the hotel might bring in people from outside the village, from another country even, because they are cheaper. Again, there is leakage from the local community.
There may be another negative impact of employment creation in tourism. What do you think that could be? Another negative impact?
Finally, there may be a social impact of the new jobs. Fishermen and farmers are very independent. They manage their own lives. If they become gardeners or cleaners, they may develop a different view of themselves. Will the impact be positive or negative? What do you think?
There is another issue relating to different lifestyles. Tourists often do not have the same lifestyle as the locals. They demand different facilities, in many cases, including swimming pools and golf courses. Sometimes, facilities get better for everybody, including the local community. But often, tourists have priority over locals for water and electricity supply. What is the social impact of this aspect?
Tourists spend money in the local community, and some of that will go back to the government in the form of tax, so the national government will benefit from local tourism. But this is not a complete gain either. Why not? What is the negative side of tourism for national governments?
This is the terrible irony of some tourism. Tourists may actually destroy the things they came to see and enjoy. A lot of tourism is sightseeing, but what if the sights are damaged by the tourists who have come to see them? A small, quiet, beautiful fishing village can become a noisy, busy, ugly tourist town.
The effect can be even worse where the environment is particularly fragile. Can you think of a good example of a fragile environment that can be damaged by tourism?
What about the social impact on the original community? Tourism often divides local communities. In what way can tourism divide a community?
For all these reasons, tourism must be managed … and that's what you are here to learn about.

Presenter: **Theme 10: Nutrition and Health, Food – The New Poison?**
Lesson 1: Vocabulary
A Listen to some words.
Voice: meat
potatoes
eggs
palm tree
salmon
sheep
iron
vegetable
A, B, C, D and E

Presenter: **B Listen to two students doing the quiz.**
Student 1: What are you doing?
Student 2: This quiz on food hygiene.
Student 1: Oh, great. How are you doing?
Student 2: Well, I haven't started yet, really.
Student 1: Why not?
Student 2: I don't understand all the questions.
Student 1: For example?
Student 2: Well, Question 1, for a start.
Student 1: Question 1. *What makes food harmful?* What's wrong with that?
Student 2: What does *harmful* mean?

Student 1: It means it can hurt you, harm you, make you ill. I suppose they want you to say *bacteria*.
Student 2: What is *batkeria*?
Student 1: Bacteria. It means tiny, living creatures that you find in the air, or in water or, of course, in food. It's plural. *Bacterium, bacteria.*
Student 2: Right. Question 3. *Unsafe*. That's the opposite of safe, yes?
Student 1: That's right.
Student 2: So it means *dangerous*?
Student 1: Well, not as strong as *dangerous*, just not safe.
Student 2: OK. Question 5 – *store*. I thought *store* was a shop.
Student 1: It has two meanings. When it's a verb, it means: 'to keep for some time'.
Student 2: Right. Question 7 – *handling* comes from handle, is that right?
Student 1: Yes.
Student 2: Handle on a door?
Student 1: No, *handle* as a verb. Touch with your hands. In this case, it means prepare, cook.
Student 2: Oh, I see. OK, last one. *Defrost.* I suppose *de* means *not* or *un*?
Student 1: Yes, that's right.
Student 2: So it is the opposite of *frost*. I don't know that verb.
Student 1: No, it's a bit strange. It's the opposite of *freeze*.
Student 2: So *defrost* means *'unfreeze'*?
Student 1: Exactly.
Student 2: Right. Now we can do the quiz …

Presenter: Lesson 2: Listening review (1)
B Listen to the introduction to the lecture. Complete the outline notes.

Male lecturer: Today, I'm going to talk about food hygiene. I'm going to tell you about the factors that must be present for food to be harmful. There are three of them. They are bacteria, temperature and time. Then I'm going to talk about looking after food, which means, firstly, storing it correctly, and secondly, handling it correctly. Finally, I'm going to explain the importance of the use-by date on food.

Presenter: C Listen to the first part of the lecture and make notes.

Male lecturer: OK. So, first, when does food become harmful? There are basically three factors. Firstly, there must be harmful bacteria or microorganisms in or on the food. Microorganisms are tiny living creatures that are invisible to the naked eye. Actually, most bacteria are not harmful. In fact, the human body needs bacteria to work properly. But a small number of bacteria can cause illness and even death. The number of bacteria can grow very rapidly because they multiply. In other words, one bacterium becomes two, then four, then eight, and so on. Secondly, temperature. Bacteria multiply when food is between four and 60 degrees centigrade. This is called the Danger Zone for food. Below four degrees, bacteria cannot multiply or increase in numbers to a dangerous level. Above 60 degrees centigrade, most bacteria are killed. Finally, time. Bacteria need time to multiply, but not very much time. If we leave food in the Danger Zone for more than two hours, the bacteria can reach a harmful level.

Presenter: D Listen again and check your answers.
[REPEAT OF LESSON 2 EXERCISE C]

Presenter: E Listen to the second part of the lecture.

Male lecturer: How can you be sure that food is safe? It is impossible to be absolutely sure, because you cannot see bacteria. Some people think that food containing harmful bacteria always looks or smells funny, but this is not true. One very dangerous microorganism, which causes the fatal illness botulism, produces no changes in food that we can see or smell. But the vast majority of food you buy nowadays is safe, so if you store it correctly, handle it correctly and use it before the use-by date, you can be confident it is safe. However, there is a very simple rule about food. If you are not sure for some reason that food is safe, throw it away. In other words, if in doubt, throw it out! OK, so first you must store food correctly. Firstly, this means keeping fresh food in a refrigerator that is operating at the correct temperature – that is, below four degrees centigrade. It also means storing food correctly when you take it out of the refrigerator. Cover it to protect it from new bacteria, and don't leave it standing for more than two hours. Finally, it means storing food correctly when you take it out of the house, for a picnic, for example. I remember once I went on a wadi trip and the host brought the food in shopping bags. There was meat and fish and eggs, all in the car in temperatures up to 40 degrees. We drove for about two hours. I didn't eat anything, but other people did and several of them had bad stomachaches the next day. Anyway, getting back to the point. Put food in a cool box and put ice in the cool box. A general rule is this: if there is still ice in the box when you open it, the food is safe to eat. So we've seen that we must store food correctly. Now let's consider handling food correctly. But what is the correct way to handle food? You must ensure that you don't transfer bacteria from your hands onto the food, so wash your hands before starting to prepare food. You must also ensure that you don't transfer bacteria from one piece of food onto another piece of food, so wash your hands after handling food. And remember to wash fresh fruit and vegetables before you eat them. There will be millions of bacteria on the surface, even though you can't see them.

Presenter: F 3 Listen to the third part of the lecture.

Male lecturer: Some people have called food 'the new poison', and it's true that food poisoning has increased all over the world in recent years. Why has food poisoning increased? Perhaps it is because people use modern household appliances wrongly in some cases. For example, the freezer is a wonderful invention that enables you to keep food like meat for several months without it going bad. The meat is quite safe in the freezer, but you must be very careful when you take it out to cook it. As you know, low temperatures do not kill bacteria, they just stop them multiplying, so when you take the meat out of the freezer, bacteria can start to damage the food immediately. You must defrost the meat in a safe way and then cook it for the correct time at the correct temperature. What is the correct way to defrost meat? What do you think? … Any other ideas? … Anyone else? Come on, don't be shy. … OK. The very best way to defrost meat is to put it in the refrigerator overnight. If you just leave the meat standing at room temperature, bacteria on the outside of the meat start to multiply before the inside of the meat has defrosted. If you defrost in a

microwave, there might still be ice in parts of the food, and those parts will not cook properly and kill the bacteria.
What other modern invention causes problems with food hygiene? Well, the microwave is a wonderful invention, if it is used correctly. We can make hot meals in a few seconds. But are these meals safe? The answer is yes, if they have cooked properly all the way through, but you must turn food regularly in a microwave to make sure every part is cooked. With liquid foods, like soup, you must stir the liquid several times during cooking. Finally, what must you always do when you have finished cooking something in a microwave? Any ideas? … Anyone else? … What do you think? … Right. So, when you have finished cooking something in a microwave, you must leave the food to stand for a few minutes to spread the heat.
So to sum up. Most food that we buy in a shop is safe, but we must store it correctly and handle it correctly. There is one other thing we must do. I mentioned it at the very beginning. Does anyone remember? … We must eat it by the use-by date. That's the date printed on the top or the bottom or the side. Always check the use-by date, and if you have kept the food too long, throw it away.
OK, in the next lecture we are going to look at some facts and figures on food poisoning. We are also going to learn the Food Code, or how to be safe in the kitchen.

Presenter: **Lesson 3: Listening review (2)**
A 2 Listen and check your answers.

Voice:
all over the world
cause and effect
for thousands of years
getting back to the point
in other words
it all started with
it is fair to say that
it is important to understand
it is only recently that
let me say straight away
on the one hand
so to sum up
the majority of people
the rest of her life
to put it another way

Presenter: **B 1 Listen again to parts of the lecture in Lesson 2. Find a good way to continue in the yellow box.**

Male lecturer:
1 Then I'm going to talk about looking after food, which means, firstly, storing it correctly, and secondly
2 There are basically three factors.
3 Actually, most bacteria are not harmful. In fact,
4 The number of bacteria can grow very rapidly, because they multiply. In other words,
5 If you are not sure for some reason that food is safe, throw it away. In other words,
6 Finally, it means storing food correctly when you take it out of the house, for a picnic, for example. I remember once
7 So we've seen that we must store food correctly.
8 Why has food poisoning increased? Perhaps it is because people use modern household appliances wrongly in some cases. For example,
9 So to sum up.
10 OK, in the next lecture

Presenter: **B 2 Listen to the way each part continues and check your answers.**

Male lecturer:
1 Then I'm going to talk about looking after food, which means, firstly, storing it correctly, and secondly, handling it correctly.
2 There are basically three factors. Firstly, there must be harmful bacteria or microorganisms in or on the food.
3 Actually, most bacteria are not harmful. In fact, the human body needs bacteria to work properly.
4 The number of bacteria can grow very rapidly, because they multiply. In other words, one bacterium becomes two, then four, then eight, and so on.
5 If you are not sure for some reason that food is safe, throw it away. In other words, if in doubt, throw it out!
6 Finally, it means storing food correctly when you take it out of the house, for a picnic, for example. I remember once I went on a wadi trip and the host brought the food in shopping bags. Anyway, getting back to the point.
7 So we've seen that we must store food correctly. Now let's consider handling food correctly.
8 Why has food poisoning increased? Perhaps it is because people use modern household appliances wrongly in some cases. For example, the freezer is a wonderful invention that enables you to keep food like meat for several months without it going bad.
9 So to sum up. Most food that we buy in a shop is safe, but we must store it correctly and handle it correctly.
10 OK, in the next lecture we are going to look at some facts and figures on food poisoning.

Presenter: **Lesson 4: Listening review (3)**
B Listen to the introduction to the lecture. Complete the graph with the missing information.

Male lecturer:
Last week, we talked about food hygiene and I explained the importance of storing and handling food properly. After the lecture, several students came up to me and asked how important this subject really was. OK, they said, of course it was important to be careful with food, but you didn't have to go mad about it. After all, they didn't know anybody who had died from food poisoning. Surely, you just got a stomachache and that was that? Well, I'm pleased that your experience of food poisoning has not been too bad, but let me say straight away that food poisoning *is* a very serious danger, especially in a hot country, and you must constantly guard against it. OK, I hear you say, food poisoning is dangerous, but it isn't very common. It's true that it isn't the *most* common cause of accidental death. In most countries, that is road accidents. In the US, for example, they accounted for over 40,000 deaths in 2002. It isn't even the second most common cause, which is falls from ladders and high places. But it is the third most common cause of accidental death in the US, with nearly 10,000 deaths in 2002. That's nearly 11% of all accidental deaths in the country and more than drowning and fires put together. And in many countries, the trend is upwards, as more and more people store food wrongly in refrigerators and freezers, cook it wrongly in microwaves and keep it past its use-by date.

Presenter: **C 2 Listen again and check your answers.**

Male lecturer: After the lecture, several students came up to me and asked how important this subject really was. OK, they said, of course it was important to be careful with food, but you didn't have to go mad about it. After all, they didn't know anybody who had died from food poisoning. Surely, you just got a stomachache and that was that? Well, I'm pleased that your experience of food poisoning has not been too bad, but let me say straight away that food poisoning *is* a very serious danger, especially in a hot country, and you must constantly guard against it. OK, I hear you say, food poisoning is dangerous, but it isn't very common. It's true that it isn't the *most* common cause of accidental death. In most countries, that is road accidents.

Presenter: **D Listen to the final part of the lecture. When the lecturer stops, predict the next word. Then listen and check your ideas.**

Male lecturer: OK, so food poisoning is really [PAUSE] serious. You must protect yourself from food that is [PAUSE] unsafe. You cannot always tell that food is [PAUSE] unsafe from the way it [PAUSE] looks or the way it [PAUSE] smells. But there are ways to protect [PAUSE] yourself from eating unsafe [PAUSE] food. In the last lecture, I mentioned the most important [PAUSE] ones. But how can you [PAUSE] remember [PAUSE] them? I have devised a simple set of [PAUSE] rules. I call them the Food [PAUSE] Code. You just have to remember the four [PAUSE] Cs.
You must keep food [PAUSE] cold.
You must keep it [PAUSE] clean.
You must cook it [PAUSE] properly.
You must check that it has not gone past its use-by [PAUSE] date.